ROYAL
PURSUIT

To My Mother

ROYAL
PURSUIT

THE PALACE, THE PRESS
AND THE PEOPLE

DOUGLAS KEAY

SEVERN
SH
HOUSE

First published in 1983 by Severn House Publishers,
4 Brook Street, London W1Y 1AA

British Library Cataloguing in Publication Data

    Royal Pursuit
    1. Windsor, House of   2. Journalism – Great
    – Social aspects   Britain
    I. Title
    072 PN4784.R/

    ISBN 0 7278 3015 5

Typeset by Tarmigan Publicity Ltd, 7 Wakley Street,
London EC1V 7LT

Printed in Great Britain by Anchor Press Ltd, and bound
by Wm. Brendon & Son Ltd, both of Tiptree, Essex.

CONTENTS

FOREWORD

Not long after I began my research, a distinguished Fleet Street Editor made this prophesy: "I don't know what you're going to put in your book but I'm afraid, whatever you write, you're bound to make enemies – either among the media or at Buckingham Palace."

I hope he wasn't right – not least because my bread and butter comes from one, and my respect goes out to both.

In fact, my intention all along has been to examine and report on the sometimes turbulent, often amusing, but invariably fragile relations between Buckingham Palace and the media, without necessarily coming down on the side of one more than the other. And if this makes it sound as if I've sat on the fence, dangling my legs, for much of the time – well, some might argue that that's not such a bad vantage point from which to observe what's going on.

Besides talking at length with fellow journalists who report on the Royal scene – all of whom, without exception, were extremely generous with anecdotes of their own personal experiences – I have been fortunate enough to travel as an accredited correspondent on several Royal tours, both in Britain and abroad, during the last ten years, and have been privileged to interview a number of members of the Royal Family, including Prince Philip and Prince Charles – though not, I should add, in connection with this book.

When I first approached Buckingham Palace in January 1982 with the notion of writing a book about "Palace, Press and People" the response was, to say the least, not very encouraging. The following was the key sentence in the Palace's reply to my request for co-operation: "While a book on this subject might well have a degree of public interest, it is not one which our organisation sees as necessary, or even desirable – so I fear there would be no reason to suppose that we could make any special exception to the rules" (of access) "to which we usually adhere."

In the ensuing months, however, I did receive an invaluable amount of help and background information (within the rules), from

Mr. Michael Shea, the Queen's Press Secretary, and from his colleagues working in the Press Office at Buckingham Palace. But it needs to be stressed that much of the detail contained in the following pages, including the great bulk of the material about the working conditions and traditions operating inside Buckingham Palace, did not emanate from him but was gathered piecemeal over a period of several years from a variety of sources.

The reasons, quite apart from legally binding contracts, for the strong reluctance – nay, polite refusal – of those in the employ of Her Majesty to divulge what, to the outsider, might appear interesting but completely innocuous details about Royal family life were pointed out to me in a conversation with Sir William Heseltine, Deputy Private Secretary to the Queen:

"I think that anybody who by virtue of office is admitted to a great deal of intimacy with somebody else wants to go on being able to do their job without prejudicing it by being the source of a whole lot of information which the principle figure might prefer not to have made public."

It may surprise some to learn – especially those convinced that the Press believes in personal freedom – that some reporters from some newspapers felt themselves to be under a similar constraint when disagreements between Palace and Press reached the stage of making headlines.

Fortunately, at the time of going to the printers, the Palace and the Press appear to have arrived at some accommodation with one another, so that there are no longer accusations of intrusion winging from Palace and Press Council in the direction of Fleet Street, and no reporters and photographers flying out to Eleuthera to grab pictures of a pregnant Princess of Wales. How long this state of affairs will continue is anybody's guess. Nor can it be vouchsafed that there are not more scoops and scandals to come. Even while I was in the process of writing this book, the Queen's bedroom was invaded, the Queen's personal detective resigned, Prince Andrew made friends with Koo Stark, and Princess Diana – according, at least, to one gossip columnist – came near to refusing to go on the Royal tour of Australia and New Zealand.

For reasons already given, a number of those I have spoken to in the course of my research have requested to remain anonymous. Others asked that their contributions be entirely off-the-record. Notwithstanding, I would like to place on record my gratitude to as many as possible of those who have given so generously of their time, their thoughts, their anecdotes. I list their names below, without detailing the nature of their assistance whether great or small, and express my thanks to all of them: –

Ronald Allison, Charles Anson, Harry Arnold, Philip Arnold, Sarah

Brennan, Dennis Beaven, Ron Bell, Iris Burton, Richard Cawston, David Chipp, Terence Clarke, Anthony Carthew, Vic Chapman, John Dauth, Douglas Dumbrell, Peter Dimmock, John Dixon, Arthur Edwards, Grania Forbes, Terry Fincher, Jayne Fincher, Diana Goodman, Tim Graham, James Gray, Kent Gavin, John Haslam, Anthony Holden, Warwick Hutchings, Sir William Heseltine, I.P.C. Reference Library, Tim King, Robert Lacey, Norman Luck, Stephen Lynas, Serge Lemoine, Kenneth Lennox, Cliff Morgan, Anne Neal, David Nicholas, John Osman, Jane Owen, Jane Reed, John Shelley, Graeme Wicks, Steve Wood, Ashley Walton, Anne Wall, Christopher Ward, James Whitaker. I should like to make special mention of I.P.C. Magazines Ltd., and of *Woman's Own* in particular, which has commissioned me over a period of some twelve years to write features and profiles about the Royal Family, amongst other articles, and has helped enable me to accompany members of the Royal Family on overseas tours.

For her friendship, encouragement and professional advice I should like especially to thank Carole Blake, my agent. My thanks are also due to Edwin Buckhalter, my publisher, and David Harsent, whose skilful editing has led to several improvements in the manuscript. I am greatly indebted to Penny Whately-Smith and Anne Agnew who burned many hours of midnight oil transferring my minute handwriting into legible typescript. To my wife, Marianne, I owe a multitude of thanks for her support and her patience. Most of all I am indebted to those friends I hope I still have at the Palace and in the Press — not to forget, most importantly of all, the Royal Family itself, without whose existence this book could never have been written.

PROLOGUE

In the early hours of Monday, February 21, 1983 Queen Elizabeth II was asleep on board the Royal Yacht 'Britannia' as it progressed sedately northwards through calm Mexican waters from Puerto Vallarta towards the fishing port of La Paz.

Behind lay a tiring but pleasurable Royal tour. Her Majesty and the Duke of Edinburgh had visited Jamaica, the Cayman Islands, and Mexico – now La Paz would be the last port of call. Ahead lay what would prove to be a somewhat adventurous journey through parts of California, the Sunshine State of America, with an itinerary thrown out of kilter by some of the worst storms known in years, and marred by the tragic death in a car accident of three United States secret servicemen assigned to Royal protection duties.

Breakfast aboard 'Britannia' is usually served at about eight o'clock. But on this particular day, a good hour before then, Members of the Queen's Household were up, dressed, and about, attending to correspondence, planning the day's programme, and relaying and receiving communications passing between the Royal Yacht and Buckingham Palace.

In London it was already three o'clock in the afternoon. At Buckingham Palace other Members of the Queen's Household had returned from lunch while, a mile and a half away in Fleet Street, newspaper editors were preparing for four o'clock conferences with their staffs to plan the contents of the next day's issues.

Shortly after seven a.m. (Pacific time) or three p.m. (Greenwich Mean Time), a call came through to 'Britannia' for Sir Philip Moore, the Queen's Private Secretary. At the other end of the radio link was Sir William Heseltine, the Queen's Deputy Private Secretary, speaking from his ground floor office in the north-east wing of the Palace.

The conversation between the two men, close advisers to the Queen as well as being good personal friends, lasted several minutes and ranged over a number of topics. The chief subject however was the revelations of a former employee at Buckingham Palace published that morning in *The Sun* — Britain's largest selling daily newspaper with some twelve million readers.

Across the centre pages of the newspaper were the words: 'World exclusive: The astonishing inside secrets of the fun-loving Royals'. An even larger headline read 'QUEEN KOO'S ROMPS AT THE PALACE.'

The source of the revelations that followed — alleging goings-on at the Palace between Prince Andrew and his girlfriend, actress Koo Stark — was, *The Sun* told its readers, Kiernan Kenny, a 20-year-old stores officer who had worked in the Royal Household for two and a half years. He had left Buckingham Palace service three weeks before and would be telling readers, "what really happens on the other side of the Palace walls."

As will be shown in later chapters, *The Sun* and Buckingham Palace have by no means always been in agreement about what should and what should not be written about members of the Royal Family, but in this case, the Palace insisted from the outset that the principal fault lay with the man and not the newspaper.

On taking up his appointment at Buckingham Palace, Kiernan Kenny, like everyone working in that august building, had been required to sign an 'undertaking of confidence' as a condition of employment. By this, he agreed not to disclose any information he might come by during Royal service.

While most aboard 'Britannia' were asleep, Palace staff in London had extracted Kenny's contract from the files and, with the advantage of the eight hour time difference, lawyers had carefully considered the legal position.

When the call was placed to 'Britannia' it was to inform the Queen's Private Secretary, Sir Philip Moore, that it would be perfectly possible for an application to be made to the courts that very day to procure an injunction preventing Mr Kenny from publishing anything further about his two years of employment at the Palace. Indeed the advice from London, offered to the Queen through her Private Secretary, was that such an application should be made. The fact that Prince Charles' Private Secretary, the Honourable Edward Adeane, had previously followed a highly successful career as a lawyer and specialising in libel, was a factor not unconnected with the advice given.

But the Queen, even though she may have been sorely tempted to do so at times, had never applied for such an injunction before. Indeed, since British courts are nominally the Sovereign's courts, it might have seemed that legal difficulties could arise.

There was a precedent: in 1849 Prince Albert, Queen Victoria's husband, had obtained an injunction to prevent a Mr Strange from publishing etchings and drawings which the Prince and the Queen had made of their children.

In the event, it transpired that in this contemporary case the application could be made in the name of someone other than the Queen – namely Mr Russell Wood, Deputy Treasurer of the Queen's Household, who technically had been Kenny's employer. But speed was essential in making a decision.

Shortly after breakfast, when he was called to the Queen's presence, Sir Philip Moore outlined what had happened in London, and after quiet consultation with her Private Secretary and others of her Household, including her Press Secretary, Mr Michael Shea, the Queen concurred with the decision that Mr Wood should apply for an injunction.

Shortly afterwards, sitting in private at the Royal Courts of Justice in London, some six thousand miles away, Mr Justice Hodgson heard Counsel's application and granted an injunction against Mr Kenny and against News Group Newspapers, publishers of *The Sun*.

The next day's instalment of Mr Kenny's recollections, promoted in advance with the line: "When barefoot Di buttered my toast", was dropped. But the paper ran a front page headline in huge letters: QUEEN GAGS THE SUN.

That same day the Palace moved the matter a step further. Mr Russell Wood took out a writ seeking to order News Group and Mr Kenny to divulge the profits resulting from the publication of Kenny's story.

The rest of Fleet Street stood by, intrigued. What was to be the final outcome? Was this to be the stand-up battle that many had predicted was bound to be staged one day between the Palace and the Press? Had the Queen's patience finally been exhausted, and was she determined now to put a stop, once-for-all, to Press invasion of the family's privacy?

In America, where the Queen and Prince Philip were to start a ten day tour in less than one week's time, *Good Housekeeping* magazine was serialising the memoirs of Stephen Barry, Prince Charles' former valet – memoirs he had not been given Palace permission to publish. The sensation-gathering *National Enquirer* was shortly to print an article about "some of the secret quirks of the Queen – as revealed exclusively to the *Enquirer* by a former aide and confirmed by other Palace insiders."

Neither account was ever likely to be published in Britain, partly for fear of legal action by the Palace, though both did appear in Australian publications just one month later, coinciding with the highly publicised tour of that country by the Prince and Princess of Wales.

Matters might indeed be seen to have been getting out of hand.

"The Royal Hunt of the Sun", as *The Observer* headlined the Palace's legal action, was not directed against Britain's most popular newspaper so much as against the idea that yet another former employee at Buckingham Palace could, with impunity, walk into a newspaper office and sell his story. In the case of Kenny, it was thought that he got £2000 and a holiday in Spain. Stephen Barry in America received over £100,000.

But once the point had been made and the disclosures stopped through an injunction, the Queen and her advisers were quite content to settle out of court for a sum of £4000. (Sir William Heseltine can take credit for suggesting the money should be donated to a Fleet Street charity, the Newspaper Press Fund). At the same time *The Sun* cannot have been too unhappy, either, to have increased its circulation by some 54,000 as a result of one article, and to have received publicity worth an estimated one million pounds in advertising terms.

More than anything, the action and reaction over Kiernan Kenny's tale illustrated very well the often ultra-sensitive relationship that has existed for some years now between Buckingham Palace and certain sections of the British media. Freedom to express, and a right to privacy. Circulation and the Crown. These are considerations that are being constantly weighed and balanced, with the mass of the public – avid readers and loyal subjects both – probably being the arbiters in the final analysis.

As the ripples of the story spread, the American media showed ever-growing interest and curiosity about what one of its members termed 'the spat' between the Palace and a former employee. Perhaps it was just as well (and perhaps deliberate) that the matter was settled out of court before the Queen was many days into her tour of California and a meeting with the President of the United States.

Peter McKay, of the *Daily Mail*, reporting on the Royal tour, wrote that the Queen, wise to the ways of the Press, "knows that although *The Sun* is an obviously rapscallion newspaper, other, more sober newspapers are also obliged to report a row of this magnitude."

The showdown had been on the cards for years, but when 'revelations' like the Blunt, Fagan and Trestrail affairs had occured, wrote Mr McKay, there was little the Royals could do about it. This time there was a course of action open, and it had been taken.

It happened that just a few weeks later – and on the very same day that Prince Andrew's name was once again in the headlines with reports of his cavorting in Barbados surf with three young women – the Prince and Princess of Wales were drinking with members of the media in the unlikely setting of a motel lounge bar in the small town of Alice Springs in Australia's Northern Territory.

The Reception, admittance by *Entrée Card* only, was the standard meeting between visiting Royalty and representatives of the local and overseas Press and television which takes place at the start of every major royal tour outside Britain. In this case it marked the start of the Prince and Princess of Wales' six week tour of Australia and New Zealand in March and April, 1983.

A main purpose of these occasions is to get Palace-media relations off to a good start before the weeks of travelling begin, and invariably the purpose is achieved. But on this occasion there was added importance; it would be the first time that the 21-year-old Princess of Wales would be meeting members of the British and Commonwealth Press, so to speak, *en masse* and face to face.

Present in the large room, cleared of tables and chairs, were several of Fleet Street's highly paid 'Royal-watchers'. A few of them were men and women who, in the past, had caused the Pri . much distress by photographing her in a bikini when she was five months' pregnant, by reporting that she was suffering from anorexia nervosa, by – most recently – reducing her to the point of tears by their attentions on the Austrian ski-slopes.

The faces, as well as the names of several of these journalists, were well known to the Princess. She had posed for their photographs or more often talked to them, sometimes on the telephone, in the months leading up to the announcement of her engagement to the Prince of Wales when she was still Lady Diana Spencer. Since that time there had been scant opportunity to communicate, formally or informally, and relationships, once friendly, had very much deteriorated between Princess and Press.

Both, then, could be excused for showing signs of nervousness as Princess Diana entered the room of the motel with the Prince of Wales. For a moment, there was hesitation. But then as the Princess circulated in one direction and the Prince in another, moving between semi-circles of mooning journalists, laughter and conviviality sprang up like flowers.

Conversations between Royalty and the media on such occasions are, by mutual consent, strictly off the record. But it is breaking no rules to report that, though there were good-humoured jibes and jests thrown out in the general direction of some individuals, the atmosphere was relaxed and friendly, and the Princess carried all before her quite splendidly, displaying both charm and diplomacy.

Prince Charles is well used to dealing with the media – though some of its members can still make him nervous or irritated, or both. He has long recognised that Press, television, and radio have a job to do, as does he. Both he and they, in their ways, are paid to do it. The Princess of Wales had had less time to understand this, but she was learning fast. She was also learning, at the start of the Australian tour, that as a Princess of Wales she, along with every other member of

14

the Royal Family, has a role to play in a national, and an international sense.

As they left the Reception after an hour of relaxation before the onset of hard work, one or two journalists might have reflected on a comment made by Robert Lacey, published in *Time* magazine just five weeks before, on the eve of the Queen's tour of America:

"One must not reveal too much of the mystery because the Royals have faults, dishonesties, nastinesses like anyone else. A lot of us happen to think that the illusions and idealisation which surround this family is quite a healthy thing. Every society needs vehicles for its dreams."

1. H.Q – BUCKINGHAM PALACE

"The vast building, with its stately rooms and endless corridors and passages . . . seemed pervaded by a curious musty smell that assails me whenever I enter its portals. I was never happy there."
The Duke of Windsor, 'A King's Story'

"The role of Buckingham Palace is essentially that of a small government department . . . and in modern times it has also become convenient for the monarch to live there."
Robert Lacey, 'Majesty'

"This isn't ours. It's a tied cottage."
Prince Philip, quoted in 'The Book of Royal Lists'

Entering the gates of Buckingham Palace for the first time creates a similar sensation to stepping through one of those metal doorframes used at airports for security checks. Most people feel self-conscious, nervous, and very aware that people are watching. The difference between the two occurrences is mainly to do with pride smudged with smugness. Many pass through airport security screens but not all that number of people, you tell yourself, actually get the chance to drive right up to the Queen's front door.

Visitors and Royalty alike, on informal occasions, use the gate on the right. While tourists standing on the pavement peer inside the car, curious to see whether you're anyone important, the two policemen at the gate approach. One asks your name and business, the other checks the name against his list of forthcoming visitors. If terrorists or Palace intruders have been active recently, the underside of your car may be inspected for bombs, by means of a mirror on a trolley. Pass friend.

The feeling on the first occasion is such, for any but the most hardened anti-monarchist, that as you ease your car across the wide expanse of granite red gravel there comes an almost irresistible urge to scoot around the forecourt as if on a dodgem at a fairground.

Instead, of course, you drive as solemnly as if steering a hearse to park beside the Renault 5s, Rovers, and Fiestas — belonging to privileged workers at the Palace — that are lined up against the wall.

By habit, (and somewhat unnecessarily considering where you are) you lock your car and crunch the fifty yards or so to what you have been told is the Privy Purse Door, all too conscious of the inquisitive stares of the tourists peering through the railings.

Six crimson-carpeted steps with brass rods lead up to the Privy Purse entrance. A footman with a scarlet waistcoat and a pencil-line moustache opens the glass panelled door even as you reach for the handle. Inside, a kind of hallway. The eye is immediately drawn to a mahogany table, set against a wall, on which lies a parade of neatly lined-up and tightly rolled umbrellas; deposited there at the start of the working day by Members of the Household.

On the left of the hallway is the Footmen and Pages' room where it used to be possible to gain a brief moment *inside* Buckingham Palace merely by asking to sign the Visitors Book. The practice was ended some years ago, at about the same time as the soldiers guarding the Palace were moved inside the railings. To the right of the entrance is the waiting room. Current copies of *The Times* and the *Daily Express* are there to while away the moments till the next stage. (Nobody seems to know why it is these two papers that are always on offer.)

The furniture comprises gold painted chairs with lime green silk covers. On the walls are two paintings by the Victorian artist W.P. Frith: "Departure Scene, Paddington Station", and "Life at the Seaside".

After a wait, usually of about five minutes, (there is a toilet just round the corner if you have need), a footman comes to collect you and lead the way to the room of whomsoever you are visiting.

If you have the rare honour of an appointment with the Monarch herself you may be taken first to the office of the Queen's Private Secretary, Sir Philip Moore, on the ground floor directly below the Queen's private apartments. After pleasantries, and possibly a glass of sherry, he will in all probability escort you the rest of the way himself. Alternatively, one of the Queen's equerries will look after you. You will certainly not be allowed to wander the corridors alone!

If your appointment is with the Duke of Edinburgh, a wobbly lift will take you very slowly to the first floor where Prince Philip's study and library are situated in rooms adjacent to the Queen's. Your escort on this slow ride may offer the interesting anecdote about how the operating speed of the lift was made slower some thirty years ago when the Royal children, Prince Charles and Princess Anne, had a penchant for riding in it.

Those who have not come to Buckingham Palace to see the Queen or Prince Philip (i.e. the great majority) may nonetheless have appointments with one or other of the small band of hard working men and women in the service of the various Royal Households.

Say, for instance, you have come to see the Duke of Edinburgh's Private Secretary, Mr Brian McGrath. His office is at the far end of the corridor leading from the Privy Purse Door entrance. The footman will lead the way over the crimson patterned carpet (renewed in 1982) past the offices of the Keeper of the Privy Purse, the Chief Clerk's office, The Queen's Private Secretary's office, the Equerries' Room, the Press Secretary's office, and an office of other lesser luminaries. And as you follow the footman, whose pace gives no chance to linger, you may quite possibly overhear brief snatches of quite intriguing telephone conversations − floating through the open doors. Phrases such as: "I was speaking to the Queen about that this morning" or "I don't think the Duke of Edinburgh has anything booked for that particular morning, but I'll check."

For some reason, servants of the Crown tend to raise their voices when speaking on the telephone. Another reason their comments are so audible (and partly why, one suspects, the footman hurries you on) is that there is a long standing convention at the Palace that the doors of offices, even of the most senior people, are left ajar except when absolute privacy is essential. Another tradition is that you do not knock before entering a room.

Possibly, as you draw near to McGrath's door you may hear the most evocative Palace sound of all: the approaching yaps of a charge of Corgis. Also escorted by a footman, they sweep past, on their way to the garden to "go about their business". Nothing brings home more vividly just whose house you are in.

The public, pressing against the railings outside, have little conception of the every day life going on inside the Palace.

Those lucky enough to catch a glimpse of the Queen or a member of the Royal Family driving into the Palace may wonder why the Queen's car disappears out of sight through an archway on the far right of the building. The Grand Entrance, opposite the central archway, is used by ambassadors and on such grand occasions as the Royal Wedding. (Edward Blore's front gives the fourth side to the incomplete square of the original design.) Each of the principal occupants of the Palace uses a separate entrance nearest to his or her own front door.

The Queen uses the Garden Entrance, a fairly unimposing doorway in the north-east wing. From here she need only walk a few steps to the small lift which carries her up one floor to her private apartments. These are next door to, and continue through into, Prince Philip's apartments; but, again because it's the quickest way, he usually enters the Palace by the King's Door in the quadrangle, then turns right and climbs the wide stairway leading directly to his study and library.

Princess Anne, who retained her rooms at the front of the Palace after her marriage, uses yet another entrance known as the Quadrangle or Luggage Entrance. It is appropriately named because it is not uncommon to see the Princess lugging in from her car an armful of coats and dresses which she has used during public engagements the previous week, and lugging out a change of clothes to take back to Gatcombe Park in preparation for the following week.

Since Easter 1982, when the Prince and Princess of Wales moved into Kensington Palace, less than a mile up the road, Prince Charles tends to treat Buckingham Palace more as a business address. The Prince of Wales Office, which administers his affairs, is still situated on the ground floor of the Palace − approached, fittingly, through the Prince of Wales Door − and his private apartments, on the first floor remain very much as he left them. He moved surprisingly little furniture over to Kensington Palace; in fact his study was used for a time as an office for one of the Princess's Ladies-in-Waiting after he had left.

The Princess of Wales, when she is calling on the Queen, normally slips into the Palace either by the Garden Door or the King's Door. The stone-canopied Grand Entrance, directly facing the main central archway, is the one best known to the public and least used by the Royal Family itself. As its name implies, it is reserved for formal occasions such as State banquets, Royal Weddings, and the arrival and departure of Foreign Heads of State. Pope John Paul came and went through the Grand Entrance.

A final word about Palace doors: at the time of the Royal Wedding those who wished to send presents but preferred not to entrust them to the Post Office were asked to have them delivered to the Trade Door, Buckingham Palace. The reason for this was because every gift-wrapped package, whatever its size, had to go through a security check, and the Trade Door is the one nearest to the Palace's own Police Lodge. However, some of the more exalted sniffed at being asked to send their very expensive presents to the Prince and Princess of Wales via the *Trade* Door. So to avoid embarrassment the name was swiftly changed to the Side Door, and thus presumably it will ever more be known!

Office hours at Buckingham Palace are from nine till five-thirty, but some arrive before nine and leave well after five-thirty if the work-load is particularly heavy. The lights never all go out, though there is perhaps a tendency for some leather-topped desks to be vacated after lunch on Friday in order to allow their occupants time to journey to a weekend in the country, either at their own retreat or someone else's. The briefing for one of these weekends, incidentally, to someone not used to the style, can be confusing. A television producer invited to spend the weekend at a Private Secretary's country cottage was assured: "Oh we're completely informal at weekends. Just throw a pair of jeans and a dinner jacket into your bag."

Almost as bewildering to the uninitiated, and a source of suppressed annoyance to some who work there, are the lines of demarcation that operate within the Palace.

Employees are divided into three distinct classes. Superior among these are Members of the four Households — the Queen's, the Duke of Edinburgh's and the Prince of Wales' and Princess Anne's House-holds. Private Secretaries, Press Secretaries, and their Assistants are among those who come within this entitlement. The second category is that of Officials which includes such positions as Clerks and Office Managers. The third and largest group is the Palace Staff and into this come a wide variety of people from footmen to secretaries to washers-up. Niceties obtain between each section. For instance, each has its own separate place to eat meals. Members of the Household take lunch in a dining room while the Staff use their own canteen. Stranger than this, however, is the code of address still used between the three groups. To the Staff everyone else is 'Sir' or 'Madam', with the exception, of course, of the Queen, the Duke of Edinburgh, and other members of the Royal Family who are addressed respectively as Your Majesty or Your Royal Highness and sometimes 'Ma'am' and 'Sir'. Those designated Household and Officials have more compli-cated rules. Officials, to start with, address members of Staff as Mr, Miss, or Mrs as do Members of Household. Household, on the other hand, drop the prefix when speaking to or of Officials. An Official is addressed by his Christian name. This particularly refined and somewhat bewildering form of etiquette does not finish there. For Members of Household, in company or in private, use Christian names when addressing one another, no matter whether talking to one of the more lowly of the Palace hierarchy or the Queen's Private Secretary himself. The final irony in this ancient adjunct to snobbery is the manner of address for the Royal children. Until they reached the age of eighteen, on the express instructions of the Queen, they were always addressed within the Palace walls by their Christian names, with no prefix of Prince or Princess.

Perhaps one should not be even the least surprised that a form of class discrimination operates inside Buckingham Palace. Where else, if not there? But the fact that the Queen wanted her younger sons to be treated as much like anyone else for as long as possible might have been taken to mean that she was in favour of a more modern democratic attitude among her courtiers. It's certainly true that Prince Philip, especially in the earlier days, tried very hard to modernise certain aspects of daily life at Buckingham Palace. To an extent he succeeded, and the Duke of Edinburgh's office is still regarded as one of the most efficient. Prince Philip himself has a reputation, parallel to that of the Queen, of being the speediest in replying to internal memos.

Buckingham Palace, besides being the official residence of the Queen, the venue for State occasions, and a magnet for tourists from all over the world, is the administrative headquarters of the Monarchy. Some 320 work there, in over 600 rooms.

The Lord Chamberlain, Lord Maclean, a ruddy-complexioned former Chief Scout, is titular Head of the Royal Household though his post is largely ceremonial. His second-in-command is Lieutenant-Colonel Sir John Johnston, the Comptroller.

Then there is the Master of the Household, Vice-Admiral Sir Peter Ashmore, who is in effective control of domestic staff of which there are about fifty full-time, supplemented by part-timers at big banquets. His deputy is Lieutenant-Colonel Blair Stewart-Wilson.

The man in charge of the pages and footmen is Mr Cyril Dickman, and Miss Adrienne de Trey-White is the housekeeper. Most of the heads of departments have offices in the front of the Palace, on the ground and first floors.

In their own staff canteen, there is a bar, open from 4.30 till 8.30 p.m. Strictly speaking staff have to give three days' notice if they want to invite a guest from outside the Palace. This rule, introduced as a security precaution, has proved impracticable to operate however.

Within the Royal Household, the Queen, the Duke of Edinburgh, the Prince of Wales, and Princess Anne have their own independent administrations. Chief of these, of course, is the Queen's Household, employing altogether some twenty-one people, and presided over by the Rt. Hon. Sir Philip Brian Cecil Moore, P.C., G.C.V.O., C.B., C.M.G., Private Secretary to the Queen and Keeper of the Queen's Archives since 1977. The son of an Indian Civil Servant, he won a scholarship from Cheltenham College to Oxford where he became a double blue in hockey and rugby. He played rugby for England. In the opposing team, playing for Wales, was Cliff Morgan, now Head of B.B.C. Television Outside Broadcasts and the man responsible for 'Royal Liaison' at the B.B.C. In his time the Queen's Private

Secretary has held the posts of Principal Private Secretary to the First Lord of the Admiralty, Deputy High Commissioner, Singapore, and Chief of Public Relations at the Ministry of Defence. He was appointed Assistant Private Secretary to the Queen in 1966, during a period when the popularity of the monachy as an institution was not as high as it is now, and when the services of a senior Civil Servant with experience in public relations may have seemed particuarly appropriate.

Sir Philip's immediate superior at the Palace was Lieutenant-Colonel Sir Michael Adeane, now Baron Adeane of Stamfordham, who had been Private Secretary to the Queen since her Coronation Year in 1953. The two men came from quite different backgrounds. Adeane's grandfather, Lord Stamfordham, was Private Secretary to Queen Victoria. At thirteen, when at Eton, Adeane himself was Page of Honour to King George V and he became Assistant Private Secretary to King George VI in 1937 when he was only twenty-six. Although the two men got on well together, one observer recalls Adeane giving his Assistant "quite a tough time".

Lord Adeane retired from the Palace in 1972, at the age of 62, and was created a life peer the same year. Six years later, in May 1978, his son, Edward, was officially chosen by Prince Charles to become his Private Secretary, the appointment meaning, apart from anything else, that the Adeane family had already achieved a century of service to the Royal Family.

The Hon. Edward Adeane, a man small in stature like his father, is of a retiring nature, fond of ornithology. But he holds strong views, particularly in matters concerning the dignity of the Royal Family. When, in March 1982 news leaked out that a "baby boutique" had presented the Princess of Wales with a cot and other nursery fittings, reported to be worth more than £1000, it was Adeane who took the unusual step of personally telephoning the owner of the shop to express displeasure at what the Palace evidently considered was advertising. "He sounded like a schoolmaster and he made me feel like a naughty schoolgirl," was the reported reaction of the joint owner of the shop, Mrs Eleanor Cresner, who also told reporters there had been no intention whatsoever to publicise the gift.

Adeane is, in fact, a lawyer by training. Educated at Eton and Cambridge, he gave up a very successful practice at the Bar, specialising in libel cases, in order to work for the Prince of Wales. Included in his list of clients were Lady Falkender, *The Times,* and *Playboy* magazine.

Among the special privileges afforded to Members of the Royal Household are the use of the Buckingham Palace swimming pool, and the adjacent squash court. Another facility, by prior booking, but available to all who work at the Palace, is a round of golf on the nine hole course at Windsor Castle, which was laid down by King Edward VII. (Before he lost patience with the game altogether, the King had any bunker he landed in *moved!*)

Neither the pool nor the squash court are used as much as they used to be, either by the Royal Family themselves or by the Household, though a surge of renewed interest was noticeable when the Princess of Wales, before her marriage, started using the pool. There are no written rules; custom and good manners suggest that if you happen to be doing your ten lengths or whatever and a member of the Royal Family arrives for a dip, you stay in; but if you arrive to find the Princess, or any other Family member, already there you stay *out* unless invited *in*. The squash court, where Prince Philip was playing when he heard news that his wife had given birth to their first child, is nowadays used mostly by the younger members of the Family. Two or three years ago the young Lord Linley, Princess Margaret and Lord Snowdon's son, was given a severe ticking off by a squash fanatic who discovered him knocking up a ball while still wearing his cowboy boots!

The one time both the pool and the squash court are out-of-bounds is when a distinguished guest is staying at Buckingham Palace. The explanation is simple. Access to both recreation areas requires passing through the Belgian Suite, which are, by tradition, the rooms reserved for visiting Heads of State. Both Prince Andrew and Prince Edward, incidentally, were born in one of the bedrooms of the Belgian Suite.

Until January 1st 1982, for many of the Royal Household, the working day began with breakfast, no charge, at Buckingham Palace. The practice was generally thought to make for rather a congenial start to the morning. Bachelors who might otherwise have deemed it too tiresome to shake out a packet of cornflakes before leaving home, gleefully rubbed hands at the daily morning glory of devilled kidneys on silver salvers, of scrambled eggs and kedgeree, of piping hot coffee served by uniformed footmen. Even the married men, no doubt with a twinge of conscience, left wives and children to their normal diet of toast and tea on Formica-topped kitchen tables in order to hurry to the house at the top of the Mall for their much grander breakfast.

A great deal of useful work was done at these breakfasts. There was a catching-up on news, an exchange of ideas, a consulting of diaries to arrange meetings. It was an excellent time to discuss a perhaps ticklish point with one of the Private Secretaries.

It was a very sad day for the Household therefore when a stop was put to these breakfasts, on grounds of economy, from January 1st 1982. It seemed such a bad way to start the New Year. Even more depressing to some people was the threat of withdrawal of cakes and sandwiches from the traditional afternoon tea-break taken in the Equerries' Room. Only a spirited last-ditch stand by a lady Member of the Household saved the day. Future generations, unless there are more economy measures to come, will have her to thank for the fact that they can bite into a cucumber sandwich as well as take tea from cups bearing the monogram of George VI — most things last a long time at Buckingham Palace, and nothing is wasted.

The Equerries' Room, incidentally, is where Members also fore-gather for a drink before lunch. The actual meal is taken in another room, some way distant, where the only place unofficially reserved is that of the Master of the Household. He has a small silver bell at his setting. The menu is written in French, if the Court is in residence, and not at all when the Court is out of London. The charge for lunch is £1.00. Beer is free, but spirits you pay for.

If these small insights into the daily work pattern of the Royal Household suggest a pampered existence then it is to mislead unin-tentionally. Anyone who has witnessed Members of the Royal Household at work, inside or outside the Palace, knows that their jobs are no sinecures. Indeed, many senior Civil Servants, whose responsibilities are probably nearest comparable, might find the breadth of knowledge required, the degree of skill in diplomacy, and the sheer pressure of work undertaken, altogether quite daunting. In the company of strangers, or even with those they know of only by repute, the Queen's most senior servants appear at the same time affable yet distant, friendly but never *too* friendly. In private, amongst themselves, one or two of them have a rip-roaring sense of fun. But nearly all of them would wish to remain totally anonymous as far as the general public is concerned. They would prefer to be written about, if at all, only after they were dead.

To the outsider, one or two of the accepted Palace customs may appear somewhat out-of-date, smacking of the feudal. For example, there seems to be no very good reason why someone employed by Prince Charles, a friend of many years' standing, should not have been invited to the Prince's eve-of-wedding party simply because he happens to be an Official and not a Member of the Household. Or why Margaret Macdonald, the Queen's dresser for 30 years (and nursery maid to Princess Elizabeth before that), should address male members as 'Sir' even though she must be aware that they regard her, one of the Queen's closest companions, with awesome respect.

But the nuances of Palace life are like a maze, where an outsider can easily become totally confused and lost. And, as in many matters concerning the Royal Family, very little enlightenment is offered to the outsider by those who know their way around. Charming and courteous as the Queen's closest advisers invariably are, they seldom regard it, quite reasonably, as being in any way part of their job to impart knowledge to the media. That heavy responsibility falls to another department within the Royal Household, namely the Press Office, known best to the public outside through the much-quoted prefix: "According to a Buckingham Palace spokesman . . ."

2. "A PALACE SPOKESMAN SAID . . ."

"I am grateful to destiny that I have not been chosen as public relations officer to Buckingham Palace which is in truth a nightmare task."
Harold Nicolson, 'Monarchy'

"The British royal family is an adman's dream. A unique selling proposition with a pliable market strongly pre-disposed towards the product."
Andrew Duncan, 'The Reality of Monarchy'

"The idea that Michael Shea is universally unpopular in Fleet Street is, I hope, absurd."
Michael Shea, the Queen's Press Secretary, in conversation with the author.

For the world's media, the fount of information about Britain's Royal Family − though not the only source by any means − is the Press Office at Buckingham Palace, presided over since 1978 by a genial career diplomat who writes thrillers in his spare time.

Michael Shea, the son of a Clydebank marine engineer, takes trouble to spell out his widowed mother's full name in his own entry in 'Who's Who': Mary Dalrymple Davidson MacAuslan. The name has the ring and resonance of a character in a Scottish novel, and the Queen's Press Secretary himself has the looks and demeanour reminiscent of a minister of the Kirk or a domini at a Highland school. Erect, bespectacled, with a lock of steel grey hair that he habitually brushes from his forehead, he speaks with a refined Edinburgh accent. The Queen is said to enjoy having a 45-year-old Scot at her Court whose hobby is sailing rather than shooting and whose conversational range is wider than that of some of her other courtiers.

Fleet Street has never been totally convinced that a Foreign Office diplomat had the right kind of background to understand its demands and way of thinking. Most editors would probably have been happier to see a journalist appointed. Respect may have increased once reporters realised he made as much if not more money from his books than some of Fleet Street's best-paid men. Shea's salary, in accordance with his grading as a Foreign Office Counsellor, is between £18,525 and £22,201 (plus a London weighting allowance of £1,087), which is paid monthly on a Foreign Office cheque issued through the Palace Privy Purse. It does not seem a very high remuneration for the job he does, and may be at least part of the reason why the Queen, not long after his appointment, installed her Press Secretary, his Norwegian wife and their two children in a handsome four floored house in Pimlico, bought for between £170,000 and £200,000. Shea was careful to point out at the time that no new money had changed hands because the Queen had sold another grace-and-favour residence in Hampstead, named The King's House. The house in Pimlico was more suitable, being nearer to Buckingham Palace.

The job of handling "the P.R. account of the Royals" — a description Shea would *not* give to his task — must count as one of the most demanding and important at the Palace, calling as it does for more than an average amount of patience, stamina, well-aimed outrage, diplomacy, trust, quick thinking, smooth talking and, not least, an ability to withstand without wilting the requests, questions and complaints, that wing in not only from the Press (below stairs), but also from the Queen, (literally upstairs), and other members of the Royal Family.

In her earliest days of marriage, (after the honeymoon and before the arrival of Prince William), it was not unknown for the Princess of Wales to return to the Palace from a public engagement and make it exceedingly plain that she had not been altogether satisifed with the prior arrangements made to keep the Press, photographers in particular, at a respectful distance, and her adoring public under control. "What is not always appreciated," reflected the slightly miffed person responsible for pre-planning some of the Princess's engagements at that time, "is that you can make arrangements for people to stand in certain positions, but on the actual day they do not always do so, not for very long anyway."

The function of the Palace Press Office is not spelled out in any directive — "its role is self-evident," says Shea slightly dismissively. However, some time ago, a guideline prepared internally for newcomers to the Press Office began with the words: "The Press Office do not tell lies ever, nor do we knowingly mislead. We do infrequently, much less frequently than we're accused of, refuse to answer questions or confirm speculation if we've got good reason for doing so.''

Leaving aside for the moment the frequently debated question of whether the Palace Press Office is basically a public relations organisation, there essentially to burnish the image of the monarchy, there is no doubt that most of the work involves *replying* to questions from the Press (which is not always the same as *answering*) supplying information on a wide variety of topics including forthcoming royal events, making arrangements for Press and television to cover these events, both in Britain and overseas and, as Shea puts it, "co-ordinating facilities to maximise the amount of coverage that a royal event can get without inconveniencing either the Royal Family or members of the public." Increasingly in the past few years, the Press Office believes, it is the public that have been inconvenienced rather than the Queen by the activities of the Press and this, it appears, is something which particularly annoys Michael Shea. Anyone who has witnessed this Scotsman, his jaw jutting, his pace purposeful, striding between penned-up groups of reporters and photographers in the minutes leading up to the arrival of a member of the Royal Family is left in no doubt that, while he will help all he can with sorting out last minute media problems, he will not tolerate any departure from what is "acceptable".

He often looks pre-occupied, as well he might with both Press and Palace demands to satisfy, but he seldom shows anger. There was, however, one legendary occasion when his wrath led him to use language that is fairly common in Fleet Street, and not altogether unknown in royal circles either. This was during the Queen's state visit to Morocco in 1980 when the extraordinary behaviour of the host, King Hassan, drove his visitors from Britain to distraction. After days of contending with schedules that were cancelled or changed at the last moment, of being sent to the wrong place at the wrong time, and being kept waiting for a King who might or might not turn up, Keith Graves, B.B.C. television newsman, protested to the Queen's Press Secretary that in all his very considerable experience of reporting major events around the world he had never been so f — d about by anyone. "*You've* been f — d about," responded a visibly shaken Shea, "the *Queen's* been f — d about. *I've* been f — d about!" At this point the very familiar figure of Harry Arnold of *The Sun* appeared in the small circle of newsmen who had gathered round. Arnold clearly remembers Shea's look of worried dismay, presumably at the thought of what *The Sun* might publish the next day. But situations such as this tend to bind Palace representatives and Press together. A day or so later, London newspapers reported that the Queen appeared none too pleased at the way she had been treated by

King Hassan. And television pictures of her tapping a foot as she sat patiently waiting for the King to arrive told a whole story.

A fact of constant surprise to journalists from overseas, and of absolute astonishment to representatives of the visiting American media, who are used to everything on a much more massive scale, is the size of the department at Buckingham Palace that cares for the public and private image of the best known family in the world. In addition to the Press Secretary, there are just two Assistant Press Secretaries to the Queen and four Lady Clerks. In all they occupy four rooms, three on the ground floor of the north-east wing and one small room on the first floor close to the Queen's private apartments. Shea agrees it is not a very conveniently organised arrangement — "ideally, the Press Office ought to be one big room with one ante-room for the boss-man as it were." Adding, "and it should be close to the front door." (It is somewhat surprising that journalists, of all people, are allowed to walk through the length of one side of the Palace in order to reach the Press Office.)

As it is, Shea has the largest room — as large as that of any of the Queen's Private Secretaries — with a window looking onto regal rows of geraniums in the summer, and tulips in the spring. On two corners of the handsome desk stand table lamps with fluted silk shades, and to his right as he works (often in shirt sleeves but never without a tie) is a box of slightly antiquated looking electronic tricks, incorporating a 'phone to the outside world and a transmission to the inside, with direct lines to the Queen, Prince Philip, and Prince Charles — as well as to their Private Secretaries. In addition, there is a device whereby Shea can conduct a telephone conversation with the handpiece resting on a sort of cradle. To the person calling in from outside, this has the effect of making him sound as if he is speaking from the deep end of an empty swimming pool. Asking the patient and polite Palace switchboard (the number is not ex-directory) for the Queen's Press Secretary by name does not, however, guarantee that he will answer personally. Each call is automatically routed to all the Press Office staff. A light shows up on their 'phones and if the person being buzzed does not answer someone else will pick up the call. Shea "takes the top stuff and crisis manages" but on questions of fact anyone may answer.

One of the problems of a small staff is giving the media a 24 hour service. The Press Office are the only people at the Palace to carry "bleepers" for instant summons during hectic times. But even when things are quiet, a duty Press Secretary may be disturbed at home several times during the night with calls from Australia or America re-routed through the Palace. Being roused from a deep sleep to answer a question about what facilities will be given to the Princess of Wales to breast feed her child during an overseas tour — as happened to one person in the Press Office — calls for an ability to return to full consciousness very rapidly. "Say the first thing that comes into your head and you are likely to find yourself quoted by newspapers and radio around the world by the morning."

The normal working day at the Palace begins at nine — though the chief residents have already been up for over an hour. The Queen, who gets up at about a quarter to eight, will have read letters from friends, their envelopes specially initialled to distinguish them from all other mail delivered to the Palace, and probably made a start on the more difficult of the two *Daily Telegraph* crosswords. Over breakfast she may have listened to B.B.C. Radio's 'Today' programme and had a telephone conversation with Lord Porchester, her racing manager.

One floor below, the various members of the Household will be arriving at their offices, after driving or training-in from Wimbledon, Pimlico, or walking from St. James', round the corner almost, where some of them have grace-and-favour homes.

Michael Shea and his colleagues will have read all the morning newspapers before arriving at their offices. They will have tuned into radio and breakfast television for an updating on world events and briefed themselves on speeches made in either of the Houses of Parliament during a late-night sitting. Quite apart from any follow-up enquiries from Fleet Street, they can be quite certain that the Queen will be conversant with the latest major political happenings around the world.

Among the first tasks each morning is the preparation of a Press Summary for the Queen's personal benefit. This comprises a sheet of paper marked off into columns, one for each of the eight national dailies. (The communist *Morning Star* does not figure.) The top half of the page tells the number of paragraphs in each paper given over to reporting official Royal engagements of the previous day, plus "other major news items", such as "Prince Charles has hired Argentinian born horseman to look after polo ponies." The bottom half of the page rules off in parallel the eight papers and gives the number of the page containing a story about the Royal Family: SUN. 7 — p (picture) "The Princess of Wales nearly gets a parking ticket/ shopping for birthday card." It comes as no surprise that the list starts with *The Times,* continues with the *Daily Telegraph* and finishes with the *Daily Star.* The Queen doesn't read all the papers every day from cover to cover — she literally hasn't the time — and she doesn't read the gossip. What is likely to be of particular interest to her is the kind of space and treatment given by the provincial Press to an out-of-London visit by herself or another member of the Royal Family the previous day. The success or otherwise of such a visit is gauged to a large extent by local Press reaction.

A major part of the job of the Press Secretry to the Queen is to act as a filter, working in both directions, between senior members of the Royal Family and the media. Sometimes the Queen is as interested in the Press, and the sort of thing it's getting up to, as the Press is in knowing what's going on behind the scenes at Buckingham Palace. A blatant instance, which we will examine more closely later, was the story in the *Sunday Mirror* alleging a middle-of-the-night rendezvous between Lady Diana and Prince Charles, before their engagement, on the Royal train in a railway siding. It was one of the few occasions when, to quote one Court official, the Queen "blew her top".

In common with most of her family, the Queen regards the media as having a vital role to play in the presentation of the monarchy to people in Britain and around the world. And despite the invented stories that appear in newspapers from time to time — some of which are so ludicrous they make her laugh — she probably has more faith in the Press as a whole than some of her closest advisers would appear to have. Or perhaps it is that she and Prince Charles rely on the ultra-cautiousness and, on occasion, slight sniffiness towards the Press of some senior members of the Royal Household to ward off examination and access considered too close.

Shea and his colleagues have direct access to members of the Royal Family, but their Private Secretaries are in closer daily contact and do not always see the necessity for the Press to be kept fully informed about some things that may seem to be of legitimate public interest. Shea enjoys a close and friendly working relationship with Sir Philip Moore and the Hon. Edward Adeane, Private Secretaries to the Queen and Prince Charles respectively, but in the past it has been known for relationships between others to be strained to the point where communication was confined to the writing of crisp memos. Perhaps sensibly, perhaps not, an attitude of deep suspicion, even of dismissiveness, towards a large part of the Press obtains among a few of the Queen's advisers. It is engendered, one suspects, not so much by personal animosity towards individuals, (most national newspapers editors are, after all, made very welcome guests at Palace parties), but by an inbuilt desire, common among the senior ranks of the medical and legal professions as well, to remain as private and anonymous as possible.

At times one is almost forced to the conclusion that these people would really prefer that all reporting on the activities of the Royal Family was confined to the few lines handed out each day from the Palace in the Court Circular and printed under the Royal Coat of Arms in *The Times* and the *Daily Telegraph*. In today's world that could never be — people are too hungry for information of all kinds, and information about the Royal Family, colourful and personal, as well as straight reporting of public appearances, has helped give it greater popularity than it has ever known. As things are, Michael Shea and the Queen's two Assistant Press Secretaries, Vic Chapman and John Haslam, act not only as filters but also as buffers between Palace and Press. "I have extremely good relations with editors," says Shea. "I'm unpopular with a small number of photographers and a couple of journalists. At times they'd love to be criticising the Family, but can't. So they kick me as the spokesman." In the twenty-two years since Harold Nicolson, the official biographer of King George V, described the job of public relations officer to Buckingham Palace as "a nightmare task", times have changed. But apparently not all that much. As it is, by far the largest part of the work of the Press Office is concerned with the day-to-day mechanics of arranging facilities for the media and issuing accreditation passes.

One of the least requested pieces of written information available from the Palace Press Office is the one headed: "History of the Office of Press Secretary to the Sovereign". It happens to be among the more interesting.

"The Office of Court Circular, or Court Newsman," it reads, "began during the reign of King George III. The King, being much annoyed at the inaccuracies in the papers as to the Royal movements, took the advice of the chief Metropolitan Magistrate, and appointed a Court Newsman. His duty was to distribute daily to the morning papers a document supplied from the Court, and called the 'Court Circular'".

The annual salary of the Court Newsman in 1866 was £45, debited against the Lord Chamberlain's department. No record of the Court Newsman's duties has been found earlier than 1899 when it was his job to attend personally at Buckingham Palace daily, afternoon and evening, when Queen Victoria was in London, and once a day, Sundays included, when Her Majesty was away from London. He was to attend at Windsor Castle whenever summoned by the Master of the Household. And "after levees and Drawing Rooms, he was given the invitation cards for the purpose of making lists to deliver at the offices of various newspapers".

These tedious tasks cannot have been valued very highly at the Palace for in 1909 the salary of the Court Newsman was reduced to £20 per annum, though he was allowed to sell information, "on his own responsibility", to newspapers.

Between the world wars, up to 1931, the Palace employed its first full-time Press Secretary, but then the post was abolished altogether until 1944 when Captain Sir Lewis Ritchie, K.C.V.O., R.N. took on the job for three years. After him came the redoubtable Commander Sir Richard Colville, K.C.V.O., C.B., D.S.C., R.N. who served King George V and Queen Elizabeth II until his retirement in 1968, and who became a legend both in Fleet Street and at the Palace.

Colville, an old Harrovian, had no training in public relations. Indeed he did not see his job in that light at all. He told a Canadian journalist who, somewhat naively, asked to be shown round Buckingham Palace: "I am *not* what you North Americans would call a public relations officer." Andrew Duncan, in his book *Reality of Monarchy,* wrote that "Colville seemed to think most other people, particularly the Press, were tradesmen." This was perhaps being a little harsh on him for, in part at least, Commander Colville (who died in 1975) was probably reflecting the wishes of the young Queen at the time — the fifties and early nineteen sixties. Her very strong desire then was to preserve her privacy, even to the detriment of her popularity in the country. Colville distrusted the media, and fed them the minimum of information. "My job is for the most part to keep stories about the Queen out of the Press," he once said.

It was just as well then, for the media, the Royal Family and the public as well, that Colville's successor as Press Secretary was someone of a totally different nature, background, and outlook.

Bill Heseltine (Sir William Heseltine as he has since become) is an Australian schoolmaster's son from Fremantle. He had been attached to the Royal Household in 1960 on a temporary basis as an Assistant Press Secretary, working directly to Colville. He had come to the post highly recommended by the enthusiastic monarchist Prime Minister of Australia, Sir Robert Menzies, whose Private Secretary he had been for four years between 1955 – 59. Heseltine returned to Canberra after two years of tasting Court life to become Acting Official Secretary to the Governor-General, and when he was asked back to the Palace, on Colville's retirement, he returned ambitious with refreshing ideas of his own. Fortunately most of them coincided with those of the Queen, and of the Duke of Edinburgh. Heseltine didn't deliberately set out to be different from Colville, he just *was* different, and had different running orders from the Queen and Prince Philip from those Sir Richard had been given.

Basically, the difference lay in a reappraisal of what the monarch's role should be in the "swinging sixties". In essence it was to be one of communication. Communication with her subjects, in Britain and throughout the Commonwealth. This was to be achieved through the media and, more important, through personal contact where possible. His own initial contact with individual members of the Royal Family had made Heseltine aware of the simple fact that the Queen actually laughed — that she was really quite a cheerful person. It was not the image the public had of her at that time. And Prince Philip was neither the boor nor the frustrated womaniser the gossip columns sometimes hinted he was. Every single member of the Royal Family was a much more substantial character than he or she appeared to the Press and, Heseltine bravely argued, if people could learn what they were really like they'd write more accurately about them. In other words, though he didn't actually say this, it would be harder for the Press to make up stories about members of the Royal Family.

Having already decided herself that it was time for *some* change, the Queen went along with Heseltine's ideas, though somewhat hesitantly at first. She gave two informal, off the record, press receptions at the Palace – similar get-togethers had been staged for several years on Royal tours overseas. She allowed her eldest son, who was still at university, to be interviewed on radio by Jack de Manio, a friend of Prince Charles' equerry and future Private Secretary, David Checketts. There was never any question of the Queen herself giving an interview – but she did finally agree to taking the greatest risk of all, from a public relations point of view and allowed film cameras to follow her and her family around for practically a whole year. As it turned out, the resultant film, *Royal Family,* shown umpteen times both on B.B.C., I.T.V., and throughout the world, was an astonishing success – though, as its producer, Richard Cawston, relates in a later chapter, it so nearly might have been an almost complete failure.

There is no doubt that Bill Heseltine, with the strong and necessary backing of Prince Philip and Lord Mountbatten among others, managed to unlock and swing open the exceedingly solid gates guarding the Royal Family's isolation to allow the public a glimpse of a real flesh-and-blood family doing an important job of work. The gates remained open for a time. But in the last few years, some would argue, they have been gradually closing once more. Or if not closing, barricades have been erected across the opening – as they have been in so many other areas of public domain – so that the contact is only superficially close.

One of the younger members of the Royal Household, viewing *Royal Family* for the first time only recently, remarked on the degree of co-operation given. "Today you wouldn't be allowed to do half the things that were allowed in that film," he said. Perhaps not. Perhaps the Queen feels there is no longer the necessity – as there was in 1969 when the film was made – to show the Royal Family 'warts and all'. (Cynics would claim not a blemish, let alone a wart, was shown.) Perhaps a Royal Wedding and a Royal Tour with a baby Prince has obviated that need.

After five years as Press Secretary, Bill Heseltine was elevated to the post of Assistant Private Secretary to the Queen, and when the present Private Secretary, Sir Philip Moore, retires in the not too distant future it is Sir William who is strongly tipped to succeed him.

After Bill Heseltine came Robin Ludlow, a surprising choice in that he was the first bona fide Pressman (albeit on the sales management and promotion side) to be appointed to the position of Press Secretary since 1918. He came from the *Economist* and, according to an interview given some seven years after he left the Palace, "I saw myself as a newspaperman and so had no fear of the media."

His role, he believed, was not only that of adviser to the Queen on all matters relating to the Press "but I also saw myself as the representative of the Press within the Palace". A mole within the organisation! The very concept would have been enough to give the Palace administrators palpitations. Of course, Ludlow was in no sense a mole. He genuinely thought it would be a good idea to have someone close to the Queen who had personal experience of working in the Press and who could channel his views to the highest level.

Perhaps he did not go about things in quite the right way. (The only difference between Palace politics and ordinary office politics, joked one of the Household, is that at the Palace the knives are solid silver.) After only thirteen months in the job, Ludlow resigned and went back into the world of full-time public relations. Afterwards he admitted that friction had existed between himself and other Palace administrators. "We had disagreements, and I resigned." he said, quickly adding that there were no ill-feelings upon his departure on either side.

Such is the confidence and trust required of those in positions of great responsibility at Buckingham Palace that sometimes vacancies are filled by relatives of the previous occupants of the post. But even when there are no family or long service connections, the Queen and her advisers prefer to scout out potential recruits long before any approach, formal or informal, is made. It is possible for a person to be under friendly surveillance for several months without his or her being aware of the fact. In other cases the person may be in almost daily contact with Court circles and be on first-name terms with senior Members of Household.

Ronald Allison, for instance, had been the B.B.C.'s Court Correspondent for four years (as well as being a sports reporter and commentator) when he was approached to take over from Ludlow as the Queen's Press Secretary. He did the job excellently for five years, before leaving to set up his own public relations company and eventually to become Head of Sport and Outside Broadcasts at Thames Television. He was in overall charge of I.T.V.'s coverage of the Royal Wedding and still does the occasional piece of royal commentary, when his invaluable experience allows him to slip in asides such as "Unless things have altered, which I very much doubt, what is probably going on inside the Palace at this very moment is ..."

Michael Shea was writing fiction long before he followed Ron Allison to the Palace. His first book, 'Sonntag', was published in

1971. It was followed by such titles as 'The Dollar Covenant', 'A Long Time Sleeping', and 'The Master Players'. All of them thrillers, and all written under the pseudonym of Michael Sinclair. Shea, cautious by nature and training, was extremely anxious not be thought by anyone to be using his position to enhance his writing career. Thus the editor of a woman's magazine who was prepared to pay more than she might otherwise have done for a series of Shea short stories was more than a little put out when he insisted they should appear under the by-line of Sinclair and no mention be made of the fact that the author was Press Secretary to the Queen! Since then the Foreign Office has relaxed its conventions. Shea's latest novel, 'Tomorrow's Men', published in Autumn 1982, came out under his own name. Now Shea is pushing ahead with an ambitious plan for a television series, and works of non-fiction to follow on his books about Britain's off-shore islands and maritime England.

As in the upper reaches of the Civil Service, few senior people leave Buckingham Palace without the prospect of lucrative or prestigious offers to come − a couple of directorships at least. But as a professional writer Shea knows he must rely mainly on the power of his own invention. Not that he is near retirement age. At 45 he has some way to go in what is still his main career, that of a Foreign Office diplomat.

In the past the normal term of office for a Press Secretary has been about five years. The assumption that the Queen personally wishes Shea to stay on beyond this time (he actually completed five years in May 1983) is evidence of the very high regard she has for him.

For his part, the job seems to fit Shea like a kid glove. At times he positively purrs, and his respect for the Crown and its representatives can at times be almost overwhelming.

Some eight years ago, when he held the position of Deputy Director-General, British Information Services in New York, Shea was asked to join the party accompanying the Prince of Wales on a tour of the United States. He was to give support to one of the Queen's Assistant Press Secretaries at that time, a personable young Australian named John Dauth, who was acting as Press Secretary to Prince Charles.

In an exhausting cross-country tour of ten cities in eleven days the Royal party had reached Atlantic City, Georgia, and after some problems (half-expected) about Press access to the State Governor's house had run into some unfriendliness (most unexpected) at, of all places, the headquarters of the English Speaking Union. A group of reporters was having an altercation with a very large, black sergeant of police who was barring the way up a hill to the building where the Prince of Wales was taking afternoon tea with some Anglophiles.

John Dauth, ever fleet, came pounding down the hill to see if he could sort matters out. He was soon joined by his colleague from the British Information Services. After listening courteously to the policeman, Dauth said he would take the responsibility on himself. The reporters *could* go up to the house. But the sergeant still said they could not, and addressed himself quite aggressively to Mr Dauth, who is not a tall man. Finally, Michael Shea drew himself up to his quite respectable height and inquired of the policeman: "You *do* realise who you're talking to, don't you? Mr Dauth is the Assistant Press Secretary to the Queen." The sergeant appeared neither impressed nor unimpressed. He merely continued staring down at Mr Dauth. "All I knows," he said in his rich southern accent, "is that I's a gentleman, and I just hopes I's talking to a gentleman." Dauth appeared lost for words. But he got his way in the end. The reporters went to the top of the hill.

Only a matter of months later, Shea was summoned to Buckingham Palace and confirmed in the position of Press Secretary to the Queen, with John Dauth as one of his Assistants. There was no connection between the two events, though the fact that Shea had experience of being on two Royal tours (he accompanied the Queen's party on her tour of America in 1976) must have stood in his favour when being considered for the post. Also, presumably, the fact that he had done his National Service in the Intelligence Corps, worked in the Cabinet Office and served as Head of Chancery in Bucharest. A little surprisingly, perhaps, for one who has a reputation of never missing the salient parts of a pre-briefing, the Queen was apparently unaware that Shea had been educated at Gordonstoun when she interviewed him as a candidate for the job of Press Secretary. But at the luncheon afterwards, when he was introduced to members of the Royal Family, Prince Charles remarked on the fact. Others heard him call across to Shea — "We'll outnumber the Old Etonians yet!"

John Dauth worked in compatible harness with Michael Shea until 1981, sharing with him and the other members of the Press Office the work that evolved after the Queen's Silver Jubilee Year of 1977, and dealing with the continuous stream of rumours and speculations about the Prince of Wales' matrimonial prospects. The Queen personally asked him to stay on beyond his allotted time and he finally went back to his native Australia to take up a senior post in the Department of Foreign Affairs. (He is now stationed in Iran.) He returned briefly to London in 1981 to attend the Royal Wedding as one of the Prince of Wales' personal guests.

By custom, one of the two Assistant Press Secretaries is usually a diplomat assigned from a Commonwealth country, normally on a two years' posting and invariably with little or no experience of dealing with the media and even less knowledge of how the Palace bureaucracy operates. In the past, one or two of these men have found the experience daunting, frustrating, and at times very nearly unbearable, despite the privileges and prestige offered by the job.

Sometimes, one suspects, the governments that accede to the call from the Queen's Private Secretary (Press Secretaries come into his bailiwick) to detach one of their diplomats for service to the Queen at her Palace in London, are not entirely acquainted with the special requirements needed of a candidate. It is, to be fair, a request that comes only once every six years or so, for, again by custom, Australia, New Zealand and Canada take it in turn to supply a candidate. (A Ghanain held the post temporarily, for two months, in 1959, and then there was a move much more recently, backed by Prince Charles, for another black person to take up the position, but in the end this came to nothing.)

The present incumbent, Vic Chapman, appointed in August 1982, is married with two children from his wife's previous marriage, but his three predecessors were all single men, making their way up the diplomatic ladder in their own countries. Not all of them found it easy to adapt to a different kind of job where, as one of them put it, "you spend a great deal of your time trying to reply to questions from the media to which you just don't know the answers, and almost as much chivvying photographers into a fixed position at an outside event like some commissionaire at a cinema". The person who said this would be the first to agree that there is much more to the job than *that*, but unquestionably a posting to Buckingham Palace does not always turn out to be quite so glamorous as envious friends back home imagined it would be.

There are many compensations, however, and privileges others would give their eye-teeth to be granted. The Queen and the Duke of Edinburgh for instance, go out of their way to make these Commonwealth visitors feel welcome. Usually they take up their appointment in September, and, in the week or two before this, the Queen personally invites each newcomer to join her and the Duke on the Royal Yacht 'Britannia' for the traditional cruise between the Western Isles of Scotland on the way to Balmoral for the Royal Family holiday.

Again, when she hears that a member of her Household has been ill or generally under the weather, the Queen will drop the person a note, and occasionally invite him for lunch in her private apartments.

Until a few years ago, the Queen's Press Secretary and the Assistant Press Secretaries were rarely quoted by name in the newspapers. Any response to a journalist's question was attributed to "a Buckingham Palace spokesman". This anonymity protected individuals and also meant that, if the Press Secretary himself was not available, others in the Press Office could answer on his behalf.

Then, as relationships between Palace and Press became slightly less cautious on both sides and a sort of camaraderie developed, newspapers began quoting Palace officials by name. At first there were mild protests from the Palace, but gradually the practice became almost acceptable and Press Secretaries did not seem to mind too much seeing their names in print, even though it led to John Dauth being nicknamed Dauth the Mouth in an unfriendly gossip column, and Warwick Hutchings, the mild mannered New Zealander who succeeded him, being described by one newspaper as "an arrogant Antipodean".

There were drawbacks to being identifiable. In April 1982, the Toronto Star, one of Canada's largest newspapers, claimed that Michael Shea, in conversation with their reporter Lynda Hurst, had responded to her observation about the Queen sometimes looking po-faced with: "Oh, you mean her piggy-face?" The exchange allegedly took place late in the evening at a banquet given by the Queen in Ottawa in celebration of Canada's Constitution, and within a short time the story had sprung across the Atlantic to appear in *The Sun* under the headline: HER MISS PIGGY FACE LOOK. *Palace in tizzy over shock name given to the Queen;* alongside was a large very unflattering picture of the Queen. The *Daily Mirror,* the day before, had come out with a front page story under the headline: "The curious case of Miss Piggyface, the Queen and her Press Secretary". Alongside was a picture of "Miss Piggy", the famous fat lady in the television show "The Muppets", wearing a tiara, and below a picture of the Queen, also wearing a tiara.

Asked to comment on the report at the time Shea told the *Mirror:* "I'm sorry, it was late at night, and I can't quite remember." He went on to say, as quoted: "I am told the phrase is an expression that is used in the family about the Queen. I don't want to deny that. But to the best of my knowledge I didn't mention it to Miss Hurst." (Later he was to deny ever using the phrase at all − "it is just not in my vocabulary, and nobody in the Royal Family uses it either. What's more, the meal did not take place 'late at night' but at five in the afternoon!") But *The Sun,* never one of Shea's favourite newspapers, presumably felt it could not let him off the hook. It ran a leader suggesting he ought to be given the sack.

"Did you know the Queen has a nickname? It's Miss Piggy Face! For this information we are obliged to, of all people, Mr. Michael Shea, the Queen's own Press Secretary and a prize muppet in his own right. His job is to protect the image of the Queen. On this showing, he ought to be given a right royal redundancy notice . . . Like Queen Victoria, the Queen is entitled to say: 'We are not amused'. More likely, knowing her good nature, she will shrug off the incident as just one of those things. But an office boy who gave that kind of cheek to the boss would be out through the door fast. So it's a fair

question: Does Buckingham Palace really need Mr. Shea?"

Evidently the answer was a decisive 'Yes'.

A day or so later, the Princess of Wales popped her head round Michael Shea's office door. She was carrying a large toy Miss Piggy, which had been handed to her on a walkabout by a child admirer. "I think you should have this," the Princess said, with that delightful smile of hers. Miss Piggy was placed on the mantelpiece to the side of Shea's desk where she still lolls today. A constant reminder that Press Secretaries as well as Press reporters can sometimes find themselves in a lot of hot water . . .

3. PRIVACY – THE ROYAL INSISTENCE

"The thought occurs to me that one of the most inconvenient developments since the days of my boyhood has been the disappearance of privacy."
The Duke of Windsor, 'A King's Story'

"A Subject and a Sovereign are clean different things"
King Charles I

"Weren't any of the editors, journalists and TV producers who so intrude on his privacy ever themselves 22?"
Sir John Junor, Editor-in-Chief of the Sunday Express, commenting on reports of Prince Andrew's holiday in Antigua in the company of actress Koo Stark

"I wish you would go away," said the Queen. Her remonstration – in January 1981 – was directed towards a cold cluster of photographers and reporters hanging about on the perimeter of Sandringham House, the Queen's private estate in Norfolk. It was a rare occurrence for the Queen actually to speak to journalists, except on properly pre-arranged occasions, and the small group looked slightly sheepish and drew back. A moment or two later, after the Queen had passed by, they conferred with one another to make sure they would be quoting the Sovereign correctly, and more importantly in unison, then dispersed to 'phone in their stories.

In this way another skirmish in the long and seemingly endless battle between Fleet Street and the Royal Family over areas of privacy was duly recorded.

Part of the reason for the Queen's anger was the fact that she was leading a pony, astride which was her three-year-old grandson, Peter. The clicking of cameras and general commotion might easily have startled the animal. But the Queen was also angry − had been for some days − because of what seemed an over-abundance of photographers in the near vicinity of one of her private houses during the five week New Year holiday. This is a time when, by tradition, the Royal Family escapes from public duties and is supposed to be able to relax beyond the range of long focus lenses.

During August 1982 when Pressmen 'staked out' Balmoral − to use the description the Royal Family itself uses − Prince Charles was photographed on a number of occasions. Once, stretched out on a river bank, wearing fishing gear and reading a paperback − "Most Secret War" by R.V. Jones. On the same day he was photographed unawares kissing his aunt, Princess Margaret, on the cheek at the door of a timber lodge on the Balmoral estate. A few days earlier Nanny Barnes had been spotted, and photographed, wheeling a pram containing the baby Prince William: even though he was not visible. And *Paris Match* ran a picture of the Princess of Wales hiding in a hut and anxiously peeping over the parapet of a window apparently to see whether the coast was clear.

Such incidents, which she regards as indefensible intrusions into privacy, infuriate the Queen. At the same time, she has always been loath to take action to prevent them. She told her eldest son during a recent summer holiday that he was "silly" going to the same places time and again when photographers with long range lenses lay in wait. She lightly rebuked him for being "so predictable". But though he has a fairly strong aversion to being snapped unawares, Prince Charles has an even stronger dislike of having his movements dictated by photographers and reporters. He feels, with justification, that he has every right to go where he pleases on private family land on a private family holiday. The Queen, along with other members of her family, shares this attitude. At Sandringham, with advance notice of where photographers are lurking, she refuses to enter and leave by a different gate each time merely in order to avoid them. Why should she?

It might be thought that with 20,000 acres of land surrounding Sandringham, and miles of hill, woodland and heather encircling Balmoral, that there would be plenty of space for the Royal Family to escape the attentions of the Press without surrendering more than a fraction of freedom. However, two of the main problems about maintaining seclusion at both Royal homes concern two of the Queen's highways. At Balmoral a public road runs for a good distance alongside the River Dee, parallel almost all the way with a stretch of water where Prince Charles particularly likes to fish. And at Sandringham the stables happen to be outside the perimeter of the main estate and are approached by crossing a public road.

Reporters and photographers dashing about in cars, or waiting for hours in freezing rain, are careful to stay on public land, and not to trespass. But sometimes even this precaution is not enough protection from Royal wrath. Four days into 1981, at the conclusion of a pheasant shoot at Sandringham, Prince Charles left the Queen's side to approach a group of photographers, warmly wrapped up against the weather. "May I take this opportunity to wish you all a Happy New Year," he said. Something about his expression made them pause. "And," the Prince added, "your editors a particularly nasty one." As he turned, his gun-dog at his heels, and strolled back to rejoin the rest of the shooting party, one or two of the photographers stretched smiles and shouted after him cheerily: "A Happy New Year to you, Sir." (Photographers who 'follow the Royals' tend to think that Prince Charles rather likes them and would probably be disappointed, or disbelieving, to learn that this is not always the case. They for their part rarely hold him in anything but chummy regard.)

Earlier in the same week, a lady from *The Sun* had reported that a royal shooting party, which included Prince Charles and Prince Philip in its number, had fired a shotgun and pellets had struck her car. *The Observer* headlined a story the following Sunday: "Royal Family's fury at the siege of Sandringham" and quoted a Buckingham Palace spokesman as saying: "The Queen is finding the intrusion quite intolerable and is more than a little angry over the behaviour . . . It seems that some Fleet Street editors now think the Queen is fair game even when she has no official engagements." When the matter of the reporter's car being peppered with shot was raised *The Observer* was told: "People who were close at hand were given plenty of warning."

The next day *The Sun* came out with a leader as strong as a dreadnought leaving port, slow at first, but gathering speed:

"The Queen is said to be angry about the unusually large number of photographers outside the Royal Estate at Sandringham.

It is reported to be spoiling her Christmas holiday, which is due to last five weeks.

The Sun − along with the rest of Fleet Street, no doubt − is sorry if she is upset.

Nobody wants to ruin the Queen's well-earned holiday . . .

The Monarch is now held in higher esteem than ever − thanks partly to the major reporting role played by the popular press.

But the unfortunate − and we believe, temporary − breakdown of good relations has hardly been helped by Mr Michael Shea, Press Secretary (or should it be anti-Press Secretary?) to the Queen.

His 'contribution' has been to leak to the posh papers the information that the Queen is being hounded.

This he knows to be pure fiction.

The claim by 'a Palace spokesman' (no doubt the same Mr Shea) that the Queen is now considered 'fair game' by Fleet Street, even when on a private holiday, is misleading and mischievous.

The press is not there to persecute her.

Its natural and legitimate goal is to photograph the lady who may be the next Queen of England."

In that final sentence was the nub of the whole affair. "The next Queen of England" at the time was Lady Diana Spencer, still some six weeks away from the official announcement of her engagement to the Prince of Wales. It was she and not the Queen or Prince Charles that the journalists were trying to get a glimpse of. And in the case of those papers that might have thought 'staking out' Sandringham was demeaning, their journalists could claim that they had been sent there to report on harassment of the Monarch and not to add to the harassment themselves. (Newspapers have always been adept at justifying their actions.)

The age-old grumbling war between Palace and Press over what is private and what is of legitimate public interest (even though private) is reminiscent of a suburban row about a boundary fence. It is never likely to be settled to everyone's satisfaction.

In recent times, it is the Princess of Wales and her baby son who have attracted the attentions of a world Press hungry − on behalf of its readers it would claim − for any morsel of information or picture, no matter how out of focus. But the story of the Queen's reign these last 30 years contains several instances of what could legitimately be termed intrusion. Subjection to the long focus lens is nothing new. What is more, the Queen has not always shown tolerance towards those who offend. In 1964 she drew the attention of the Press Council − Fleet Street's self-appointed watchdog − to pictures published in the *Sunday Express* "taken surreptitiously and when the subjects were obviously unaware of the presence of photographers". The pictures were shot in the grounds of Sunninghill Park, near Windsor, where the Queen and Princess Margaret liked to go for picnics and Princess Margaret enjoyed water-skiing. The letter to the Press Council, couched in the words of the Queen's Press Secretary at the time, also took exception to the presence of two photographers on another day who were discovered by a forester "hidden in the undergrowth lying on the ground with their cameras trained on the hut where Her Royal Highness was changing her clothes."

"These two persons were escorted off the private property and were therefore prevented from taking any pictures." All this happened, it should be remembered, almost twenty years ago.

A much greater furore blew up some four years later, in October 1968, when *Paris Match* published several pages of pictures showing the Queen sitting up in bed holding her newly born youngest son, Prince Edward, in her arms. Their publication caused many an "Oh, la, la'' among readers of the French magazine, but the Queen, after the initial shock, was intrigued, more than anything, to discover just how the photographs had ended up where they had.

Prince Edward had been born in the Belgian Suite, on the ground floor of Buckingham Palace, on March 10 1964. The pictures had been taken soon after, some by Prince Philip and some by Princess Anne, using one of the Queen's cameras. They were really rather good. But how had they arrived in the offices of *Paris Match* all of four years later? (The Queen learned about their publication as she travelled back to London in the Royal train after her summer holiday at Balmoral.)

Initially, suspicion fell on the relative of a well loved Royal servant who had recently died. Possibly this was why the statement issued by the Palace in response to Press enquiries was exceedingly restrained: "Since the pictures are of such a personal kind, the Queen would naturally prefer that they had not been published. For that reason, we are unable to approve their future publication.'' It was hoped that this mild warning would be enough to prevent the pictures being printed in Britain at least. It wasn't. The *Daily Express,* which had a tie-up with *Paris Match,* decided to publish. The other papers held up their editorials, if not their inky hands, in horror at this; even though, unbeknown to most people, only a day or so earlier, one of the papers had made an unsuccessful bid to buy the pictures itself. The Press Council began an investigation into "the circumstances surrounding their publication'' and as 'Insight'-type teams began stirring the muddy waters even more, the *Daily Express* went to the extent of buying a full page of advertising space in *The Times* to demonstrate to the world its clear conscience. The advertisement pointed out that, short of 'lifting' the pictures by photographing the pages of *Paris Match* or photographing earlier editions of the *Express,* the other newspapers were helpless. "'Holier than thou' *could* be termed 'sour grapes''' sniffed the advertisement in its last line.

One or two continental magazines did copy the pages and refuse to pay a fee, believing the pictures to be stolen in the first place. But no-one, including the Queen, yet had an answer to the original question: Who had filched the family pictures taken privately of the Queen sitting up in bed in Buckingham Palace?

It was some time before the story − and even then not the whole story − was pieced together in Andrew Duncan's highly readable *The Reality of Monarchy.* Apparently the practice at the time was for the Royal Family to send their rolls of exposed film to a well-known camera shop in London for processing, usually in the safe-keeping of a detective who stationed himself outside the dark room while the photos were developed. Once he had been handed a sealed packet of prints he returned to the Palace and delivered them to their owners, who no doubt inspected them with the same mixture of admiration and disappointment as anyone else who takes 'snaps'.

Some were placed in albums, others discarded or shoved out of sight in *bureaux.* For some reason, it had never occurred to anyone that copies could have been taken, or that anyone would stoop so low as to do such a thing – until a stack some three inches high of pictures taken over a period of years appeared at the London office of a man who had 'got them from a friend who was acting for someone else'. The final courier was a mild mannered man from a suburban semi-detached who was whisked over to Paris, and, in a small cafe near the Gare du Nord, paid nearly £5000 for his pile of rather ordinary pictures, some of which were to appear in Australia, Canada, the American magazine *Life,* as well as throughout Europe.

An interesting aspect of the whole affair is the fact that no-one at the Palace lodged a complaint with the Press Council about the publication in Britain of pictures of the Queen and the baby Prince Edward. And in the end the Press Council found itself rejecting the complaints that were made by five people, all men, including a Squadron Leader Carling from Letchworth in Hertfordshire; a Mr R.T. Henderson, of Blairston Cottage, Alloway, Ayr; and, interestingly, a Mr John Morehen of 24a The Cloisters, Windsor Castle.

What gives the whole episode added interest after so many years is speculation as to whether Buckingham Palace reaction would be the same today as it was then. If some of the pictures that Prince Charles and his close relatives have taken of his wife and son were somehow to land up on the desk of a Fleet Street or television news editor, what would happen? Would the editor publish and risk being damned, especially if he knew the pictures were about to be, or had already been, published abroad? Would he surreptitiously seek permission to publish by sending the pictures round to the Palace for identification? (This is what the editor of the *Daily Express* did with the pictures of baby Prince Edward.) Would he immediately inform the police, without first ensuring he retained copies of the pictures? Would Buckingham Palace refrain from lodging any complaint with the Press Council, merely issuing a statement instead to the effect that the Prince and Princess would have preferred the pictures were not published? The reply to each and all of these questions would surely be, to use a favourite response of Palace Officials: ''The likelihood of any of that happening is not very high.''

The nearest parallel to the Prince Edward incident was the publication in Germany of extracts from some of the essays Prince Charles had written while a 16-year-old pupil at Gordounstoun. The exercise book containing essays had evidently been pinched by a fellow pupil from a pile on a form-master's desk and sold for £7.00 to an ex-pupil who had 'upped' the price to £100 when he resold them to a Scottish journalist. They were eventually bought by *Der Stern* for £1000 and published under the misleading headline "The Confessions of Prince Charles". Mostly they were well thought out comments on a variety of well-worn topics, the kind of thing done by intelligent teenagers in any school. In one of them Charles argued the case for a free press, something he has done repeatedly as an adult. He wrote that a free press was essential in democratic society "to protect people from the Government in many ways, to let them know what is going on – perhaps behind their backs".

However, he did not mean to infer approval of intrusion into private lives – anybody's private life – without very good reason indeed.

The Press Council, an august but almost toothless watchdog, takes up its position in all matters of privacy – "whether that of Royal Persons or of commoners" – from its Declaration of Principle dated April 1976.

The Declaration begins firmly enough: "The Press Council exists primarily to protect the freedom of the Press, the maintenance of which in our democratic society has never been more important than now."

However, in a subsequent clause, the Council declares avowed support for a policy "which accords with the practice of responsible journalists."

Thus:

"The publication of information about the private lives or concerns of individuals without their consent is only acceptable if there is a legitimate public interest overriding the right of privacy."

It is that sentence which starts up the arguments in Fleet Street. As if in anticipation, the Declaration points out: "'Of interest to the public' is not synonymous with 'in the public interest'." Equally it might be said, 'of interest to the public' sells newspapers and magazines whereas 'in the public interest' sometimes smacks of axe-grinding or even propaganda.

Prince Andrew's decision, against Buckingham Palace advice, to board a plane for a holiday in Antigua accompanied by an actress who had appeared in soft-porn films, was definitely of interest to the public. (Whether it was in the long term best interests of Prince Andrew is another matter.) The relentless pursuit by the media of the Princess of Wales before her engagement, on the other hand, could be argued to have been in the public interest, though by no means everyone would agree. Mrs Shand Kydd, Diana's mother, wrote to *The Times:* "Fanciful speculation, if it is in good taste, is one thing, but this can be very embarrassing. Lies are quite another matter and, by their very nature, hurtful and inexcusable."

Mrs Shand Kydd's protest came soon after a report in the *Sunday Mirror* of two late-night rendezvous between the Prince of Wales and Lady Diana, as she was then, on board the Royal train "as it stood in secluded sidings in Wiltshire." (The Queen demanded a retraction of this 'totally false story'. But none was given.) A few days later, after she had been quoted as saying "I'd like to marry soon," Lady Diana was in tears as she denied ever having made such a comment. And Mrs Shand Kydd, in her letter to *The Times,* asked the editors of Fleet Street "whether, in the execution of their jobs, they consider it necessary or fair to harass my daughter daily, from dawn until well after dusk? Is it fair to ask any human being, regardless of circumstances, to be treated in this way? The freedom of the press was granted by law, by public demand, for very good reasons. But when these privileges are abused, can the press command any respect, or expect to be shown any respect?"

Fleet Street's response to such criticisms usually takes the form of self-defence. If Lady Diana Spencer was to become a future Queen of Britain, and the signs were increasingly that she was, then the public had a right to learn as much about her as possible. (This is never much of a defence against downright lies.)

Buckingham Palace pleads, in the case of Prince Andrews's girl-friends as well as Princess Diana before her engagement, that there is not much it can do in the way of protection unless or until the person actually comes under the wing, so to speak, of a member of the Royal Family. A model, who was thought to be a girlfriend of Prince Andrew but wasn't, 'phoned up the Palace in great distress to say she was being besieged in her flat by newspapermen. She was told that unfortunately there was very little the Palace could do in the way of practical help.

Prince Charles, well before Diana came on the scene, was aware of the problems of what it was like to be a working girl who danced with the Prince of Wales, or even just stood near his car at a polo match. "I can cope with this sort of Press attention and I'm protected by an organisation and staff. But the girls concerned are not, and it's very difficult if they have a job." Just one of the methods he used (a technique adopted since by his younger brothers) was to arrive at a party with one girl, or in a group, while the girl he was really interested in was already safely inside mingling with other guests.

In the case of the young lady who ultimately was to become his wife, Prince Charles took extra care that they were never seen together − or, at least, never seen together through the lens of a camera. His own family, like most families, were happy to watch the relationship grow at its own pace and in its own way. On a walk before lunch at Balmoral, for instance, Prince Philip and Prince

Edward, shotguns crooked in their arms, would lead the way, followed by Charles and Diana, with a Private Secretary, a police officer, and possibly one or two house guests a few paces behind. Without anything being said, Philip and Edward might move ahead to search out something to shoot, while Charles and Diana would take the opportunity to strike out at a tangent over the heather, leaving the rest of the party to continue its perambulation and conversation in quiet unconcern.

It was really only when Lady Diana was back at her flat in London and working at the kindergarten in Pimlico that she came under the full blast of Fleet Street's attention. And on the whole, to start with at least, she did not seem to mind too much. Perhaps it was the novelty, perhaps her own inexperience in the ways of the Press. Certainly she was taken aback when she saw what happens when photographed against the light — "I don't want to be remembered for not wearing a petticoat!" (The famous photograph, taken outside the kindergarten in Pimlico, showed very clearly the outline of her legs under her thin skirt.) But she was friendly, she was fun. Amost overnight, pictures of her on television and in the papers endeared the nineteen-year-old Lady Diana to a worldwide public — not unimportant, if you are to be Queen. Even one or two reporters and television technicians covering the story of the Royal Romance went home at the end of a very long day's work dizzy with fatigue and in a whirl of fantasy. The Prince of Wales was a very lucky man indeed if this was the girl he was going to marry.

However, once the excitement of the engagement was over the beginning of a change in attitude was detectable. Lady Diana no longer seemed to enjoy, or be very willing to put up with having lenses poked in her direction. At least that was the conclusion drawn by some photographers. Perhaps they failed to appreciate fully that relationships were almost bound to change once Lady Di — the name, to this day, many of them use — became engaged and moved into the restrictive world of Royalty. Perhaps she, in turn, was not prepared to face the inescapable fact that the world's press would be *more* interested in her, not *less,* as the day of the Royal Wedding approached. Whatever the reason, a close friend of the Royal Family agrees: "It did seem as if she withstood the pressure rather better in the days before she was affianced than afterwards."

No-one could fault the way in which Diana carried out public engagements. Indeed, reporters were loudest in their praise. They paid Lady Diana, by their standards, the highest compliments possible, comparing her friendliness to a crowd with that of Queen Elizabeth the Queen Mother, and her elegance and charm with that of Princess Alexandra. But because she showed such composure they may have momentarily forgotten that she was still only nineteen, and not trained since childhood to the rôle she was about to undertake. The Royal Wedding – surely the most gloriously happy event to take place in Britain for decades – put all thought aside of any mild reassessment of her personality.

Later, after it became known that the Princess of Wales was pregnant, concern grew within the Palace about the strain being placed on her by media attention. Even before this, however, there had been indications of the Princess's true feelings.

It was Prince Charles himself who proposed that accredited photographers and television news cameras should be invited to Balmoral one day in September 1981 – not long after the honeymoon voyage in 'Britannia' – so that they should have an opportunity to take pictures, in controlled circumstances, of a very happy couple. It was an opportunity that Fleet Street had been hoping – indeed, asking – for. The resultant pictures of the Prince and Princess, both wearing tartan and both looking deliriously happy, were published and televised in practically every country in the world and brought great pleasure to millions. Even the Princess's slightly barbed rejoinder to Pressmen who had presented her with a bouquet of flowers – "Thank you very much. I suppose these will go down on your expenses" – was taken as a joke in the spirit of the happy occasion. But what Fleet Street never discovered was that the original timing of the photo-session had been put back by twenty four hours in order that Prince Charles could talk the proposal over with his wife and be assured of *her* agreement.

The photo-call achieved its purpose. It was the kind of deal Fleet Street had often maintained it wanted from the Palace: a short, pre-arranged photo-call in exchange for an unwritten promise to call off the royal watchers. And it worked. The Prince and Princess were left alone to enjoy the rest of their holiday unmolested by prying eyes. To be sure, Diana wasn't always enamoured by the amount of time her husband spent thigh-deep in river-water casting after salmon, and it has been said that her new relatives' preoccupation with dogs – wet Labrador and waddling Corgi – drove her almost to distraction at times. But these were the kind of conflicting priorities that either partner in a new marriage has to adjust to.

What, in the coming months, the Princess found much harder to tolerate, was 'The Return of the Press' – like so many scalp-hunting Red Indians rising up on the skyline in an old John Wayne western. Apparently she had felt prepared for the attention that she knew she would receive during the few months leading up to her wedding. According to friends, however, she was convinced that once she and the Prince of Wales had flown back from Egypt at the conclusion of their honeymoon cruise, Press and public interest would quickly wane. The fact is that it did not, and she found this hard to take.

In October, together with Prince Charles, she undertook her first major tour. Three days in Wales in icy-cold, blustery wet weather. She wore all the wrong clothes for the climate, but all the right clothes for a Princess. She was a stunning success both with public and Press. Everyone commented on her smile and her stamina, but what nobody — including herself — fully realised was the extent to which her enthusiasm and desire to please had drained her strength.

She returned to Buckingham Palace physically and mentally exhausted, and those responsible for arranging her programme of public events realised they would have to be careful not to place such heavy burdens on her in future. Though she was much younger than several other members of the Royal Family, she almost totally lacked their experience of appearing in public for hours, sometimes almost days, on end.

Just over a month after their return from Wales — on November 5 — Buckingham Palace announced that the Prince and Princess of Wales were expecting their first child in the following June. The news, not totally unexpected, had Fleet Street and foreign picture editors drumming their fingers on their desk tops (an excitable lot, on the whole, picture editors) as they worked out where and how they could get pictures of the pregnant Princess. Public interest, which had never really died down, had now increased considerably. But opportunities for satisfying people's curiosity were not great.

In the late summer of 1981, Charles and Diana moved into Highgrove, their Gloucestershire country home which the Prince had purchased the year before and in which he had camped out for many a weekend while workmen tried to renovate the house and make it fit for a bride.

Despite the drawback of living in a house which was, perhaps, too small to accommodate a family and a staff, and the even greater disadvantage of its being too visible from public road and footpath, Prince Charles was extremely contented in his early days at Highgrove. Friends remarked on how much more relaxed, more self-confident even, he became when he was there compared with when he was staying at Buckingham Palace, or even Balmoral which has always been a favourite home for him. At Highgrove he showed the pride common to all first-time houseowners, and when he was joined by his bride his joy was seen to be complete.

As far as the Princess of Wales was concerned, however, there was one large ugly black cloud on the horizon. The Press. Long focus lenses, operated from hundreds of yards away, picked her out as she stood on the terrace. Wide-angle lenses snatched pictures of her when she called at the paper shop in the local town. She was *not* going to have her life ruined by photographers. She was *not* going to change her lifestyle completely just because she had married the Heir to the

Throne.

Practically everyone, including those who bought the newspapers that published the pictures, sympathised with Princess Diana. "Leave the poor girl alone," was the expression used by many well wishers as, incongruously, they avidly read the latest titbits of news.

No-one realised better than members of the Royal Family, the Queen and Prince Charles in particular, how vital it was that Princess Diana's new life should not get off to a bad start. Her relations with the media must not be allowed to reach permanent impairment. Yet matters were already in danger of getting seriously out of hand.

At the customary informal daily meetings inside Buckingham Palace between the various heads of departments the problem was talked over, as usual, in moderate terms while coffee cups were slowly stirred. At the same time a feeling of apprehension was unmistakable. It was quite clear to Michael Shea that both the Queen and Prince Charles expected something to be done. No complaint was made specifically by the Princess of Wales herself, but her feelings were well known. The problem was, as it so often is, how do you tell the media what to do − or in this case what not to do − without appearing to impinge on a jealously guarded freedom? No-one at the Palace has ever been so unwise as to try to lay down strict rules on how a newspaper should relate Royal news to its readers, or seek to obliterate public interest in the Royal Family's activities. But there are times when feelings are made plain, and proposals are put forward for consideration. The Palace always takes care not to insist, only to explain. It invites, it doesn't summon. In truth, it's actually quite wary of Fleet Street, despite the impression it sometimes manages to convey to Pressmen of being flintingly superior or almost unassailable.

Although the wisdom of appointing a diplomat to the post of Press Secretary had been questioned by some of Fleet Street's old hands, it was now that Shea's Foreign Office training would come to the fore, along with his experience in Public Relations in New York where he had learned the maxim that a PR man doesn't attempt to call the tune until he is fairly sure he can make people dance to it. He had tried unsuccessfully, by dint of 'phone calls and carefully selected luncheon dates, to persuade editors to reduce at least the amount of attention they were paying the Princess of Wales, to give her a chance to have a modicum of privacy. Now he intended to suggest taking a stronger course of action, one which had not been employed at the Palace for 24 years.

The proposal that Michael Shea placed before the Queen in the last week of November 1981 was that he should invite the editors of all Britain's national newspapers, along with those in charge of BBC and ITV news services, to a meeting at Buckingham Palace.

The purpose of the meeting would be to make clear to everyone the Queen's increasing concern at the impact the activities of photographers was having on the Princess of Wales. The hope was that a forum for frank and open discussion would result in a decision by editors to desist from such activities for at least a decent interval.

When Fleet Street's editors had last been invited to the Palace *en masse* it was to be told – almost threatened – that if they continued to print a seemingly endless stream of stories, many of them trivial and unfounded, about the Prince of Wales' first term at Cheam preparatory school, then the Queen would be forced to take her young son away from boarding school and have him educated privately by tutors – something she would have been most loath to do. Furthermore, her Press Secretary of the time made it clear that if Her Majesty were to be forced to take such action then the blame would lie firmly at the door of the Press. Soberly, the editors went away to reconsider and, having considered, left the boy Prince more or less alone for the rest of his four years at Cheam.

However, since that time – the 1950s – some Fleet Street newspapers had become more cavalier in their attitude to the Royal Family. Shea could not be confident of a successful outcome of his meeting, or even sure that his invitation would be readily accepted by one and all. After all, the Princess of Wales was twenty, not eleven as her husband had been. She was beautiful and she was more newsworthy. The public, and not only the photographers, grabbed every opportunity of seeing a new picture of her.

The Queen, who is not usually one to ponder long before making up her mind, gave her Press Secretary the go-ahead. The meeting was to be arranged if possible for the second week in December. Shea ventured another proposal. Though he didn't intend to inform the editors beforehand, would Her Majesty be agreeable to their joining her for refreshments after the meeting? He thought an informal chat over gins and tonics might greatly contribute to a successful outcome. The Queen said she would be happy to meet the editors, especially if it would help. Thus it was, shortly before mid-day on December 8 1981, that the editors of Britain's national daily and Sunday newspapers, with a combined readership approaching 40 million, began arriving at the Palace. Also there were David Chipp, Editor-in-Chief of the Press Association, David Nicholas, Editor of Independent Television News, and Peter Woon, Head of BBC news.

Michael Shea had taken the wise precaution of sounding out his idea for a meeting with one or two specific editors before approaching the others. Disparity of view exists between editors as well as between newspapers. It is not always a simple matter to shepherd them into the same pen. Experts in the field of public relations – an area that most of Fleet Street regards with extreme caution – will tell you from experience that if the editors of the liberal minded *Observer* and the more conservative *Sunday Express* agree to attend a conference then the editors of the other Sunday papers are likely to come too. Similarly, if you can engage the *Daily Mail's* interest then the curiosity of the *Daily Express* and the *Daily Mirror* will be aroused. The *Guardian* is not so likely to be influenced by what other papers are doing, and may easily decide it is beneath its dignity to do the same anyway. *The Sun,* the tabloid with the largest circulation of any newspaper in Britain, is likely to make up its own mind.

In this case only *The Sun* was not represented. Michael Shea heard it said that its editor, Kelvin MacKenzie, did not wish to be on first-name terms with the Press Secretary to the Queen. He did not know if this was true – he still does not know for Mr MacKenzie declines to discuss the Palace meeting – but Shea was led to understand that in any case the editor of *The Sun* had a pre-arranged meeting with his proprietor, Rupert Murdoch, on December 8 and so would be unable to accept an invitation to the Palace.

The meeting went ahead anyway, without Mr MacKenzie, in the 1844 Room, on the garden side of the building. The Queen's Press Secretary in welcoming his distinguished visitors explained the reason behind the invitation – on the 'phone each had been asked to the Palace merely "to discuss an unspecified problem", though most guessed what it was. Shea pointed out there was considerable anxiety among those who loved and cared for the Princess of Wales about the pressure of a constant surveillance of her private life by photographers. She had coped splendidly with her public duties, said Mr Shea; and she had survived very well in the run-up to the engagement to the Prince of Wales when the Palace had not been able to provide any protection; but there was concern that her present feeling of beleaguerment would permanently affect her attitude and that of her husband when they were playing an even more important role in the life of the country.

The editors sitting around the table listened attentively. Harold Evans, then the editor of *The Times,* pulled out a notebook the moment Shea started speaking and took down his words in a highly professional rate of shorthand. The bright young Christopher Ward, then editor of the *Daily Express,* thinking the briefing was off the record sat with his hands on the table "trying to look as if I wasn't secretly tape-recording". When someone asked if the meeting was on or off the record Shea said he left it to the editors to decide, though he was obviously relying on some discretion.

It was also made clear that there was no suggestion whatsoever of any sort of edict being issued by the Queen or anyone else. The purpose of the meeting was solely to make clear the concern felt. The Princess herself had not requested the meeting. She was happy with the pictures that had been published. But undoubtedly the strain of being constantly under scrutiny, in her private life as well as while carrying out public duties, was causing excessive strain on a woman of twenty who was expecting her first child. "I was particularly keen," says Shea, "to stress that the Princess of Wales would be around longer than anyone sitting at the table, and it would be a great pity if her future attitude towards the media were to be conditioned by the recent behaviour of certain sections of the Press."

David Nicholas, editor of Independent Television News, was not alone in thinking that the Queen's Press Secretary handled the meeting most skilfully. "He made it clear that he was not tub-thumping but was saying, in effect, 'I have a problem and I wish to share it to see if something can't be worked out.' It seemed to me exactly the right approach, and he got on the whole a reasonable response."

Christopher Ward thought the unspoken fear underlying Shea's words was that as a result of the Press interest which had deteriorated into harassment, the Princess might even lose her baby. "Looking back — I've got three children and a young wife — I don't believe there was anyone in that room who was a husband or a father who didn't have some sympathy for Diana at that particular time. It had got to the stage where interest in her had got out of all proportion to editorial worth."

The only moment of potential discord came when the then editor of the *News of the World,* Barry Askew, suggested that what Michael Shea might really be saying was that the Princess of Wales was about to have a nervous breakdown, and would break down if the Press didn't cease its attentions. Shea replied that he had not suggested anything of the sort. In fact, it was exactly that kind of speculation that he didn't wish to arouse. The Princess was in perfect health. Sir John Junor, Editor-in-Chief of the *Sunday Express,* a doyen of Fleet Street who has not always found favour with the Royal Family during his distinguished career, rounded on Askew like a galleon turning into the wind. He maintained that no-one could doubt what Mr Shea was saying. He was talking about privacy and only privacy. He was not talking about the mental state of the Princess of Wales. The meeting ended with no demands being made and no decisions taken.

Mr Askew — who won the prestigious Journalist of the Year Award in 1971 but was subsequently celebrated as 'the beast of Bouverie Street' by the magazine *Private Eye* after he became editor of the *News of the World* in 1981 — joined the other editors in walking through to the adjacent room. There, as Michael Shea had been pleased to announce only a minute earlier, the Queen was waiting to greet them. (An added attraction was the arrival of Prince

Andrew, whom Shea hadn't known was coming.)

Footmen circulated with huge silver trays covered with sparkling glasses of refreshment – whisky and soda, dry and medium-dry sherry, orange juice, tomato juice, gin and tonic – all in the large proportions for which Buckingham Palace hospitality is famous.

Christopher Ward was introduced to Prince Andrew. "I say, are you the youngest editor in Fleet Street?" Mr Ward glanced around the room and guessed, at thirty-nine, that he probably was. "Jolly good. Keep it up." said the Prince, and bounded out of the room and out of sight down a corridor.*

Meanwhile the Queen engaged in lively conversation with the editors of her country's national newspapers, some of which she had enjoyed reading almost since childhood, and some of which she hardly ever saw but abhorred for the things their gossip writers sometimes wrote. She afforded everyone the opportunity of informal, easy conversation without making it apparent where her preferences lay. She had met quite a few of the editors before, either through official tours of their offices or television studios, or when they had been among the guests at the small informal luncheons given regularly by the Queen and Prince Philip at the Palace. (A cause of some surprise to the Queen's Press Secretary, when the leaders of Fleet Street arrived for the meeting, was that a number apparently did not know one another, except by name and reputation. Shea found himself making introductions.)

The Queen agreed with her Press Secretary beforehand that she would not bring up the subject of media treatment of the Princess of Wales unless it was raised by the editors themselves. In this way, presumably, it could not be said afterwards that the Queen herself had introduced it as a topic for discussion. However it was not long before one or two editors tested the temperature of the water. They found it to be bearable, for the moment. The Queen's views on the subject of Press coverage of her daughter-in-law's activities were clearly those expounded by her Press Secretary earlier. She was seeking understanding and hoping that common sense would prevail. And she added a personal touch by recalling the months when she was pregnant with her first child. She pointed out that in addition to being married fairly recently, having to carry out public engagements and grow accustomed to a new lifestyle – not to mention morning sickness – Diana would much prefer that she did not also have to contend with photographers peeping into her private life. "Desist" was the Queen's desire, but coming from the monarch it must have

---

* Mr Ward was ousted from the editorial chair at the *Daily Express* sixteen months later, in April 1983, and replaced by Sir Larry Lamb, former editor of *The Sun*.

seemed very like a command.

Barry Askew considered the Queen discussed the subject "with disarming frankness." However he was less happy with the way some of his Fleet Street colleagues later reported a dialogue that took place between himself and the Sovereign.

Askew has recalled his own "deeply respectful" conversation with the Queen, in which he began by saying he believed the British Monarchy to be not only one of the few remaining but the most popular in the world, one for which he personally had the deepest respect.

The Queen expressed her thanks to the editor of the *News of the World* (as Askew was at the time) for saying so.

"But the popularity, Ma'am," Askew continued, "depends on the exposure of the monarchy to the people with whom it is so popular, and the media clearly have a crucial role to play in letting the people see the Royal Family."

The Queen affirmed and thanked Mr Askew once more.

Then, according to Askew's very clear memory of the conversation, he referred to Michael Shea's earlier complaint to the editors that the Princess of Wales was even pursued by photographers when she went to the village shop in Tetbury, near Highgrove, to buy wine gums.

Mr Askew: "Would it not be better to send a servant to the shop for Princess Diana's sweets?"

Her Majesty: "Mr Askew, that was a most pompous remark."

Laughter from those within earshot. A smile from the Queen. More or less end of conversation, as Askew recalls. If any single word offended the Queen, he was to tell the media magazine *Campaign* later, it was the word 'servant'. But with a sense of grievance approximating to that of a biter bit, he contested the accuracy of one paper which said he had "insulted" the Queen, and another which maintained that she had reproved him. Less than a month later he was removed from the editorship of the *News of the World* by the paper's proprietor, Rupert Murdoch – though Askew is certain the sacking had nothing to do with his comments at the Palace. "I've had dialogues with Murdoch throughout the height of the publicity surrounding the Princess," he told Julian Allitt of *Campaign,* "and he has made remarks indicating that he is not an uncritical supporter of royalty."

Askew was stoutly defended by Paul Johnson in the *Spectator:* "Let me deplore the snobbish jeers which came from some other Fleet Street editors and their sycophantic claques when Barry Askew of the *New of the World* was rebuked by the Queen for being 'pompous'.

"Askew, I suspect, was much more in touch with his readers'

thoughts than the others . . . Askew was merely asking the question most of his readers would have liked to ask if they had been there, and there is no better definition of a popular journalist than that.''

Askew received a "warm letter of thanks" from Michael Shea for his attendance at the Palace — as did all the other editors — and Shea in turn received "warm" letters from the editors. The *Daily Mirror,* in its comment column, said it thought Buckingham Palace's request to Britain's editors to ease the strain on the Princess of Wales — "who is suffering from her own popularity" — was " a fair request at this time and the *Daily Mirror* will respect it.'' To the *Daily Telegraph* it seemed "a wholly reasonable request" — though "it is never easy to determine where the line between legitimate public interest (and so the attentions of our profession) and vulgar, hurtful intrusion is transgressed." Peter McKay in the *Daily Express* wrote: "Now that the Queen has made known her feelings it would be a foolhardy editor indeed who ignored her request." And the editor of the *Express*'s sister paper, the *Daily Star* told *The Times* that "we will be taking a very hard look at any pictures supplied to us in the future. We must take notice of what the Palace has said." This was perhaps the most honest and realistic reaction of all to the highly unusual meeting of editors, for where is the editor worth his salt — and his circulation — who, sight unseen, can give a firm promise about what his reaction will be to an item of news?

In fact, the Palace did have grounds for optimism. After they returned to their respective offices, several editors conferred once more — this time on the 'phone — and reached a consensus that not only would they instruct their staff to 'lay off' Princess Diana but if presented with pictures taken by freelance photographers which they considered intrusive they would decline to buy them. Having agreed, they could all sleep easy. As one editor said: "There's this competitive thing in Fleet Street whereby it doesn't matter if you miss a story so long as no-one else has got it.''

In the meantime, Michael Shea was well pleased with Fleet Street's response to his meeting. So, too, was the Queen. Christmas and the New Year passed quietly at Sandringham.

The truce lasted precisely seventy-two days.

There then occurred what many people still regard as the greatest intrusion into Royal privacy of all time, while others feel it was a fairly harmless happening with repercussions out of all proportion to its importance.

The sequence of events — or exposures, for that is what they were — that led to the subsequent uproar in Palace, Press and Parliament came to be known simply as 'The Bikini Pictures'.

The story of how these pictures came to be taken has never been fully told — partly because at the time one of the reporters involved was forbidden by his editor to talk to the *Sunday Times* Insight team. But the tale should be told. Partly, because in any examination of Palace-Press relations it has its place. Partly, because it demonstrates that a royal reporter's life is by no means always an easy one. And partly, because — well, because it just happens to be rather a good story . . .

4. THE BIKINI PICTURES

"We all do have some measure of morbid or prurient curiosity about the lives of others. But this does not mean that we respect those who purvey such information any more than those who use prostitutes necessarily respect the ladies of whose services they avail themselves."
Lord Shawcross, 'The Press and the People' 1975

"The real culprits are the public, the *hypocrites lecteurs,* who first enjoy the pictures and then denounce them enjoyably."
Honor Tracy, Daily Telegraph columnist, February 1982

"It is better to be looked over than to be overlooked."
Attributed to Mae West

James Whitaker stands 5' 10½" tall, and weighs in at 14½ stone. He has the chubby cheeks of a cherub and the disarming smile of a child who knows he's been naughty but will probably get away with it. In dress he favours grey flannels and a blue blazer with four brass buttons on each cuff – as does Prince Charles, though the Prince has five buttons, with crests.

Whitaker's attitude to the Royal Family is not unlike that of a large proportion of the British public; that is to say he is almost passionately loyal to the idea of monarchy and at the same time incurably curious about what individual members of the Royal Family get up to in their spare time. In Whitaker's case the curiosity is of a professional nature and probably nets him something well over £30,000 a year. His favourite without doubt is the Princess of Wales. He used regularly to send her bouquets of red roses but ever since her engagement to Prince Charles, the chase over, he feels a lot of the fun has gone out of 'royal watching'. Nevertheless he did attend the Royal Wedding, though not as a personal guest of the bride or bridegroom, wearing morning dress and a grey topper, and, as always, carrying a pair of binoculars — the better to see details. If he didn't do what he does, Whitaker could easily get a job as an extra in the Ascot scene of My Fair Lady. Despite what some members of Buckingham Palace Press Office are occasionally wont to say about him, he is not such a bad fellow.

Harry Arnold is also a cheerful chap. Whereas James Whitaker is fairly tall, Harry is short and dapper, with a resemblance to a London taxi-driver.

James was born in October 1940. Harry is a year younger. He dresses nattily, often in brown suits, brown shoes, cream shirt and brown striped tie. He wears a gold ring on a finger of each hand, and spectacles that go brownish-grey in strong sunlight. He, too, is a loyal supporter of the Monarchy, while at the same time being politically left of centre. He remembers being taken to London as a boy to watch the funeral procession of Queen Mary, and proudly receiving his monogrammed coronation mug and spoon as an 11-year-old schoolboy in 1953.

James can go one better. In 1971 he accompanied his late father — at that time chairman and managing director of Sperry U.K. and Europe — to Buckingham Palace to watch the Queen invest him with the Order of M.B.E.

Harry and James, Arnold and Whitaker. These then were the men — their names put together sounding like a respectable firm of solicitors in an English market town — who, in February 1982, set out for the Bahamas on Mission Impossible: to discover and photograph the Prince and Princess of Wales on their private holiday; and who, just three days later, returned to have calumny heaped about their ears like a sackful of coal because of the fuzzy pictures published by their respective editors, in The Sun and the Daily Star (as well as in other papers and magazines around the world) of a pregnant Princess in a red bikini.

According to James Whitaker, had the Palace shown more co-operation earlier, the journey to the Bahamas could have been rendered unnecessary and the pictures need never have been taken. With hindsight — that which makes newspapermen rheumy-eyed — and in one respect at least, he now wishes he had never left home.

Harry Arnold feels more or less the same, but expresses no remorse. "I would not be shocked if someone photographed my wife when she was pregnant. Even if she was wearing a bikini. It would be a memento of a stage in your child's life that was very important between you."

Following the meeting of the Fleet Street editors at the Palace in December it seemed that a truce had been all but signed. The Queen and her family, including the "beleaguered" Princess of Wales could depart for Windsor for Christmas and then to Sandringham, or in

Charles and Diana's case, Highgrove, safe in the knowledge that they would be left in peace to enjoy their winter holiday. The reporters and photographers, who presumably also like to be with their families for Christmas — they have a much shorter break than the 'royals' have — could move on afterwards to other tasks and stories. The editors had, more or less, given their word.

However, since the Royal Wedding and before, pictures of the Royal Family, and of the Princess of Wales especially, had become like a drug both to Fleet Street and, to a less measurable extent, to newspaper readers. Deprived of their "fix" for any appreciable length of time, they became twitchy. It also needs to be said that the period immediately after Christmas does not usually produce an abundance of news stories. Information, however brief, about how Charles and Diana were spending their time would have been welcome on Fleet Street news desks, particularly if there were pictures to go with the words.

As part of his job, James Whitaker was in regular touch with Michael Shea at Buckingham Palace, asking if there was any possibility of a photo-call at either Sandringham or Highgrove where the Prince and Princess of Wales could pose for a number of invited photographers for a limited amount of time — probably no longer than fifteen minutes. This arrangement had worked very well at Balmoral the previous autumn when Charles and Diana had invited photographers to take their pictures, in a well controlled situation, mainly as recompense for the hard times the Press had had chasing them, most unsuccessfully, during their honeymoon. The pictures taken at Balmoral had been reproduced in newspapers and magazines around the world and had cheered up many a breakfast table. But it was perhaps too much to ask for a similar facility to be granted again so soon. Whitaker recalls Michael Shea saying he was working on the possibility of a photo-call — it did, after all, depend on the wishes of the Prince and Princess themselves — but he was making no promises.

Some time in January, Whitaker discovered from an undercover contact at Heathrow airport that Charles and Diana would be flying to the Bahamas for an away-from-it-all holiday in the sun. They would be leaving at the beginning of February. He even learned the flight number and the seat allocations. However this newsworthy snippet did not appear in his paper. Instead, some days later, the readers of *The Sun,* courtesy of Harry Arnold (and to the annoyance of James Whitaker) were entertained with the news that the Royal couple were flying to the Caribbean.

Once the news was out, Fleet Street editors had to decide whether or not to put teams of photographers and reporters on the story. For the majority the decision was quickly made. The Prince and Princess were going on a private holiday. The Princess was almost five months pregnant. The Palace had made a request, which was repeated, to leave the young couple in peace. Most papers and both television news services decided independently not to cover the story.

However, Whitaker's editor was of a different mind. He informed Shea on the 'phone that he intended sending his reporter to the Bahamas. And when the Press Secretary briskly made it quite clear that if he did so there would be absolutely no co-operation forthcoming from anyone on the island the response was: "Well, in that case they'll just have to do background stories." There is some debate about whether or not *The Sun* decided to send their intrepid reporter and photographer on the remarkable assignment only after discovering that the *Star* was sending a team. (Fleet Street can be just as secretive about its internal workings as Buckingham Palace.)

Suffice it to say, on February 16 1982, two reporters and two photographers exchanged the cold of London for the baking heat of Nassau, where they changed planes for the short hop to the island of Eleuthera and a hotel with the alluring name of 'The Winding Beach Resort'. Harry Arnold was accompanied by Arthur Edwards, a staff photographer with *The Sun* and a veteran of many Royal assignments. In the past he and Whitaker had worked well together as a team when James was employed on *The Sun* for three years.* But the business of *The Sun* breaking the news of Charles and Diana's forthcoming holiday had soured relationships somewhat. James was convinced that his erstwhile friends Harry and Arthur were intent on scooping him if they could, and he was just as intent that they shouldn't. "We were still on speaking terms, but only just," he recalls. Kenneth Lennox, a Scot, was the *Star's* photographer and from the moment he and James checked into their hotel they were working out possible ways of procuring pictures of the Prince and Princess of Wales *and* − almost more difficult − getting any pictures and text back to London in a hurry.

They began at a disadvantage. Arthur Edwards had been on this sort of jaunt before and knew the lie of the land. The villa where Charles and Diana were to stay − they were due to fly in from London that evening − belonged to Lord and Lady Brabourne, the late Lord Mountbatten's son-in-law and daughter. In his bachelor days Charles had spent more than one happy holiday there. After his exhausting tour of South America in 1978 he had stopped off at the villa for a few days of recuperation. Amanda Knatchbull, Lord and Lady Brabourne's daughter, was also there on holiday, and for a

---

* Following an old Fleet Street tradition of switching employers at frequent intervals, Whitaker moved from *The Sun* to the *Daily Star* in 1978, and from there to the *Daily Mirror* in August 1982.

short while it had seemed a romance might blossosm — which would have delighted no-one more than the girl's grandfather, Lord Mountbatten. However, the relationship remained no more than a friendship. Charles had been a guest of the Brabournes in the Bahamas in 1977 and 1975, as well as in 1978, so he knew as well as Arthur Edwards what the chances were of someone snatching a picture of him and the Princess of Wales. They were slight.

The Brabourne house is not on the island of Eleuthera itself but on the adjacent much smaller island of Windermere. The two are connected at the narrowest point by a bridge and separated by a stretch of water that is about half a mile at its widest. Windermere is only about 1¼ miles long by half a mile across. Practically all the houses are holiday homes for the well-to-do, and at the height of the season the immigrant population probably numbers no more than forty. But, as might be expected, those who go there to swim, water-ski, and laze on the sandy beaches do not expect to have their privacy violated. Any visitor who turns out to be a journalist is liable to be treated very crustily, and any reporter or photographer who manages to get onto the island when a member of Britain's Royal Family is there will find his stay is likely to be extremely short. Partly for this reason, Windermere has always been regarded as an ideal holiday hideaway. Harry and James, and Arthur and Kenny (the two photographers) were under no illusion as to the task their editors had set them. The climate was warm. It might soon become very hot indeed.

Faced with a difficult if not unsurmountable problem, journalists on the whole tend to collaborate with one another rather than run the risk of being the ones that *didn't* get the story. Usually, provided they already know and trust one another sufficiently, they pool ideas and information. Only on the last lap, so to speak, might one or other make a spurt, pick up an extra tit-bit or quote, and race to the line (in their case a telephone line and the first edition of their newspaper) ahead of the opposition. On big stories, and especially on foreign territory, they often hunt as a pack. Real scoops are rare and usually fall, often by chance, to the loner.

At first James Whitaker was undecided whether to team up with Harry Arnold. Their respective papers were bitter rivals, but Arthur Edwards was the only one among the four who knew where to go in order to stand any chance of getting pictures of the Prince and Princess.

Whitaker's mind was made up for him in the end when Harry and Arthur made the surprise announcement that they were checking out of the hotel to go to another. This appeared deeply significant to James, despite Harry telling him the only reason was because they couldn't keep on their rooms at the 'Winding Beach Resort' for

64

another night. James' suspicions grew when Arthur Edwards, a genuinely generous man, pointed out a path that would lead to a photographic vantage point — a path that James subsequently discovered led directly to a police post!

So much for collaboration!

When Arthur suggested — things by now becoming distinctly edgy — that it would be better for everyone if they split up into two parties, Harry and Arthur, James and Kenny, it seemed to James at any rate that battle was about to be joined. This was to be one of those famous Fleet Street wars between rival newspapers. Not, in this case, fought out in boardrooms and involving editors, circulation managers, and cheque book journalism, but a real old fashioned duel between two gladiators as to who would first wire back to London a set of pictures of a pregnant Princess of Wales.

Looking back, possibly with the censure of the Queen still dinning in his memory, Whitaker has mixed feelings about the outcome of the day's work. But at the time, unquestionably, he regarded what he did simply as work, even work of historic importance as it turned out, and he set about his task with schoolboy enthusiasm and great attention to detail. Listening to him, the whole episode of the Bikini pictures begins to sound a bit like a Laurel and Hardy comedy — James naturally playing the role of the fatter partner — with a touch of *The Day of the Jackal* thrown in.

On their own now, and determined to out-manoeuvre their rivals, James and Kenny decided to take the risk of landing on Windermere Island to spy out the land. The risk was not as great as it would have been only a matter of a few hours later. It was just after midday when James drove their hired car across the one bridge linking Eleuthera with Windermere and the Prince and Princess of Wales were still hundreds of miles away, tucking into a meal and a glass of wine somewhere over the Atlantic. They were not due at the Brabourne's house until about 7 p.m.

At least an hour before then, however, Windermere would to all intents and purposes be sealed off from the outside world with the Bahamian police stopping all vehicles entering and leaving by the bridge and vetting the occupants. Police launches would guard the waters round the island and all hired boats would be checked to make sure they were not carrying photographers and reporters. (In addition to the men from *The Sun* and the *Star* at least twenty other newsmen had flown in to Eleuthera from America and Europe, including one man from a German group of magazines who had already done a deal with the *Star* in London to buy all their pictures.)

All this James knew or guessed. He reckoned that he and Kenny had approximately five hours to 'recce' the island and achieve their objective, which was not to spy out the house where Charles and

Diana would be staying, but to decide which of the beaches on the island they would be most likely to be using. They were prepared for a wait of several days, never dreaming they would strike lucky on the very first day of Charles and Diana's holiday.

As they drove around the island, both now changed from their London winter suits into shorts and sports shirts, they took care to appear as much like holiday-makers as possible. They used one of Kenny's expensive armoury of cameras to take seaside snaps of one another posing against rocks and under palm trees. James took a dip in the warm waters and noted the strength of the current. Kenny commented on how good the light was from a photographer's point of view, though he was a bit concerned about the heat haze at certain times of the day. That would not be good if he was shooting from a great distance away from his subjects, as both he and James assumed he would be. James saw no possibility of their being able to remain on the island, or to return once Charles and Diana were in residence. They would be turfed out and probably put on a plane back to England before Kenny had managed to shoot a single frame. The pictures, they decided, would have to be taken from a vantage point in Eleuthera, looking across the water to Windermere. It was just as well, in that case, that the beach they felt fairly certain that Charles and Diana would use was an idyllic sandy cove only a short walk from the villa where the Royal couple would be staying. It was a public beach, popular with families with children, but not overcrowded, and with a small jetty. Directly opposite, across the water, was a thin stretch of uninhabited beach, and behind it what looked thick green scrub and forest reaching down almost to the water's edge. There were no distinguishable landmarks, and no way of gauging from where James was standing how far back the scrub stretched before reaching the road.

With almost military-like foresight, James and Kenny drove from Charles and Diana's beach, as they already called it, to the bridge connecting Windermere with Eleuthera, measuring the distance on the car's mileometer down to a tenth of a mile.

Once back on Eleuthera they turned left, and measured out the same distance on the equivalent stretch of road, parallel to the one on Windermere. This brought them to a point where all that they could see was dense scrub with, they assumed, the beach somewhere on the other side of it. They returned to their hotel to make preparations for the next day.

Good lines of communication are as important to a reporter as they are to a commander in the field. There is no point in getting a story or a picture unless you have made sure beforehand that you can transmit them back to your newspaper office. So, with no time to waste, James began ringing round the airfields – he was amazed to find there were no fewer than three on the tiny island – to see if he could hire, or share the hire, of a charter to Nassau. This was the nearest point, he thought, from which any pictures could be 'wired' back to London. His suspicions were immediately roused when he discovered that a plane had already been booked for the next day in the name of Edwards. Had Arthur Edwards already stolen the march on him? Was our intrepid reporter in danger of being scooped? As it was to turn out, the Edwards who had made this particular booking was innocent of all duplicity, or knowledge, in the matter. But just to be on the safe side, James booked a place on two charter flights, one leaving at 2 p.m. and the other an hour or so before the one booked in the name of Edwards.

The next stage in the preparation was to acquire essential equipment: a compass, a duffle bag, and two plastic litre bottles to carry life-saving water. James guessed that the thick scrub separating the road from the beach would prove a formidable obstacle – just how formidable he had no way of knowing. But he reckoned, despite his weight, that he was in better physical condition than either Harry Arnold or Arthur Edwards and that he and Kenny Lennox would have superiority in stamina at least. Their plans laid, the two men retired early to their beds after only a short stop at the bar.

They were up again at 4.30 a.m. They left the hotel at 4.50. It got light – Whitaker has a sharp memory for numbers – at 5.58. They journeyed the two or three miles along the coastal road to the point where they planned to enter the thick scrub, drove the car off the road and hid it under some trees. Then, with a final glance up the road to make sure no-one had spotted them, they plunged into the tangle of spiky thorn and bush, some of which was over six feet high. Whitaker can recall only one experience more diabolical than the struggle down to the beach – the journey back!

It took two hours and twenty minutes for him and Kenny Lennox to fight their way through the almost impenetrable barrier of swamp and vegetation. When, finally, they heard first the sound of lapping waves and then stepped onto the hot sands of the narrow beach they were practically exhausted. They were also slightly out in their calculations and still had some way to walk before arriving at a position opposite Charles and Diana's beach. It would have been much more comfortable to wade the rest of the way along the edge of the sea, but they were afraid of being seen from Windermere by a patrolling policeman. So, with sweat and blood on their scratched faces, arms and legs, the two men moved back into cover and struggled onwards.

At about 7.15 a.m. James spotted two figures some way ahead. His first thought was that they were two detectives, put there by Prince Charles to prevent precisely what he and Kenny were attempting to do. But when he focused his binoculars on the two men a smile spread across his chubby face. He recognised the large bulk of Arthur Edwards and the smaller frame of his companion, the ubiquitous Harry Arnold. It took about half an hour to catch up with them. By this time they were sitting on the ground like boy scouts after a hard trek. Harry's first words to James were: "How will you have your eggs for breakfast, boiled or scrambled?"

After only a brief chat with their colleagues, who were after all still their rivals, James and Kenny pushed on, until they reached a point where they reckoned they were in an ideal position to get their pictures. Harry and Arthur caught up with them about half an hour later and pitched camp only a few yards away. Even so, the vegetation was so dense that the two camps were practically invisible to one another.

It was now about 8.10 a.m.

Among the camera equipment Kenny Lennox had brought with him was a massive 1200 metre lens which, with a 'dumper' attachment, doubled the range. This he mounted on a tripod and lashed against a tree to keep it as steady as possible.

He checked and double checked all his equipment, as all good photographers do, while James, like a sniper, trained his binoculars on the opposite shore. All they could do now was settle down and wait, and hope that something would happen.

At 9.45 a.m. their patience was rewarded. The Prince of Wales and Lord Romsey, Earl Mountbatten's grandson, suddenly appeared, wandering down on to the beach chatting to one another like the couple of mates that they were – Lord Romsey had been Charles' close friend since schooldays at Gordonstoun. Before either of them was married, Charles and Penelope, now Romsey's attractive blonde wife, had gone out together occasionally. And Charles and Diana had been guests of the Romseys at their Hampshire home, Broadlands, on the first night of their honeymoon.

A small power boat was already being warmed up. The two men took it in turn to water ski – totally oblivious of the cameras trained on them from half a mile away. The detective accompanying Prince Charles on this occasion was Inspector Colin Trimming – known to Fleet Street as 'Shoestring' – who had previously been Princess Anne's police officer. He, too, water skiied – though with much less élan than the experienced Prince Charles and Lord Romsey, who, or so it appeared to those on the other bank, were hugely enjoying the detective's discomfiture.

It was all good stuff. Kenny took several shots. But both he and James realised these were not the pictures their editors had sent them all this way to get. Perhaps they would have to fight their way through the jungle again the following morning if the Princess of Wales failed to make an appearance today. They shut their minds to the terrible prospect and kept looking out across the water to the far off beach.

Then, shortly before eleven o'clock, their patience and extreme discomfort were rewarded. The Princess of Wales, accompanied by Lady Romsey, strolled onto the beach. Like the peeping Toms they undoubtedly were, James and Kenny watched as Prince Charles drew up sun loungers for the ladies. Diana sat on the edge of one of these beach chairs, and as she did so the square of light oriental material that she was wearing over her swimsuit slipped open to reveal a red bikini. James could hardly believe his eyes. "Fantastic," a favourite word of his, was how he describes his reaction. A moment later, however, he had adjusted his attitude. He became nervous. He did not want to show Diana as being noticeably pregnant. He didn't think his readers would like her to be seen thus. It would have been better he thought, and his own presence somehow less offensive, if the Princess had been wearing a one-piece swimsuit. In such a way do the minds of some reporters work.

Meanwhile Kenny Lennox concentrated simply on shooting pictures and, a few yards away, Arthur Edwards was likewise engrossed. James had previously made an arrangement with his photographer that as soon as he had got what they both considered *the* picture, James would put all the rolls of film so far exposed into his duffle bag and set off for the airport, leaving Kenny to carry on taking pictures for as long as the Prince and Princess remained in sight.

It was by now approaching noon, and the time factor was critical if the pictures were to appear in the next morning's papers back home in Britain. It was already nearly five o'clock in the afternoon in London. Preparation of the first edition of Whitaker's paper, the *Daily Star,* would by now be well advanced. Yet another vital factor in the calculations was the fact that the charter plane to Nassau, on which James had booked a seat, was due to take off from Governor's Harbour in just over two hours.

Even as these problems of logistics were racing through his brain, James saw the Princess of Wales get up from her seat, slip off her wrap and, holding the hand of Lord Romsey, wade out into the calm sea. He thought she looked absolutely stunning. But as Kenny's camera clicked away James was terrified they would be spotted. He was quite certain they were visible from across the water if anyone thought to look carefully. But fortunately for them Prince Charles' detective had chosen to sit in a deck chair facing inland, towards the sun's rays. He appeared to be reading a paperback, but was no doubt keeping a wary eye out for intruders.

The moment the roll of film in Kenny Lennox's camera had exposed its thirty-six frames, James took it, along with three other exposed 35mm rolls, dropped them into his duffle bag, bade his colleague a hurried farewell, and struck out into the bush.

A matter of a few minutes later, Harry Arnold, discovering that his rival had gone, also collected up his belongings and along with Arthur Edwards hurriedly departed.

The race was on.

Until this day, James Whitaker is convinced he came very near to dying as he struggled through the maze of near-jungle back to the road. The temperature was over 100°, the thorns tore at his skin. At times he became almost totally disorientated. What kept him going, beside a strong determination to survive, was the knowledge that he was in possession of some of the most sensational pictures ever taken of members of the Royal Family. And if it was at all possible he was going to do his damnedest to get them back to his newspaper office before Harry Arnold's reached his.

It took James almost an hour and a half to stumble and stagger through the undergrowth. When he finally emerged on to the road he was bleeding profusely from more than a score of deep scratches on the face and hands, and his denim shirt and trousers were torn very nearly to tatters. Of greater importance was the realisation that he had little idea of where he was, and whether he should set off to the right or the left in order to find the hired car he had left hidden in the bushes. He trusted to luck, turned right and began walking. A car came from behind and flashed past. Suddenly conscious that the police might be patrolling the road and that he ran the risk of being picked up with the incriminating film on him, James stopped just long enough to hide the four rolls inside an old tyre that was lying at the edge of the road. He quickly marked the spot with two rusted Coca-Cola tins. Then, as he began walking along the road once again another car sped past. But this one stopped a few yards further on, backed up, and drew up beside him.

"James! What are you doing here?" The occupants were from a picture agency, also flown out to get pictures of Diana and Charles. In comradely spirit they happily agreed to find James' car, after he had retrieved his film. But he steadfastly declined to tell them how he had managed to get his pictures.

By the time the car dropped him off at his hotel, James had about half an hour remaining to drive on to the airport and catch his 'plane to Nassau. First, though, he had to alert his Manchester office that the pictures were coming, and also make sure that the staff at the government-owned news agency in Nassau didn't shut up shop for the day before he had had a chance to wire his pictures.

Also staying at the hotel was the London editor of a large group of German magazines who had already done the deal with the *Daily Star* to buy second rights on any material. He saved James some time by

70

telephoning the wire service. When James arrived in Nassau with his pictures the staff were standing by to transmit. Considering the storm of criticism they were to create when published the next day, there is supreme irony in the fact that it was one of Her Majesty's own government-run services that released the pictures to the world in the first place!

Whitaker had received strict instructions on the 'phone from his office to write nothing in his caption material identifying the pictures as being of the Prince and Princess of Wales. They were to be labelled as holiday snaps of Mr and Mrs Turner – the name of the paper's editor. But as they had to be wired through New York and then on to England, the secret was out within a minute of their appearing on the machines in New York. Agencies around the world clamoured to buy.

Exhausted, but elated at the success of his mission, Whitaker wrote a hundred or so glowing words to be printed in his paper alongside the pictures, and the next day sat down and wrote a short personal note to the Princess of Wales, on Windermere, saying that if he had caused her any upset he apologised profusely. He was not altogether surprised when he received no reply.

Kenneth Lennox's pictures were printed in the third edition of the *Daily Star* on Thursday, February 18 1982. Arthur Edwards' were published in the last edition of *The Sun. (The Sun* team had discovered there was a wire service from Eleuthera, after all, and sent out their pictures from there. Even so, the *Star* beat them by two editions.)

Both papers ran the pictures. The headline in *The Sun* read: 'DI-LAND IN THE SUN'; and across an inside double page spread: 'BAHAMA MAMA'. In both papers the quality of the pictures was fuzzy, because they had been taken from such a distance away, and because of being 'wired' across the Atlantic. But they were recognisable – just – as being of the Princess of Wales, and of a pregnant Princess at that.

Within a matter of hours of the pictures appearing, Michael Shea was making the Queen's displeasure known. The pictures, and presumably the taking of them, was "in the worst possible taste". "It is apparent that these pictures were taken without' the Prince and Princess being aware of what was happening," Shea told the *Guardian.* "Such tasteless behaviour is in breach of normally accepted British Press standards in respect of the privacy of individuals."

On the same day the Director of the Press Council, Kenneth Morgan, O.B.E., wrote to the editors of *The Sun* and the *Star* inviting them to justify "what appeared to be a breach of the council's declaration on privacy". A House of Commons motion was launched by Sir John Langford-Holt, the Conservative M.P. for Shrewsbury, attacking both newspapers for "falling short of the professional standards of journalism". A straw-poll taken amongst staff, secretarial and editorial, at *Woman's Own,* Britain's largest selling women's weekly, on the day the pictures appeared, demonstrated almost unanimous disapproval of their publication. The main criticism was that the pictures were of someone who was five months pregnant. However the *Guardian* printed the reaction of someone, unnamed, who it described as "a senior Fleet Street executive involved in following royalty". According to this person the Prince and Princess of Wales are showbiz personalities. "If they can be shown getting married, they can be shown picking their noses or scratching their bums. If they are swimming it looks much better than a formally posed picture of them staring from a fireplace." This was not a view shared by the majority of the British public. Their attitude was one of outrage. The *Daily Mirror* in its Comment column denounced the pictures published in two of its closest rival papers as "squalid in conception, furtive in execution and grubby in publication". It declared, somewhat loftily perhaps: "We are not in the business of taking sneak-shots of pregnant women bathing, whether they are princesses or not." But the editorial continued with an opinion that many working in the media would approve of. "There is no shortage of people, on the Right and on the Left, who would like to see the British press in shackles. Even though it is impossible to legislate against bad taste.

"Fleet Street is right to resist them. Yet each time a newspaper behaves indefensibly it weakens the press as a whole."

Such was the furore created by the Bikini pictures that – even though the great majority of the British public had not even seen them – both The Sun and the *Star* ran rueful leaders the following morning. The *Star,* while seeking to defend its conduct, explained it had acted out of "deep affection" for the Royal couple. At the same time it was ready to apologise if it had upset the Princess.

The Sun said it could see nothing wrong in the photographs which "brought a breath of summer into the lives of millions of our readers back in chilly Britain." The paper respected Charles and Diana's right to "moments of private intimacy", but it had to balance this with its readers' "legitimate interest in the Royal Family not merely as symbols but as living breathing people".

However another paper saw fit to make mention of the very considerable amounts of money obtained by selling the pictures to foreign newspapers and magazines, several of which had been bidding for an opportunity to show their readers what a pregnant Princess of Wales looked like in a bikini.

The Sun is said to have made close to £100,000 out of foreign sales of its pictures, and bidding for the *Star's* pictures, according to the *Guardian,* reached £50,000 before a ban on any sales was personally ordered by Lord Matthews, chairman of the paper's board of directors. Lloyd Turner, editor of the *Daily Star,* apparently thought that Buckingham Palace had "dramatically over-reacted" to the publication of the pictures in his paper, but Lord Matthews took a different view. Not a newspaperman himself, he had entered the hurly-burly of Fleet Street in 1977 when his company, Trafalgar House — owners of, among many things, the Cunard liner Q.E.2 — had bought up Express Newspapers. The *Star* had been launched as a direct competitor to Mr Rupert Murdoch's *Sun,* but Lord Matthews had barely disguised his own tastes where popular journalism was concerned. Indeed he had once confessed to a journalist that he wouldn't like to see copies of the *Daily Star,* with its regular pin-ups of topless models, lying about in his own house.

A further embarrassment, as far as the Bikini pictures were concerned, might have been the fact that only two years previously he had received his peerage from the Queen. What's more, just a few days prior to the pictures being published in his newspapers, he had sat next to Prince Charles at the Centenary dinner of the Press Club and had heard the distinguished guest of honour thank journalists for the respite from attention that they had given him and his wife since the meeting of editors at Buckingham Palace in December. He had listened attentively as Prince Charles expressed the wish that this 'breather' would continue for a little bit longer and smiled when Prince Charles added: "I am very glad that the old spirit of fair play still does twitch here and there in Fleet Street".

The pictures that Lord Matthews' employees, Lennox and Whitaker, endured such discomfort to obtain were locked away in a safe in the editor's office soon after a selection had been made for publication and there, to the best of my knowledge, they remain to this day.

However, what may come as a surprise, even to Lord Matthews, is that the package contains not only those pictures that James Whitaker wired back from Nassau but also, buried among the sheets of contact prints, there is a small number of pictures of a young couple making love on the sand in the cove directly adjacent to where the Prince and Princess of Wales were enjoying themselves!

Both Whitaker and Lennox had noticed this blond man and fine figure of a woman sunbathing and swimming while across the water they waited for Prince Charles and Princess Diana to appear on the adjacent beach. At first they sunbathed in their swimsuits, but eventually discarded these. Then, after Whitaker had left with his four rolls of film, his colleague could hardly help but catch sight of the couple actually making love on the sand, only yards from the

Prince and Princess. He continued to take pictures of Diana and Charles, but could not resist pausing long enough to swing his camera to the right to take two or three shots of what must have seemed a quite extraordinarily bizarre event in the circumstances.

In statements to the Press Council the editor and staff of the *Star* made the point that Charles and Diana were on a public beach. But the Press Council, roundly castigating both papers after an inquiry into the whole affair, found that "the surreptitious taking and publishing of these long range pictures of the Princess of Wales on a beach when she was five months pregnant and wearing a bikini was a gross intrusion into her personal privacy. Whether the beach was public or private is immaterial to this offence."

The Council took *The Sun* in particular to task for an editorial in which it claimed it was "deeply sorry" if it had offended by transgressing the couple's privacy, but printed the apology alongside *republication* of the offending pictures − in editions selling in areas where the pictures wouldn't have been seen the day before!

The day after the original pictures were published, the *Guardian* claimed that the reporters on *The Sun* and the *Star* were being hastily recalled from Eleuthera as a result of the furore their pictures had caused. But James Whitaker insists it was a return rather than a recall. His objective had been achieved, and there was no point in staying on. Later he was to concede that what he had done was "very intrusive". But as a newspaperman sent out to do a job he felt some pride in having played a major role in procuring "what, after all, were some pretty historic pictures of Royalty". His one slight but nagging regret continued to be that the Princess of Wales had chosen to wear a bikini on that particular day. He thought the ensuing fuss would have been far less if the pictures had shown her wearing a one-piece costume.

Harry Arnold, quoting one of his sources, claims the Prince and Princess of Wales actually laughed when they were shown the pictures in the newspapers.

Only a few days after he returned to London from the Bahamas (he received no bonus of any sort for his 'scoop' incidentally) Whitaker was sent by his paper to report on a Press reception for Elizabeth Taylor, who was about to open in London in *The Little Foxes*.

Alan Rusbridger of the *Guardian* wrote in his paper the following day: "Outside the London Palladium, and Nikons are raining on to the pavement. The crowd is ten-deep and bodyguards are leap-frogging the bonnet of a Rolls Royce.

"Inside the London Palladium, Mr James Whitaker of the *Daily Star* has dressed for the occasion. He sports a white rose in his button-hole − perhaps plucked from the Bahamian undergrowth, where he has recently crawled in search of Princess Diana.'' James beamed when he read it.

5. THE ROYAL WATCHERS – REPORTERS

"Honesty and integrity are vital factors in reporting and often get submerged in the general rush for sensationalism."
Prince Charles, addressing the Indian Institute of Technology, New Delhi, November 1980

"Editors and reporters, we're all alike in this: if the Royals are nice to us we all roll over on our backs and want our tummies rubbed."
James Whitaker

"In the provincial press, coverage as usual has been 100 per cent nice, and in the national press 95 per cent pleasant."
A Buckingham Palace spokesman commenting on the Royal year for The Guardian, December 1982

"I simply treat the Press as though they were children."
The Princess of Wales

"Without Press coverage, the Royal Family would be little more than rich overdressed people in big houses."
Suzanne Lowry, Sunday Times, January 23, 1983

On most weekday mornings, between the hours of ten and eleven, an attractive-looking young woman with thick dark hair and a rosy complexion arrives at Buckingham Palace and enters through the Privy Purse door. In her handbag she carries a laminated plastic pass from the Royal Household – even though she is not a member of the Household, or employed in any way by Buckingham Palace.

The pass, which expires in February 1985, shows her code number and her personal accreditation as No.1. It replaces a much more elaborate affair enfolded in red Morocco leather and signed by the

Queen's Press Secretary, which requested that the holder 'may be offered all the necessary facilities to enable her to perform her duties'.

Both passes are much-prized possessions for each shows its owner to be an accredited Court Correspondent. At present only five journalists hold such cards. Four of them report on Royal events for the B.B.C., Independent Television News and Independent Radio News. The fifth member of the exclusive little club is Grania Forbes, Court Correspondent of the Press Association; she who calls on the Palace between the hours of ten and eleven.

In Knightsbridge and county circles where *The Times* and the *Daily Telegraph* are perused each morning, not least for news of who has died, who has been born, and who has done neither but has decided to get married, Grania Forbes is 'that nice gal' (she was 'that chit of a girl' when she took the job) who strings together beads of information for the jewel-box known as the Court Circular. Compared with journeymen like Whitaker and Arnold, she is 'la crème-de-la-crème' – though still a journalist and therefore not *quite* to be trusted.

Grania has been the Press Association Court Correspondent since 1977, but the news agency that employs her has been going for over 100 years. Its staff of some 160 supplies a twenty-four hour service of news: photographic and feature material on all manner of items, that goes out on teleprinter machines to newspapers and radio and television stations throughout the length and breadth of Britain. The Palace has one of the machines tucked away in a corridor.

As with most titled jobs in journalism, the role of Court Correspondent has gradually altered over the years. For a long time the man holding the job (Grania was the first woman to be appointed to the post) was little more than a postman picking up official messages at the Palace and delivering them to Fleet Street. Discretion was the essential ingredient of his make-up. A reporter's nose for news was not required. Today Grania Forbes, and her editor David Chipp, work on a somewhat different principle. To them a reporter is always, first and foremost, a reporter – even if, as has happened on occasions, the priority results in conflict with the Palace.

The first Court reporter for the P.A. was a character known as George 'Royal' Smith, who doubled as registrar of births and deaths for Finchley and Friern Barnet and, who for a time at any rate, sold insurance. He held the job for 33 years, from 1894, and when he died King George V sent his widow a personally signed letter of condolence.

Perhaps the King knew of 'Royal' Smith's greatest coup which for persistence, resourcefulness and cheek would take some beating, even today.

When the Peace of Vereeningen was signed, ending the Boer War in South Africa, Smith trundled down to Windsor to pick up what he believed would be the inevitable proclamation of King Edward VII on this historical event.

However, on arriving at the Castle, he was informed, somewhat sniffily by Lord Knollys, the King's Private Secretary, that His Majesty had not prepared a statement for the nation and was, in fact, taking tea with a lady in Windsor Great Park and was unlikely to return for some time.

"I'll wait," announced the resolute Smith, throwing back his coat tails and taking a seat. The wait lasted for several hours and he passed part of the time scribbling a few paragraphs. When Lord Knollys returned at dinner time, to throw him out, Smith presented him with a draft Royal Proclamation. "Perhaps you would be good enough to submit this to His Majesty?" he said.

Knollys took the piece of paper and went away, only to return a few minutes later with it signed "Edward R.I." . . .

Though not expecting to be quite as lucky as Mr Smith on that occasion, Court Correspondents have always enjoyed a privileged position compared with others who scrabble after Royal news. In return they have been expected to be discreet, respectful, and above all respectable. The men who preceded Grania Forbes stood out among their colleagues in Fleet Street for their sartorial elegance, if for nothing else. A dark suit, a bowler hat and an umbrella were essential when calling at the Palace, even on as mundane an errand as collecting the list of forthcoming Royal engagements.

On February 6th 1952 Alan Wheatley was shown into Commander Colville's office and found the Monarch's Press Secretary studiously bent over a bound volume of *The Times*. Without even looking up Colville murmured: "By the way, the King is dead." Wheatley looked suitably startled. Evidently the news of King George VI's death had been 'phoned to the Press Association a few minutes before and put out on the teleprinter tapes, so it was ironic that he, the acting Court Correspondent, was probably the last newsman in Fleet Street to know of the King's death.

At the same time, something very similar happened to Godfrey Talbot, the first B.B.C. reporter to be issued with a warrant card as 'the British Broadcasting Corporation observer accredited to Buckingham Palace'. When he arrived at his office in Broadcasting House on Wednesday, February 6, the 'phone was ringing. He picked it up and recognised the voice of Commander Colville at the other end.

"Godfrey, *when* are you going to announce it over the air? What *is* going on?"

"Announce what?" asked Talbot.

"The King is dead. It is on the tapes, and has been for some time.

We are waiting for the B.B.C. Will you please see why your people are delaying?"

The news had indeed arrived at Broadcasting House, but apparently no-one was certain of the proper procedure to be followed by the B.B.C. − then, even more than now, the 'voice of Britain' when dealing with national calamity.

A file labelled 'Demise of Crown' was located, but it contained mostly notes of policy meetings and advice to announcers on how to act 'during grave illness of Royalty'. Meetings were hurriedly convened to formulate the words of grief, while at Buckingham Palace, officials continued drumming fingers on desk-tops to the sound of interminable dance music coming from the wireless . . .

Eventually, at 11.15 a.m., a good half hour after Fleet Street had received the news, John Snagge's voice told radio listeners: "It is with the greatest sorrow that we make the following announce-ment . . ."* And as soon as the carefully worded statement had been read out the whole of the B.B.C. went off the air, in Britain at least, apart from the news bulletins at one and six o'clock together with a special announcement that all persons were expected to wear mourning for the King.

Talbot, on his way to Buckingham Palace to find out about the new Queen's homecoming (Princess Elizabeth was on a tour of Africa when her father died) stopped off in Jermyn Street to acquire a black tie, and a new bowler hat.**

A large part of a Press Association Court Correspondent's working life consists of collecting and collating official announce-ments from Buckingham Palace. Dates of forthcoming visits and events, attendance at investitures, news of appointments and trans-fers within the Royal Household, births, deaths, and marriages. As the P.A. provides a service for the provincial as well as the national media, the Court Correspondent finds him- or herself tapping out paragraphs of little interest to the country as a whole but of great interest to a particular locality. Whereas in many cases other Fleet Street reporters will give a Royal visit a miss, the P.A. reporter very often trails in the wake of a Royal party to a northern factory, or a hospital in Devon, making sure to spell the names of the local dignitaries correctly in a report that is always factual and never gossipy.

---

* The Overseas Services of the B.B.C. were less inhibited than their colleagues up the road in Portland Place. Their announcers broke in with the news of the King's death whenever there was a gap. Indonesia was in fact the first country in the world to hear the news from the B.B.C.

** "Ten Seconds from Now" by Godfrey Talbot (Hutchinson 1973)

This regular day-to-day contact with those in Royal circles obviously has its advantages. Members of the Royal Family come to know, often to like, Court Correspondents. Indeed one of them, Ronald Allison, a journalist who coupled sports reporting with court reporting for the B.B.C. (he was known to his colleagues as Court and Sport) was eventually invited by the Queen to become her Press Secretary.

When the Princess of Wales visited a children's play group in South-East London, Grania Forbes was among the reporters hoping to find a paragraph. Also there, among the spectators, was her young son, Edward, in the charge of his nanny. Purely by chance, the Princess stopped to speak to them. The following week, covering a tour of University College Hospital and engrossed in noting names of nurses and patients, the boy's mother heard a familiar voice at her shoulder. "You've got the most super baby. It's lovely to know what he looks like," said Princess Diana.

Sometimes, when stepping out of a car or a train to face yet another sea of unknown faces, a Royal Prince or Princess is quite glad to spot a familiar face in the crowd and will make a point of having a word, if only to calm nerves all round. This friendly practice can have its disadvantages, however. Ron Bell, the Press Association's Court photographer, has missed out on some of his pictures through this kind of Royal exchange. While he has been standing erect, camera lowered, to receive the banter of Prince Philip or Prince Charles, his colleagues (and professional rivals) have been clicking merrily away.

Compared with their more freewheeling, buccaneering comrades, who, after all, are not blessed with passes requesting 'all the necessary facilities to be offered', Court Correspondents are required to be circumspect in their dealings with the Palace. It is in the nature of their job so to be. At the same time, to all but the most sycophantic, there are moments when the true reporter's insatiable appetite for news has to be curbed to a cruel degree. For while it hands out information to its favoured friends, the official source is sometimes apt to place its other hand over the reporter's mouth.

On the night the Duke of Gloucester died (he was one of King George VI's younger brothers) the Press Association's Court Correspondent at the time, Douglas Dumbrell, was rung up by a member of the Duke's Household at around seven, to be informed of the event. He was also told that the death wouldn't be announced until 9 o'clock the following morning, and Dumbrell would have to stay silent till then. No amount of persuading would alter the official's decision.

On other occasions Dumbrell was more fortunate. One evening in March 1974, he and his wife, Stella, went along to a reception being

Top left: The Princess of Wales, head lowered against the attentions of professional and amateur photographers, on the ski slopes in Austria. January 1983.

Top right: Prince Andrew, sporting buckle-belt and jeans, whose romances have received as much publicity in the last year as did those of his aunt, Princess Margaret, some 25 years ago.

Below: Photographers were invited inside Balmoral Castle to take pictures marking the Queen's Silver Jubilee 1977.

Above: The Princess of Wales faces one battery of photographers while a second waits, cameras trained, for her to turn.

Above: Proud parents show off their son, Prince William, at the start of the Royal tour of New Zealand. April 1983.
Below: Watching the traditional fly-past that follows Trooping the Colour. June 1983.

Above: The Prince and Princess of Wales with baby Prince William pose for photographers at the beginning of their 1983 Australian tour, immediately after a 30-hour flight from London to Alice Springs.
Below: Almost alone on the side of Ayers Rock in central Australia, Charles and Diana, watched from below by sightseers and Pressmen alike.

held in the City at which Princess Anne was the guest of honour. Afterwards they followed the Princess's car down Ludgate Circus and up Fleet Street, then went to Dumbrell's office for a supper snack in the canteen on the top floor. A matter of minutes later a messenger came looking for any 'off-duty' reporters. A Royal car had been shot at! Dumbrell knew that only one car from the Royal mews was out that night – the Queen and Prince Philip were in Indonesia on the last lap of a two month long tour, and none of the other members of the Royal Family had evening engagements.

Abandoning his plaice and chips, Dumbrell raced to Buckingham Palace. His accreditation pass got him past the police barriers but once inside the Palace he wandered from room to room on the ground floor without finding anyone to speak to. Thinking perhaps it would be presumptious to venture upstairs, he walked out of the Privy Purse door and went round the corner to No. 3 Buckingham Gate where – unknown to all but a few – there was a telephone in the hallway used from time to time by reporters rushing news from the Palace. In his usual calm manner he dialled 930 4832 and, put through to a voice he recognised, explained that he had been looking for someone to tell him what had happened. "Oh, we're all in Princess Anne's room, you'd better come over," said the lady at the other end. Dumbrell replaced the receiver and bustled back across the road where, a few minutes later, along with Daniel Counihan, the B.B.C.'s Court Correspondent, he was given a graphic account by Princess Anne herself of how, less than an hour earlier, a white car had swerved in front of the Royal limousine as it cruised up the Mall, within a few hundred yards of the Palace. A gunman had leapt out and tried to kidnap the Princess. In the ensuing struggle the Princess's bodyguard had been shot three times, her chauffeur and two passers-by once each, while Captain Phillips shielded his wife as the assailant grabbed hold of the Princess and tried to drag her from the car. At this point, the Princess related, police reinforcements arrived and the man ran off, but was soon apprehended.

Dumbrell marvelled at the courage of everyone concerned, especially the cool self-control of Princess Anne, and hurried off to file his interview. What intrigued him, when he had more time to think about it, was how the Press Association had received the news of the drama within minutes of it happening. Of a number of 'phone calls made to the agency, one of the tip-offs had come from the P.A. office in Belfast, Northern Ireland. It transpired the mother of one of the reporters there, on a visit to London, had witnessed the incident and had hurried to the 'phone to let her son know.

In the past, a good relationship between Court and Court Correspondent has relied almost entirely on trust – trust that the reporter won't publish, or even report back to his office, anything that the

Palace would prefer wasn't made widely known. But, as in most matters of trust, it has not always been certain that secrecy served the best interests of all concerned.

Not so long ago, a Court Correspondent was tipped off that an intruder had penetrated Buckingham Palace security and reached as far as the Grand Hall before being challenged. However, denied any enlightenment by the Press Office, he had decided not to enquire further or even pass on his suspicions to the Press Association's crime reporter. His fear was that if the story was reported, it might result in cranks making similar attempts to get inside the Palace. Now, with hindsight, he wonders if publishing an account of the incident instead might have led to a tightening up of security which could have prevented Michael Fagan reaching the Queen's bedroom in July 1982.

Even though it is still delicately poised, and still depends to a great extent on sound judgement and mutual trust, the relationship between Court and Court Correspondent is not as it was fifty or even twenty years ago when, in the words of one veteran, "as soon as you got inside Buckingham Palace you closed your eyes and closed your ears to anything you weren't supposed to see or hear."

Today's Court Correspondent is much more a Court reporter, a seeker after hard news as well as a recipient of Palace-approved items and information. The person most responsible for this gradual change – which has not met with unqualified and unanimous approval of courtiers – is David Chipp, aged 56, who has been Editor-in-Chief of the Press Association since 1969.

A doughty, stocky man with a penchant for coaching oarsmen and listening to Wagner, Chipp reviewed the post of Court Correspondent soon after he took up his appointment and reached the conclusion that if the Press Association, an independent profit-making organisation after all, were to pay a person to report exclusively on Royal matters then he or she should be something more than a conduit for official announcements.

He saw the job of Court Correspondent as being to report on all matters Royal that were of interest to the public, but to steer clear of certain areas – the private lives of members of the Royal Family, certainly – where not to do so might lead to charges of intrusion, irresponsibility and possibly result in withdrawal of facilities. David Chipp had been Reuters' correspondent in Peking during the mid-fifties and could refer to his experience there, where he'd desisted from reporting certain trends and occurrences after seeing colleagues thrown out of the country for filing stories that had ended up almost ignored by everyone except the Chinese, at the bottom of an inside page in a foreign newspaper. Better to keep quiet about one small revelation than miss out on the really big exposure.

The dilemma arises in deciding what is small, and more importantly, when a reporter is failing to carry out his job properly. Or, to couch the issue in practical terms, what if he is the only reporter, newspaper, or news agency, *not* to carry the story?

At the height of the paperchase of Lady Diana Spencer, David Chipp saw national newspapers brimming over with accounts of the Royal romance. It was not in the tradition of the Press Association to speculate or to harass, and yet the subscribers to the biggest news agency in the country had a right to be kept as well-informed as possible.

One day a reporter returned to the office with a story about meeting Lady Diana and, in response to one of his questions, hearing the headline-making quote "I'd like to marry soon". The next day, publicly in tears, Diana denied she'd ever said any such thing. But David Chipp checked with his reporter, and his notebook corroborated the story.

Lady Diana's mother, Mrs Shand Kydd, in a sharp letter to *The Times,* wondered how the Press could expect to be shown any respect when it harassed her daughter from dawn until well after dusk; and, quite separately and unofficially, Sir Philip Moore, the Queen's Private Secretary, demanded to know if David Chipp was still occupying the editorial chair "after his disgraceful behaviour". When the Editor-in-Chief asked to speak to the Queen's Private Secretary he was invited to the Palace and then verbally chastised.

Incensed at being treated like a junior subaltern, Chipp was almost on the point of telling Sir Philip that he intended to withdraw his Court Correspondent, but then tempers cooled and the friendship between the two men, which went back many years, was restored. Even so, the Palace had been left in no doubt that the Press Association was an independent – and fiercely proud – organisation, just as it had been some years earlier when David Chipp had caused a few Palace brows to furrow by intimating his intention to appoint Grania Forbes as Court Corespondent. But there had never *been* a woman Court Correspondent. There had never been a Court Correspondent so young – Grania was 26 when she was offered the job.

Reservations about the wisdom of making such an appointment receded when critics learned that her paternal grandfather was a colonel in the Coldstream Guards, and a Secretary of the Guards Club in London, and her father had gone to Eton.

Male colleagues in Fleet Street were more impressed by the fact that Grania was good at her job, fair and straight with rival reporters, and a person who didn't expect special treatment because she happened to be a woman in a predominately male profession. Seeing her in a pub, they wouldn't think twice about going over and asking her to buy them a drink.

In the six years that she has held the post of Court Correspondent, Grania has painstakingly built up a close relationship with members of the Queen's Household. And because it is her job to report on the whole Royal 'parish' and not to concentrate just on the odd scandal up at the rectory, she also has a much closer relationship with the scions of the monarch than have other reporters. She deals with the official announcements from Clarence House (Queen Elizabeth the Queen Mother), York House (the Duke and Duchess of Kent), Kensington Palace (Princess Margaret and Prince and Princess Michael of Kent) as well as making her daily call to Buckingham Palace. She has travelled on several overseas Royal tours, and has sometimes been deputed by her colleagues (they call her 'Head Girl') to convey their grievances to the Press Secretary accompanying the Royal Party.

But, even after years of careful attendance to Royal reporting, she occasionally senses she is still not entirely trusted by the Palace establishment. It only needs a newspaper to publish a story *not* approved of by the Palace − the business of the bikini pictures is an example − and the Press Association's Court Correspondent, along with every other journalist working on a Royal story at the time, finds the atmosphere suddenly turning frosty.

Official spokesmen can at times be quite extraordinarily obdurate, for reasons which are either not apparent or appear to be somewhat trifling. When Queen Elizabeth the Queen Mother was whisked from her dinner table at Windsor to an operating table in a London hospital one evening in the autumn of 1982, Grania Forbes was one of several reporters who had the greatest difficulty discovering details of what had actually happened to one of the most dearly loved members of the Royal Family.

In part this may have had to do with the fact that Press enquiries about both the Queen Mother and Princess Margaret are handled not by Buckingham Palace but by Clarence House. The official spokesman there is Major John Griffin, a charming gentleman, older than his Buckingham Palace counterparts, who works behind a very large desk in a rather small room.

As there are never any scandalous stories penned about the Queen Mother these (or any other) days, the Major rarely has much trouble from the Press. Those 'responsible' journalists who wish to write an article, or even a whole book, about the 83-year-old lady who has graced public life in pastel shades for over half a century, may be invited by Major Griffin to drop in at Clarence House − the rear entrance − for a generously poured pre-lunch gin and tonic, and a courteous conversation lasting the length of a 'top-up' in the first gin and tonic. If they are extraordinarily fortunate, the Queen Mother herself may make a brief appearance in the ground floor ante-room, entering through a door that on one side is a mirror, for she too enjoys an aperitif and a convivial discussion of current affairs. But these are gentle, civilised interludes in the day and, for the journalist, everything is off-the-record anyway. They in no way compare with the heavily guarded reaction to a hard news story, such as a sudden illness or an emergency operation.

It was on November 21, 1982, when the Queen Mother was giving a dinner party for a few friends at Royal Lodge, Windsor, her private home since the 1930s, that she was suddenly convulsed by a fit of choking, gasping for breath and unable to swallow. All immediate remedies failing, her Windsor physician, Dr John Clayton, was summoned, and after consulting with Dr John Batten, the Queen's physician, it was decided at 1.30 a.m. that Her Majesty should be taken immediately to King Edward VII Hospital for Officers in London for an urgent operation, to be performed by Mr Alan Fuller. Princess Margaret accompanied her mother to the hospital in the Queen Mother's car and remained close at hand until the operation had been successfully completed.

Drama indeed. But Fleet Street remained blissfully unaware of events until several hours later, when a carefully worded statement composed jointly by the Queen Mother's Private Secretary, her surgeon, and her Press Secretary, informed the world of the old lady's very unpleasant ordeal. "A 'foreign body' had lodged deep in the throat" of Queen Elizabeth the Queen Mother, the bulletin stated.

But what, Fleet Street was eager to know, had comprised the 'foreign body'? No-one would say. Grania Forbes, who had rushed to Clarence House for more details, plied Major Griffin with questions in between his lifting up and banging down the 'phone on his desk as call after call came through from reporters wanting to know every particular, from what the Queen Mother was wearing to the running-order of the previous night's menu. "Damn it, Her Majesty is not a film star. Film stars may publish their menus, but we don't," protested Major Griffin.

Could he not say, though, what had lodged so perilously in the Queen Mother's throat? Was it a piece of bread roll, or a morsel of meat, perhaps? The major, a man who by nature likes to help friends, confided to the P.A. Court Correspondent that as it happened he did know that fish had figured on the menu at Royal Lodge the previous evening. Eureka! Then Grania could report that the mysterious 'foreign body' was a fish-bone! Hold on, not so fast. First the Queen Mother's Private Secretary and the surgeon must be consulted − which meant 'phoning them at the hospital when more important considerations must surely be occupying their minds. Then, if the fish-bone theory was true, it must be decided whether the information came under the heading of 'privileged' or not. It turned out that the theory *was* true, and after some cogent argument by the highly professional Miss Forbes, the Major finally agreed that she might publish the fish-bone fact, presuming she would preface this news with the time-honoured phrase "It is understood that". But no, she could not report which kind of fish it came from. Definitely not. Actually it was a trout that had caused the near calamity, but even if it had been the more superior salmon the total ban on divulgence would have equally applied.

Recounting the background minutiae to the incident may seem like over-emphasising its importance. After all, the episode of the fish-bone turned out in the end, fortunately, to be a fairly small event in the Queen Mother's long life. But the anecdote illustrates very well a perennial problem in Royal reporting: what should be reported, and what should not; which facts should be released by official spokesmen, and which withheld.

Reporters with no specific authorisation from the Palace have — as we shall see — their own particular problems in carrying out their work, but even Court Correspondents, in their privileged position, sometimes risk strong criticism if they report facts that, on the face of it, would seem to be harmless enough. Is there any good reason, for instance, why the public should not have been allowed to know that the Queen Mother ate trout? Or, to quote another instance, that the personal detectives of the Prince and Princess of Wales were guests at the party that followed the baptism of the infant Prince William? Why should there have been a complete news blackout on the names of well known people who enjoyed themselves at Prince Andrew's twenty-first birthday party? (No, Miss Koo Stark was *not* there that night!) It is difficult not to sympathise at times when reporters complain, as they do, that the prime purpose of Palace Press Secretaries appears to be to prevent information getting out rather than to give it out.

Equally, of course, it can be said Fleet Street's appetite is insatiable and its taste sometimes questionable. And if, as has been mooted, regular 'briefings' were given by the Palace spokesmen — in the way that the Foreign Office and Number Ten Downing Street brief other specialist reporters — it seems unlikely that enough information would be forthcoming to satisfy curiosity or that the interests of both the monarchy and the people would best be served in the long run. A baffling mystique, after all the centuries and despite today's laser-like instruments of scrutiny, still shrouds the institution of monarchy, and a quiet company of soberly-suited men stand shoulder to shoulder in protection of privacy. A reporter, a veteran of many sorties, described Buckingham Palace's Press security as being "like a fortress with a number of stockades surrounding it.

Occasionally you may manage to get over and into, or even be allowed to enter, the first enclosure. But those guarding the fortress never want you to reach the keep. You're always trying to reach the keep and they, ever so amicably, are always trying to prevent you. Nobody's ever got all the way yet.''

It's an analogy likely to bring a wry, knowing smile to the faces of people inside and outside the Palace, participants in an elaborate and seemingly never-ending game of hide and seek. Most often it is played in an amicable spirit, though just now and again things can turn nasty as one side or the other threatens to stop playing altogether.

James Whitaker, who has played the Royal game – not always according to their rules – for some fourteen years likes to think of himself as a huntsman working a pack of hounds, flushing Royals from cover. He visibly perspires with pride as he lays claim to a first sighting of Diana with Charles, in September 1980, on the banks of the River Dee near Balmoral.* He used binoculars and she – dammit – kept her back to him so he couldn't properly identify her. Craftily, she employed a small make-up mirror to keep an eye on him and the two accompanying photographers, before clambering up a steep bank into some trees and out of range.

"It's very rude to go around peering at people through binoculars," said Prince Charles at a function some 18 months later to the man who was Whitaker's editor at the time. But Whitaker has rarely been deterred. Despite what individual members sometimes say about him, he is a steadfast supporter of the Royal Family; the Queen in particular has his unswerving admiration. On a Richter scale he rates her at 10, and everyone else at 2, though it is his considered view that Prince Charles is 'moving up'.

Harry Arnold, a most prolific reporter of the Royal scene and another man who makes pleasant company, is also a Royalist – "though some people may be surprised by that fact," he suggests. Over the past 5 years he has had Buckingham Palace "jumping up and down" over some of the stories he has written. Some – like the assertion that a nuclear bomb-proof shelter was being built in Prince Charles' country home in Gloucestershire – have turned out to be true. Others – like saying the Queen had ordered Prince Andrew home from his Caribbean holiday with Koo Stark – turned out not to be true.

"I am actually a Royalist not because I'm in love with the Royal Family as individuals but because I think the alternative to a

---

* He had spotted Lady Diana Spencer before, at Sandringham in January 1978, but at that time she had not been regarded by the Press as a contender in the Prince Charles marriage stakes. Her elder sister, Lady Sarah, was the favourite then.

monarchy would be awful." He admires Michael Shea — "he's one of the very few at the Palace who has the courage to ring up the Queen" — and thinks his rival, Whitaker, has ideas of self-aggrandisement. He sees the important difference between them as one of basic training. Whitaker, he says, has the approach of a gossip writer while he himself remains what he always was, a hard nosed general reporter. But then again, Whitaker is happy to describe himself as "a Master of Trivia".

Both men came to Royal reporting almost by accident. Whitaker's involvement began when he was sent to report on an inter-varsity polo match in which Prince Charles was playing for Cambridge. After the game, the organisers invited the young reporter to join them in a glass of champagne. Being offered champagne because he was doing a 'royal' story seemed infinitely more inviting than having a brown ale in a bar. Henceforth, he vowed to keep up with other people's standards whenever possible, and began reading all he could about the Royal Family. Today he never goes on an out-of-town story without first placing a big black bag of reference books in the boot of his car.

On holidays — spent mostly in the South of France or skiing in Switzerland — he bones-up on the latest Royal biographies. He has his own cross-reference system of newspaper cuttings, which comes in very useful when he writes magazine articles under any one of six pseudonyms, the most romantic-sounding of which — Victoria Austin — is borrowed from one of his three children.

Harry Arnold drifted into Royal reporting after being sent to interview the man who was going to be best man at Captain Mark Phillips's wedding. Until about six years ago, he combined stories about Royalty with reporting murder trials at the Old Bailey. He has a strong aversion to privilege for its own sake, and an abhorrence of snobbery. His disclosures about the Royal Family gross him in the region of £40,000 a year, enabling him to buy a villa apartment near St Tropez in 1983, for the holidays he enjoys with his wife and three young children — "If I stopped writing about the Royals tomorrow I'd miss some of the travel but I'd look forward to seeing a good deal more of my family." He admits to having been guilty at times of crossing the border-line between reporting what is of legitimate public interest and what amounts to intrusion, but says that reporting on the Royal Family is a bit like bringing up a child. "There aren't any perfect handbooks that tell you what to do and what not to do."

Arnold and Whitaker are probably the best known, which is by no means the same as saying they are the best loved reporters at the Palace. But there are many others in Fleet Street charged equally by their editors with finding out all they can about the Royal Family, among them long distance reporters with names resonant of a pre-war Hollywood: Steve Lynas *(Daily Mail)*, Ashley Walton *(Daily Express)* and Ann Morrow (late of the *Daily Telegraph)*, whose languid accent and fazed appearance at a Royal event has on occasion led to her being mistaken for a Lady-in-Waiting.*

All vouchsafe to the fact that writing about the day-to-day lives of Britain's Royal Family is no sinecure. In fact, of all specialised reporting jobs – on mass-selling newspapers especially – it is probably one of the hardest. Experts in other fields – politics, sport, industry, trade unions, to name just a few – are handed out far more background information than they can ever need or use, whereas Royal reporters receive the skimpiest regular diet from Buckingham Palace – hardly more than a calendar of forthcoming events. Politicians, relying on election or re-election to further their careers, are nearly always keen to talk to journalists. Royalty has no need. Public relations organisations spend huge amounts to promote a client's image. Palace Press officers accept reporters' invitations to lunch or dinner, but make a point of not returning the hospitality lest it be misconstrued – though Michael Shea does give private dinner parties for editors. It might be the view of some that the monarchy today is in essence all to do with PR, but that opinion certainly isn't entertained, or much tolerated, within the Queen's palace.

An essential part of any reporter's basic equipment is a good contact list, and despite constant attempts to track down and silence 'deep-throats' at the Palace, leakage of privileged information does occur. Harry Arnold tells of the occasion when, after *The Sun* had run a number of 'exclusive' Royal revelations, he was telephoned by Michael Shea and told there was a good deal of interest at the Palace in who his 'mole' was. "*They* think it's a Royal policeman. I think it's a Royal servant." "Actually," Arnold replied, "you can relax: you'll never find him because there are eleven of them!"

With a staff of hundreds employed at Buckingham Palace, Windsor, and the other Royal residences, it would be surprising if there were not some whose tongues could be loosened in a local pub after working hours. Others might expect to supplement their wages with hard cash for a plain tip-off. It has never been the practice of any of the Royal Family 'not to speak in front of the servants'. Such a practice would be almost intolerable, since for the greater part of their daily lives, officials and staff from various levels are usually in near attendance. The Royal Family place great trust in those who work for them, but at the same time are perfectly aware that some, usually harmless, secrets may leak out from time to time. What they

---

* John Edwards, a top feature writer on the *Daily Mail,* once asked Press Secretary Michael Shea what was the biggest problem with his job and received the reply: "Harry Arnold".

find much harder to forgive is someone 'doing a Crawfie'.* For many years now it has been a condition of Royal service that employees sign a legal document binding them to confidentiality about anything they see and hear in the course of their duties. But this did not inhibit Stephen Barry, Prince Charles' valet for twelve years, from embarking on a book about his Palace experiences (he began as a footman at the age of eighteen) and selling the serial rights in America, to *Good Housekeeping* for well over £100,000. Apparently Prince Charles read the book before publication in February, 1983, and was relieved that it contained nothing offensive about the Royal Family as a whole, and his wife in particular.** At the same time his legal advisers were prepared to take legal action if ever an attempt was made to publish or serialise the book in Britain.

In the past there have been 'reliable sources' so incensed by the inaccuracy of some newspaper reports that they have been willing to talk to trusted journalists, on and off the record, purely "in order to put the record straight". But in the last year or so certain sections of the Press have attracted such odium among individual members of the Royal Family that even the best intentioned officials dare hardly admit they even know the names of certain pressmen.

For a long time one of James Whitaker's high level sources of information – or more often, confirmation – was someone still holding a senior position at Buckingham Palace today. But since the 'tightening-up' operation that took place after the infamous 'Palace Intruder' incident in July 1982, this particular source has become, more often than not, 'unable to help'. Another of Whitaker's contacts, he is ready to admit, is a member of Earl Spencer's family (and therefore related to the Princess of Wales) whom he entertains to a lavish lunch on a fairly regular basis. Neither person is paid a

---

* Marion Crawford was governess for seventeen years to the Queen, when she was Princess Elizabeth, and to her sister, Princess Margaret Rose. After she left Palace service she wrote a book about 'The Little Princesses' and went on to write a regular column about the Royal Family in *Woman's Own* for many years. She was said to have made considerable amounts of money out of both these enterprises and eventually retired into deliberate obscurity in a bungalow outside Aberdeen.

** In April 1982, *The Sun* carried a report that Mr Barry had been "sacked by Princess Diana" after clashing with him repeatedly. The unofficial Palace view was that Barry's departure was mainly due to a change in Prince Charles' domestic requirements after his marriage. He still employs two valets, but soon after he and the Princess of Wales moved into Kensington Palace, a butler was recruited to the staff.

penny for their information and Whitaker tends to value them as sounding-boards for his own flights of speculation rather than as sources of hard fact.

Asked the obvious question: "Why don't you go to Buckingham Palace Press Office for any information you require about the Royal Family?" the response of many journalists, including at least one editor of a national newspaper, is that they too seldom receive satisfactory answers to their questions. And yet, even with a miniscule number of staff, the Press Office is available on a round-the-clock basis to deal with enquiries from the media. Stacked on a long shelf in one of the rooms are thick leather-bound volumes containing a veritable encyclopedia of facts about the Royal Family, ranging from the Queen's glove size (7) to the number of Royal swans paddling up and down the Thames. All of this reference material, painstakingly collated over a period of many years, is invaluable to those writing Royal biographies or articles about facets of Royal life. But it serves less well the reporter who has been told by his news editor to find out where Prince Andrew spent last night, or whether or not the Princess of Wales breast-fed Prince William. These are the kind of questions Fleet Street (and the foreign press who 'phone in from all parts of the world) frequently want answered. Equally, these are the requests that Buckingham Palace spokesmen — at the Queen's command — are not prepared to satisfy.*

Palace Press Officers never divulge information about the private travel arrangements made by members of the Royal Family. Very often they are ignorant of even the broad outline themselves. The Prince of Wales, in particular, jealously guards his 'off-duty' hours. In his bachelor days, he would frequently slip out of the Palace for a day or a weekend without giving his staff even an inkling where he was going. In a dire emergency about the only way of contacting him was by asking the Palace police station who always knew the whereabouts of his personal detective, and therefore of the Prince.

But word of a royal visit, even by so-called private invitation, usually leaks out, often through hotel or airline employees, and reporters can usually track down their quarry if their editors want them to. Prince Charles has tended, in any case, to follow the same pursuits in more or less the same places year after year. Between his

---

* It is not only Buckingham Palace that is sensitive about what should be revealed and what should not. Robert Lacey, author of *Majesty,* on a pre-sales promotion visit to a high-class bookshop, mentioned he would be quoting another author's description of watching the Queen feed her Corgis and receiving, as he did so, "a glimpse of the Royal knicker". He was told that if he published this anecdote the shop would refuse to stock his book.

main holidays at Sandringham over the New Year and Balmoral in early autumn, he has gone skiing in January or February, fishing in Iceland in August and played polo at every opportunity during the season. In the case of his younger brothers, Prince Andrew and Prince Edward, however, no such pattern emerged. It was quite by chance that in October 1982, Steve Wood, the *Daily Express*'s 'Royal' photographer, stumbled on one of the most headline-catching 'private travel arrangements' in years.

Mr Wood (as Prince Charles calls him) or Mr Woods (as, up till now, he has been addressed by Princess Diana) is one of Fleet Street's best known and − where the Royal Family is concerned − most persistent photographers. He was responsible for the colour version of the famous picture of Lady Diana Spencer in the 'see-through' skirt. "At first I didn't realise the back-light was making her skirt transparent. I'm afraid, as a result, she hasn't entirely trusted me from that point on."

The son of a celebrated news photographer, Henry James Wood, who took one of the first pictures of a buzz-bomb passing over London in World War II, Steve arrived in Fleet Street at the age of twenty-two after four years in art college. At thirty-seven he retains a youthful look with dark wavy hair and hazel coloured eyes dangerous with wounded innocence. He has smuggled himself into Poland and Afghanistan to bring out world exclusives for his newspaper, as well as into a banquet in Monte Carlo where he concealed a camera under his dinner jacket in order to snatch pictures of Prince Charles sitting next to Princess Caroline. Over the years he has become well known to the Royals and his rivals alike.

In the first week of October 1982, when he might have expected to be covering the Queen's four week tour of the South Pacific, Steve Wood was instead on his way to a holiday in the sun with a nurse fourteen years his junior with whom he had decided he was very much in love. "After a life of flippancy and debauchery I thought I'd try really hard to persuade this beautiful girl to settle down with me."

Accordingly he had turned down a late chance of going to the Pacific in order to keep to a booking he had already made to fly his girlfriend, Katie Hobbs, to a secret destination for a three week holiday in a five star hotel. Katie had no idea where Steve was taking her until she arrived at London Heathrow airport and passed through the Gate leading them both on board a British Airways 747 (flight BA 257) bound for Antigua and Barbados.

Being the sort of person who rarely does anything by halves, Steve had booked two First Class seats and, soon after going aboard, he presented his *Daily Express* card to the Chief Steward, requesting that after take-off he escort his lady friend to the flight deck as part of the surprise package. Steve himself fully expected to be asleep by then. He'd been working up until almost the last moment before leaving for the airport, taking pictures of the Princess of Wales and following up rumours of a relationship between Prince Andrew and an almost totally unknown actress called Koo Stark.

Only minutes after nodding off, Steve was awoken by a tapping on the shoulder and, to his considerable surprise, found himself looking up into the face of one of the Royal detectives, Inspector Padgham. The Inspector was holding the visiting card that Steve had given to the aircraft's Chief Steward.

"How did you know we were on this flight?"

In time honoured style, Mr Wood replied that he was unable to reveal his sources. After a few minutes the Inspector went away, plainly dissatisified, just as Katie returned from the flight deck.

Steve apologised, but explained that he might, after all, have to do a little work as it appeared that Princess Margaret was on the same flight – Steve had run across Inspector Padgham a number of times when photographing Princess Margaret and had assumed, wrongly as it turned out, that Padgham was still assigned as her protective police officer.

Reluctantly, since he really did not welcome the intrusion of work into his and Katie's holiday, Steve rigged up one of the cameras (three Nikons and an Instamatic) that he was carrying in a canvas bag, and descended the spiral staircase from the First Class section to tour the main First Class cabin and then the Business and Economy Class right to the rear of the aircraft. He returned to his seat a few minutes later, having drawn a blank. No sign of Princess Margaret. "It must the Duchess of something or other who's aboard," he told Katie. "In any event, no-one to spoil our holiday. The only people who would matter if they were on this flight would be Prince Andrew or Princess Diana."

Just to be sure, before he settled back into his seat, Steve set off on another tour of the aircraft, leaving his girlfriend to make a second trip to the flight deck and have a chat with the Captain.

Steve was back in his seat when Katie returned, hardly able to control her laughter. "It's Andrew!" she exclaimed. Steve refused to believe her. "True. He's on the flight deck. You must have walked right past him!"

Steve realised he had thought he vaguely recognised the faces of two of the passengers sitting in the Economy Section. Prince Andrew and Koo Stark, going on holiday together! On the same 'plane as himself and Katie. He could not believe his luck. (He verified later, from a helpful stewardess, that they had booked their seats in the names of 'Mr and Mrs Cambridge'. But this was not quite true. In fact the pseudonym was used to book Prince Andrew's seat, according to standard Royal practice. Koo Stark travelled under her own name.)

After giving the matter careful thought, Steve decided the best course of action for all concerned – Prince Andrew, Miss Stark, himself, and his newspaper – would be to make a direct approach and go for an 'arranged' picture, rather than trying to snatch a shot. (It was too much to hope that, as a newspaperman, he would volunteer to turn a blind eye to what was potentially a popular paper scoop, even though this might have been the advice of the majority of his newspaper's readers.)

Accordingly he made his way aft once more and, speaking to Inspector Padgham in front of Prince Andrew, asked if some arrangement could be made whereby he obtained his picture, but without disturbing the Prince's holiday and bringing the rest of Fleet Street racing out after him.

Steve related how, earlier in the year, he had skied in the company of Prince Edward for practically a week and had made a 'deal' with him whereby the Prince went back to London carrying all nine rolls of film that Steve had shot, thus ensuring almost complete privacy for Edward until his holiday was over. The exclusive pictures had subsequently been published in the *Daily Express* – though not as prominently as they would have been had not news of the Falklands war broken on the same day!

It was clear from what he said that Inspector Padgham was disinclined to trust the Press in general, and would strongly advise Prince Andrew against acceding to Mr Wood's request. Notwithstanding, Wood pleaded his case several times more during the long flight to Antigua. Eventually, an hour away from landing, Prince Andrew informed the photographer that he had decided not to agree to pictures being taken of himself and his companion, together or separately. As to any 'deal': "I must leave it to my detective, and he says 'No'."

While these negotiations were taking place, Koo Stark positioned an airline blanket to half-conceal her face and when Steve Wood, all other avenues closed in his estimation, began trying to shoot off pictures without permission she drew the blanket completely over her head.

It cannot have been too pleasant an hour for Prince Andrew and his companion *or* for the other passengers on the 'plane – though no doubt some secretly revelled in the totally unexpected excitement, regaling their friends afterwards with accounts of what they had witnessed. At the same time, of course, they'd be likely to condemn the actions of the man who was to bring the gossipy story to millions of others through their breakfast time newspaper.

When the jumbo-jet landed at Antigua after a seven hour flight, Steve and Katie disembarked along with other passengers who had booked to go only this far. Steve had no worthwhile pictures, he realised. But he still had an exclusive news story. Whether or not the *Daily Express* published his account of what he had seen was not up to him, but his editor. The fact that most of the other passengers on the aircraft were aware of Prince Andrew's presence meant that any one of the them might tip-off a newspaper.

The editor of the *Daily Express,* with forty-five minutes to go before the first edition went to press, took Steve Wood's understandably agitated 'phone call and then put him straight through to 'Copy'. He also instructed his enterprising photographer to 'stay with the story'. Arrangements were hurriedly made for Philip Finn, the *Express* man in New York, to join Steve Wood by flying to the far north of Canada in order to catch the next available flight to Antigua and Barbados. In the meantime Steve and Katie, who must have wondered what had hit her, obtained fourteen-day visas for the St. Vincent Islands and went to their hotel — for a few hours instead of a few weeks, as intended — to await the next 'plane to Barbados.

In Barbados they hung around for three hours in the middle of the night before catching a flight to St. Vincent. From there — they had now been joined by Philip Finn — they intended booking a flight to Mustique, which Steve had established was Prince Andrew's destination. (He and his friends were to stay in the villa owned by Princess Margaret.) Mysteriously they were turned away from that flight, and when they tried to hire a speedboat they were told it was not possible to take them to Mustique. Rightly or wrongly, they suspected the police had already put out warning notices.

A taxi driver told them of a Swedish yacht that had just arrived and might be willing to carry them between islands. Its crew — a Swede and a Dutchman — did agree, but declined to hang about, unceremoniously dropping their three passengers on the beach. The police arrived soon after. Steve later made his way, quite openly, to Princess Margaret's holiday home on the island, but was turned away by police guarding Prince Andrew and his companions.

At the local bar they dined and wined most handsomely but were told they would not be allowed a bed, so 'the three Mustiqueers' ended up sleeping on the beach under the palm trees and the stars. Steve remembers it as the most idyllic night of his life — apart from waking up in the morning to find he and Katie were covered from head to toe in insect bites!

He made one more attempt to get pictures of Prince Andrew, this time surreptitiously. Concealed in some bushes near the house, he overheard Inspector Padgham enlightening a group of local policemen, "You've got to watch these Press photographers. They could be sneaking up on you right now. They could be six feet away." Steve Wood was.

A little later he was discovered trying to take pictures, and was escorted back to the local bar. There, following a delicious lunch, he remembers looking out to sea around three in the afternoon and watching as six ocean-going yachts – "all stuffed with Press" – drew ever nearer. "I just turned to Katie and said: 'That's the end of the exclusive'."

Steve Wood's amazing good luck in being on the same 'plane as Prince Andrew, and the Prince's rotten bad luck (though how he imagined, if he did, that he wouldn't be spotted by *someone,* is hard to fathom) resulted in the *Daily Express* coming out the next day with a 'splash' story almost as sensational as that of 'the Bikini Pictures'.

The headline across almost the whole of Page One read: ANDREW'S SECRET. It was sandwiched between a picture of the Prince, in Royal Naval uniform, clenching a long-stemmed red rose between his teeth (a present from a well-wisher on his return from battle service in the Falklands) and a posed photograph of Miss Stark wearing very little.

Michael Green, in the following week's *Sunday Times,* possibly unaware that Steve Wood was a photographer and not a writer, compared the accompanying text to the "style of a rather daring lady journalist of 60 years ago".

Admittedly the *Express* did appear to be taking a somewhat coy or, more likely, careful line: "The Prince's romantic holiday shows what a modern young man he is. Ten years ago it would have been unthinkable for a Prince to have taken an actress on holiday posing as husband and wife."

The revelation was undoubtedly a scoop in Fleet Street terms, and it had rival newspapers baying after Koo during the following days. *The Sun* ran stills from some of Miss Stark's "sizzling sex films". The *Daily Mirror* published a short interview with Koo's cleaning lady under the headline "I SAW ANDREW LEAVE HER FLAT IN THE MORNING. HE ALWAYS LOOKED RATHER TIRED". And the *Daily Mail* made out that all was above board on the island of Mustique by quoting Koo's stepfather, Carl Caruso, as saying "My wife is with them under express orders from the Queen", only to have Buckingham Palace promptly deny any such authorisation.

The Queen at this time was in Australia, processing regally on the tour of her Commonwealth possessions in the South Pacific. Kept informed of what was going on, almost entirely through newspaper reports incidentally, she hardly ever made reference to her son's activities and when the subject was discussed, shortly, as a matter of interest to the Press (Australian as well as British) she apparently made light of it. The headline in the *Sunday Times* "Sailor takes girl on holiday" seemed to equate most nearly with her own views at the time. It was certainly never true, as Harry Arnold reported in_ The

Sun on on October 8, that the Queen "had ordered Prince Andrew to come home from his holiday in the sun with sizzling actress Koo Stark".

In the intervening period since October 1982, the friendship of the Prince and the actress has undergone several vicissitudes. At the time, the *Sunday People,* having conducted a nationwide poll, concluded that the majority of people felt that "Prince Andrew has done his stuff in the Falklands and if he wants to unwind with a shapely actress on a faraway island, good luck to him!"

Buckingham Palace consistently maintained the line that popular newspaper reports about Prince Andrew's private life were either untrue, exaggerated, intrusive, or mere tittle-tattle published for financial gain, and — though she would obviously prefer that emphasis was given to more important matters — the Queen was not unduly worried by them. They constituted, after all, a kind of reporting the Royal Family had come to expect.

At the same time, when Steve Wood broke the story of Andrew and Koo's holiday in Mustique, there were undoubtedly those among the Queen's Household who seriously worried about the young man's behaviour and wished that he had at least been more circumspect. A certain amount of advice was offered, and declined, but not nearly as much as he would have received if there had been one person — a Private Secretary for instance — who worked exclusively for the Prince. At that time Prince Andrew had no personal staff apart from a valet and a police officer. Buckingham Palace has always felt decidedly more comfortable when the third in line to the Throne is on his ship and safely at sea.

A postscript to the Mustique romance of Prince Andrew and Koo Stark is that on March 8 — a birthday they share — Mr Steve Wood asked Miss Katie Hobbs to marry him. At the time of writing he is still awaiting her final answer.

6. THE ROYAL WATCHERS – PHOTOGRAPHERS

"God save us from those bloody vultures"
Prince Philip, of Press photographers, on a Royal tour of the Pacific 1954

"You *are* a pest, by the very nature of that camera in your hand"
Princess Anne, to a photographer who had expressed the hope that he was not being a pest. Quoted in 'Royal Quotes'

"Unless you are actually vain, being photographed is not a particularly comfortable or enjoyable experience"
Patrick Lichfield, 'A Royal Album'

"I hate photographers. They don't allow us to live . . . That's why I can understand wild animals being pursued by men with rifles. Zoom lenses are like weapons"
Brigitte Bardot, quoted in 'Time' January 10, 1983

Essentially, where taking pictures of the Royal Family is concerned, photographers can be lined up in three ranks: the related, the relevant, and the reviled.

Lord Lichfield and Lord Snowdon are in the first rank. Thomas Patrick John Anson, 5th Earl of Lichfield, married to Lady Leonora, daughter of the Duke of Westminster, is a cousin of the Queen. The Earl of Snowdon is the former husband of the Queen's sister, Princess Margaret, and father of the Queen's nephew and niece, Viscount Linley and Lady Sarah Armstrong Jones.

Both men, through a combination of great personal charm, inventiveness, and brilliant mastery of their craft, have produced over the years a gallery of portraits and photographic records of historical events that rank alongside the great oil painters' work of past regal reigns. Others may argue about which is the better all round photographer, with Snowdon probably emerging with the reputation of being the more technically sound. But each has been responsible for some of the most beautiful pictures ever taken of the Royal Family. The portrait of Lady Diana Spencer (Snowdon) taken for *Vogue,* and the delightful study of the Prince and Princess of Wales (Lichfield) taken directly after the formal group photographs at their wedding breakfast, are just two fine examples of their work.

Another photographer with an international reputation is the lovable Norman Parkinson who lopes around the world from his island paradise home on Tobago to conjure ethereal beauty out of faces and places where sometimes little was known to exist before. He can made fashion models look like human beings, and Princesses look like goddesses.

Over the years Norman Parkinson's highly individual style of photography has resulted in quite stunning portraits of the Queen, the Queen Mother, Princess Anne and Princess Margaret. And he must have been well in the running to be asked to take the official wedding day pictures of the Prince and Princess of Wales. In the event, Lord Lichfield was given the prestigious job − though he fell down slightly by inadvertently including for public distribution a wedding day picture that Prince Charles had wished to retain for his own private album − it is the one where he bends low to kiss the outstretched hand of his bride.

As the man who has handled the sales of both men's work for many years, Mr Tom Blau, says in the foreword to one of Lord Lichfield's albums of Royal photographs: "The most coveted prize in contemporary photography in Britain is to be invited to photograph a member of the Royal Family. There is no way to achieve such an invitation except by being asked and the asking is done with a very remarkable degree of discernment and sensitivity."

Despite their close personal connection with the Royal Family, both Snowdon and Lichfield become extremely nervous about taking Royal pictures. Sometimes one helps the other. Over Christmas 1971, Lichfield was asked to take a formal photograph of the whole family at Windsor after the style of a Winterhalter painting. The problem was arranging grown-ups and children to be looking more or less in the same direction but not necessarily at the camera lens. It was Snowdon who suggested grouping everyone round a television set to watch, as it turned out, a Marx Brothers film.

Prince Philip came up with an idea for the big group picture at the Palace on Prince Charles and Lady Diana's wedding day. "It's not difficult: the other week when we were in Luxembourg for a wedding they simply gave us name cards to stand on attached to the carpet." Lichfield hadn't enough time left to write out individual name tags for the fifty-seven British and foreign Royalty who were to line up for the picture so he just placed numbers on the steps where they were to stand and compiled a list of names with their numbers adjacent. But when the Queen came to look at the list she good humouredly complained that her name wasn't on it. Naturally, as she was to be in the centre, Lichfield hadn't given her a number.*

The second category of royal photographer – the relevant – comprises those who regularly follow the 'Royals' around, turning up in the B.M.W.s and Mercedes, Cortinas and even one Rolls Royce at horse trials, polo matches, weddings and whistle-stop tours of provincial towns, to record the events of the day and, if they're lucky, catch a close-up of a Royal face that is good enough to go on the cover of a magazine, or newsworthy enough to make the front page of a newspaper.

They are a comparatively small band of brothers, numbering about fifteen in all, working either as staff photographers for newspapers or as freelancers with strong connections with picture agencies and magazines. When working they tend to look scruffier than reporters, mostly because they are so strung around with equipment and wear either much protective clothing (when it's cold and they may have to stand around for hours), or jeans and sweat shirts (when it's hot and they may have to run around a lot). They eschew ties, but always keep one handy for such formal occasions as banquets or when there's a possibility of being presented to the Queen at a reception. Whereas, on a Royal walkabout, reporters trail in the wake, photographers walk backwards in front of the Royal party. The faces of most of them (Anwar, Serge, Ron, Tim and Terry) are instantly recognisable to most members of the Royal Family through long association (along with Harry, Ken, Steve, John and Jim) but with varying degrees of delight. A photographer who has offended one day – it is not always easy to discover the reason – will find the next day that Prince Charles, or whoever, somehow manages rarely, if at all, to look in his direction. If photographers as a phalanx feel they have been unfairly treated, usually because the organisers of Royal events have failed to provide what they consider adequate access, their ultimate form of protest is to stand in a line, their cameras at their feet, as the limousine draws up and the Royal personage alights. As a ploy it invariably works because, whatever they may think privately of individual photographers or their methods, the Royal Family and its servants recognise the need for their public appearances to be recorded.

At the end of what is frequently a very long day the photographers package their exposed rolls of film, send the packets off for processing

* A Royal Album, by Lichfield (Elm Tree Books 1982)

(not knowing whether they've got any good pictures or not) 'phone their offices, 'phone their wives or girlfriends, meet up in the hotel bar with friends and rivals, then tuck into *Cordon Bleu* meals with expensive bottles of wine lined up. In common with television crews, they tend to be more than usually fond of their food. They talk shop a lot, and loudly, and one or two especially always seem surprisingly alert at the end of a day in which they will have had to think quickly and move quietly for hours at a stretch. Shoulder pressed against rival's shoulder, loose cameras crashing against neighbour's equipment, with no time to line up a shot and with hardly a second to focus, they have to take what comes, literally, and just hope that among the score of rolls of film they might shoot in a single day there is one picture that is going to win an award, or make them a fortune, or both.

Reporters complain that photographers never read briefings, so they are forever asking what they're supposed to be doing next. Photographers, sweating under the weight of their equipment, moan that reporters have a cushy job. Mostly they work together more out of necessity than choice, and generally end up the day in clusters at either end of a bar, ordering their own drinks. It's true that, physically, a Royal photographer's job is much more strenuous than a reporter's. But at the close of play, when photographers have put away their cameras and despatched their film, reporters are usually still left with their stories to write and file.

'Royal writers make contacts and Royal photographers make money' is an adage much argued over, but there is no doubt that a single picture procured in seconds can reap the person who takes it, or his employer, thousands of pounds within a day. And this is where the third category of photographer – the reviled – makes his appearance. Or, sometimes, makes sure he doesn't appear, for the reviled photographer is the one who conceals himself in bushes, or up trees, or in a stationary car, and shoots film at four frames a second on motor-drive or with a long focus lens that catches his subject unawares like a bank robber on closed circuit television.

He is reviled by the Royal Family; by the Queen in particular. He infuriates Prince Philip and Prince Charles, and so angers the Princess of Wales that her somewhat ambivalent attitude to the Press at the best of times can be adversely affected for several days afterwards.

Sandringham, and to a lesser extent Balmoral, the Queen's private houses, have been hunting grounds for the intrusive photographer for several years past. In January 1981 (when the quarry was Lady Diana Spencer, as the Princess of Wales then was); in January 1982 (the pregnant Princess of Wales); in January 1983 (Prince Andrew and Miss Koo Stark – who was not even there).

In December 1982, partly to forestall any Press complaints that special facilities had not been offered, the Prince and Princess of Wales invited representatives of both Press and television to their home in Kensington Palace to take pictures of themselves with Prince William at the age of six months. For more than twenty minutes cameras clicked and whirred in the Princess's study overlooking the Palace Gardens. Dressed in a white silk romper suit, Prince William sat first on his mother's knee and then on his father's. His yellow teething rattle was shaken and his tummy was rubbed. Both parents were relaxed and co-operated to the full. The photo-call was the first in Prince William's life and represented the kind of facility Fleet Street had always said would greatly improve Palace-Press relations. It resulted in colour pictures and film appearing in newspapers and on television around the world. Everyone ajudged the operation to have been a success. It had even proved that Prince William's hair was fair, not red as had been earlier reported in some papers.

In a letter to each of Fleet Street's editors afterwards the Queen's Press Secretary expressed the hope that in the aftermath of this very happy occasion – and since the original suggestion had come from the Princess of Wales herself – the Queen and her family would be left to enjoy their traditional New Year holiday at Sandringham unhindered by Press attention.

Within a fortnight Sandringham was 'besieged' by Pressmen – "fifty photographers and the worst harassment ever", according to Michael Shea. As quickly as they had come they disappeared. For one thing, Prince Andrew had left to return to duty with the Royal Navy; for another it was learned that the Prince and Princess of Wales were flying to Liechtenstein for a private holiday.

Once again, like flies, journalists descended in a cloud. Some were from Britain and some from continental papers. A Swiss paper hired the one helicopter licensed to operate in the area; and as its pilot set down on the snow photographers leapt out, like characters in a film about the S.A.S., took pictures of Charles and Diana as they skied, then jumped back into the aircraft and were lifted up into the sky once more.

Crowds of holidaymakers and Pressmen surrounded the Prince and Princess whenever they made an appearance. Attempts were made to spirit the couple away to remote slopes, but to little avail. Reports reached London of road blocks being set up, of skiers' passes being assiduously checked in case their owners were newspapermen. One photographer was knocked to the ground by a policeman and cut about the face. Another ran into trouble with Prince Charles' personal detective, Superintendent John Maclean, whose behaviour was compared to that of a Nazi stormtrooper.

Relationships between the Press and the Royal party deteriorated to such an unpleasant level that Vic Chapman, who looks after Prince Charles' media arrangements, was summoned from London to help sort things out – even though he was on the point of flying off to Australia to do a reconnaissance on the Prince and Princess's tour to Australia and New Zealand in March. He returned to his desk at Buckingham Palace on the Friday morning and flew off to Sydney the same night.

The Queen was 'very upset by the degree of harassment' both at Sandringham and on her son and daughter-in-law's private holiday. Michael Shea, "choosing words carefully", warned that the two episodes could lead to "a very serious reappraisal of the Royal Family's relationships with, and the facilities offered to, the Press". Until then there had been no discrimination made between the 'sensational' Press and its infringement of privacy and the media that 'appreciated and abided by the unwritten rules'.

On the day that Charles and Diana returned from their holiday, the Palace denied that the Princess of Wales had snubbed Fleet Street by refusing an invitation to present the 1983 British Press Awards. A spokesman said the Princess's decision not to accept the invitation had been taken in December. "The Princess gets hundreds of invitations and she cannot accept them all, particularly with a lengthy overseas tour coming up."

Two days earlier another request, which had been 'in the pipeline' since November, for Princess Diana to make a private tour of *Woman's Own* magazine offices was postponed because of "her very heavy programme including overseas tours". Clearly, not for the first or the last time by any means, the behaviour of a certain section of the media had contributed to a feeling of revulsion for the media as a whole.

Photographers are at a disadvantage compared with reporters in that they nearly always have to be seen in order to do their work. Remaining out of sight – even by using long range lenses – is usually impracticable for any length of time. Reporters, on the other hand, need only be seen when they want to be, and it is difficult for anyone to know for certain what kind of article or story they intend to write. The Royal Family can, and often do, ignore or laugh at many of the stories written about them, dismissing them as pure invention or unfounded speculation. But it is harder to ignore a picture, impossible to deny that the situation or the facial expression is a pure figment of a hack's imagination. The camera does lie, as everyone knows, but it can sometimes tell a truth far more forcefully than words.

Tim Graham's pictures of the Prince and Princess of Wales with their baby son, Prince William, were taken at Kensington Palace in a special session to mark the start of their visit to Australia and New

Zealand in March and April 1983. Since then they have probably been produced more often and in more places than any other single set of Royal pictures taken in the last ten years – earning Graham and the French picture agency that distribute his work overseas a huge sum in fees.* Expertly shot, with close attention to detail, they succeeded in conveying exactly the impression of young, happy parents inordinately fond of their first child, that was looked for by both the Palace and the general public.

It was a great compliment to Tim Graham, a freelance in his early thirties, to be chosen to take the pictures, and it came as something of a surprise both to him and his colleagues (who were among the first to extend congratulations) that such a prestigious commission had gone to him rather than to either one of the Lords – Snowdon or Lichfield – or possibly to Norman Parkinson. The Princess, it is said, specially asked for Graham, having a preference for informal family photos. Both she and Prince Charles were almost certainly influenced by Tim's quiet manner, which puts people at ease very quickly, and by the fact that the pictures he had taken of Prince Edward the previous year had met with general approval.

Known to his friends as 'The Squirrel', Tim is the son of a ratings surveyor with British Railways, who took his first picture with a box-brownie when he was twelve (it was of a tree in the garden, and he was amazed when it came out) and began work as an apprentice in Fleet Street at sixteen. He is married and has a baby daughter, Lucy.

His appearance – a slight stature, a winning smile, and ginger hair – is well known to individual members of the Royal Family since he's accompanied them on several overseas tours. His presence has also been included from time to time among those photographers who hang around Sandringham and Highgrove – though less noticeably after the photographic session with Prince Edward.

Graham would like to have photographed Prince Edward piloting a glider, with Balmoral in the background below. Or out walking on the flat heath around Sandringham with his gundog.

However both suggestions were turned down, the first because it would take up too much time, and the second because the Queen was in residence at Sandringham – this was January 1982 – and she would not wish to have a photographer inside the grounds (after all, there were already plenty skulking around *outside!*).

Prince Edward, who was on holiday at Sandringham, was prepared (though not that pleased) to come up to Buckingham Palace

---

* Graham declines to discuss figures, but other Royal photographers estimate the total must be at least £20,000 and possibly as much as £50,000 eventually, a portion of which Graham has donated to charity.

for a three hour photographic session and, at Graham's urging, he reluctantly agreed to bring his Labrador, Frances, with him. He would be returning to Gordonstoun, via Sandringham, the following day so would take advantage of this trip to London to have his hair cut – but not until after the pictures had been taken.

Graham had already been given a guided tour of some of the rooms at Buckingham Palace and had elected to shoot some of the pictures in the Chinese Room – he was attracted by the abundance of gilt – and others showing Prince Edward sitting at his desk in the second floor living room which he shares with his brother.*

He intended to shoot some more pictures outside in the garden, but by 11.45, with his allotted time of three hours almost expired, he found himself still inside the Palace.

Prince Edward was extremely patient and forbearing, but much less inclined than his elder brothers would have been to engage in conversation. He was more shy than either Charles or Andrew, Graham concluded, and really saw the business of being photgraphed as more or less a duty that had to be endured. About the only thing that got him to smile was to ask "Could we have just one more?"

Outside in the Palace garden, on a freezing cold day that incorporated flurries of snow, the Prince posed for several minutes leaning against a tree – and when Graham had to reload his camera, ran around in small circles to get warm. Frances, his Labrador, proved a useful subject for conversation, as Graham had guessed she would, but unfortunately was more interested in looking at the ducks on the lake than at the camera.

Graham was slightly concerned that Prince Edward was wearing black shoes with a brown jacket and brown corduroys, but when he asked the Prince if by any chance he had a brown pair he could change into he was told that these were the only ones the Prince had at the Palace! The photographer got around the small problem by scuffing leaves over Edward's feet to disguise their colour. He also noticed, as did some sharp picture editors when they inspected the prints, that the Prince's trousers had been let down for length – a point made much of when the birthday pictures were finally released on March 10, Budget Day.

A photographer who specialises in portraits and group shots of Royalty takes pictures that please both family and friends – those prints that don't please are ruthlessly crayoned-out by the subjects themselves before the public ever has a chance of seeing them. A

---

* Prince Andrew and Prince Edward share a suite of rooms on a second floor corner of Buckingham Palace. They each have a bedroom, with a communal living room, stereo, and dining table with four chairs. The big, handsome desk is used by both the Princes.

photographer who is given accreditation by the Palace, either as an individual or as a representative of an organisation, to attend Royal engagements or go on Royal tours, is always looking out for the picture that is 'different'. At the same time he is wary of causing Royal displeasure lest he prejudice possible future favours. The dilemma for editors, with photographers as with reporters, is deciding when members of the Royal Family have a right to absolute privacy and when the public has, if not a right, then a legitimate interest in knowing what is happening. When Princess Anne is riding a horse in a public competition, is that a part of her private life? When the Princess of Wales is being pulled to the top of a slope in a public ski-lift, should she not be photographed by professional photographers when amateurs are snapping all around her? Or are these questions too naive?

On November 14 1979, Ron Bell, the Press Association's Court photographer, was despatched by his office to Leicestershire to get a picture of Prince Charles. The Prince had left Sandringham only that morning to go fox-hunting with the Quorn — the only occupation of the many that he enjoys that arouses deep anger in some people who otherwise admire him.

Trying to follow a hunt in a car in unfamiliar terrain is not the easiest of assignments. After several hours of driving hither and thither without any success, Bell was ready to admit defeat. He had not glimpsed the Prince all day. With murky light fast turning to darkness, he drew up at the 'phone box in a remote country lane to ring his office. He had just picked up the receiver and was about to dial when faintly he heard the clip-clop of a horse's hooves, and looking up saw the Prince of Wales riding slowly towards him, completely on his own. He stepped out of the 'phone box and lifted his camera. Prince Charles' only reaction as the shutter clicked was an oath of one word. Bell followed him a little way up the lane where he joined other members of the Quorn. He took a couple more pictures from a distance, then swallowed hard as he watched Prince Charles detach himself from the rest of the hunt members and move towards where he stood. He felt certain he was about to receive the most fearful telling-off. Instead Prince Charles merely said: "Not you as well." And Ron, smiling weakly, said how sorry he was, but in strong defence added: "But it *is* your birthday, Sir. Many happy returns."

Twenty years ago there was only one photographer, Ray Bellisario, the son of an Italian ice cream man from Pontefract, Yorkshire who constantly gave offence to the Royal Family by snatching pictures. When he sent the Queen a specially bound copy of his book *To Tread on Royal Toes,* containing 120 photographs of the Royal Family, it was returned with a curt, unsigned note:

"The Private Secretary to the Queen is commanded to acknowledge Mr Ray Bellisario's letter of 20th November and the copy of book which accompanied it. Her Majesty does not wish to accept the book and it is therefore being returned herewith."

Bellisario, who suddenly disappeared from the photographic scene in Britain some ten years ago and was last heard of in South Africa, was said to dislike the whole idea of monarchy intensely. "I am, by nature, a Republican," he was once quoted as saying. But he made a very good living out of his specialisation and since his departure more than one other photographer has taken his place.

Men such as Ron Bell, highly respected both in Fleet Street and at the Palace, would always be wary of taking pictures which they thought might embarrass the Royal Family. At the same time attitudes on all sides have undoubtedly relaxed since the days when Bellisario's pictures gave such offence, and there is an ever increasing number of young and enthusiastic freelance photographers who have heard of the large sums of money that can be made from selling Royal pictures. Fortunately, from the point of view of established photographers, most of these young men − and a few women − retire hurt from the fray when they learn how much hassle and jostle is involved. It also becomes apparent to them that there can frequently be a very small return on an orginal investment that may run into hundreds if not thousands of pounds.

The basic equipment of a Royal photographer, as carried by Ron Bell for instance, comprises five camera bodies, two loaded with colour film and two with black and white. The fifth is a spare. Ten lenses, ranging from 24mm to 400mm are needed, and anything up to 250 rolls of film on a long overseas tour. Most Fleet Street photographers use either Nikon or Canon cameras, which are strong enough to stand up to the rough treatment they inevitably receive. Professionals also put a sturdy pair of aluminium step ladders in the boot of the car when they set out on an assignment in order to see over crowds. The total value of all this equipment can add up to £10,000 and the total weight that has to be lugged around can easily be as much as 16 kilos.*

---

* Part of the tour of Australia and the South Pacific, by the Queen and Prince Philip, in October 1982, necessitated the Press party flying by charter 'plane between islands. The weight limit on luggage was 15 kilos − at least one kilo less than the weight of camera equipment most photographers were carrying. The solution? The equipment was loaded on board the aircraft and for the next eight days its owners managed to survive by wearing the same set of clothes, washing out their smalls every night, while the rest of their personal luggage, by courtesy of the Queen, was transported on board the Royal Yacht 'Britannia'.

Rivalry between freelance photographers is, on the whole, friendly but intense. When twenty or more are penned up in an enclosure to witness a Royal event, or forced to walk backwards on a walkabout, conditions for the perfect shot are never ideal. One photographer can be lucky enough to catch the picture that counts while the man standing next to him can miss out entirely. And the system of rota and F.P. (fixed position) passes, intended to restrict the number of Press to manageable proportions does not guarantee a good picture. Frequently the best shots come to he who marauds on the edge of the crowd or preselects a vantage point others have not thought of. Being in the right place at the right time can be as important as being in focus.

When speculation about Lady Diana Spencer's engagement to Prince Charles was at its height, a freelance photographer working for *The Sun* decided to drive home via Buckingham Palace at the end of a tiring day, just in case . . . As he circled the Queen Victoria monument in front of the Palace he spotted Lady Diana's mini-Metro entering the Palace gates. (Every Pressman who had been on the story of the Royal romance was well acquainted with Diana's car.) But by the time he had finished his circle of the monument and drawn parallel with the Palace, the driver had already slipped inside the building. But the car was still visible, parked neatly on the right of the forecourt, its bonnet nosed against the Palace wall. The light was abysmal, and the distance between photographer and subject was some 100 yards, but even so he took a number of shots and raced back to *The Sun* office. The pictures were vital to the story that *The Sun* was intent on running on its front page the next morning: that the announcement of an engagement was imminent. By 2 a.m. the paper was on the streets with a world exclusive picture story − 'LADY DI GOES TO THE PALACE' − and the photographer responsible, it is said, was paid £7,000 in cash for pictures that the very next day would have been worth almost nothing.

It was on the next day − February 24 1981 − that the engagement was officially announced, at 11.00 a.m., some hours after *The Times* had scooped the world with a small story on its front page headed 'Engagement of the Prince to be announced today'.

Interestingly several people, politicians as well as close relatives, had to be let into the secret before the official announcement was made. Sir William Rees-Mogg, at that time editor of *The Times,* was tipped off at his home. He's not saying by whom though it's not hard to guess that it might have been a member of the Privy Council or an official at No. 10 Downing Street. But a freelance journalist who, perhaps not surprisingly, also wishes to remain anonymous, had strong evidence of what was about to happen some forty-eight hours before Sir William received his news. The journalist, stonewalled by the Palace Press Office ("When there is something to announce, no doubt an announcement will be made") pressed to know if the engagement would be announced without the Queen's Press Secretary being present in London. "No, and he is not expected back until next week," he was informed. Michael Shea was in fact in Oslo, with Robert Fellowes, the Queen's Assistant Private Secretary (who is married to Princess Diana's eldest sister, Lady Jane) making preparations for a forthcoming Royal visit by the Queen to Norway. Two days later, on the Sunday evening, the journalist, his news instincts prickling, telephoned the British Embassy in Oslo, and asked to speak to Mr Shea. He was told that the Queen's Press Secretary had already left for home. This should have been the clincher, but the journalist still searched for harder evidence – until it was too late for him to secure what would probably have been the greatest scoop of his career. Interestingly, Shea and Fellowes had no inkling of an impending engagement announcement when they set off for Oslo. They were sitting in a car in the centre of the Norwegian capital when they received a call on the car radio with a message to ring the Palace. This was at 10.00 on the Thursday morning. Shea's two children were due to arrive on Saturday to stay with their grandparents and he was to meet them. He had just time to do so before flying back to London to handle Press arrangements for the announcement on the Tuesday.

Properly marketed around the world, a single picture can earn a freelance photographer £50,000 or more (with his agency taking a forty or fifty per cent cut) but examples of this happening are rare. However, in a good year, one or two photographers can earn as much as £100,000 in reproduction fees for Royal pictures. Some of the top names enjoy an annual income of £50,000 and over, but in order to earn such amounts they have first to lay out thousands of pounds on equipment, a studio possibly, an efficient photo-index system, and at least one person to do the paperwork and act as office manager. A large part of their profit derives not from pictures recently taken but from those carefully filed away in cabinets, dating back many years. The expense of going on an overseas tour – which can easily add up to anything from between two and ten thousand pounds – is often not recouped, if at all, until long after the tour has ended. Royal birthdays, anniversaries, births and deaths are what invariably produce a resurgence of interest in archive material. So valuable are some of these pictures (and so unreliable some of the offices they are sent to) that photographers insure each original they send out for at least £250 – which, technically at least, sets the stock list value of some photographers' and photgraphic agencies' filing cabinets at well over £500,000.

If he were ever to allow it to be published, an extremely high price would certainly be paid for one of Patrick Lichfield's pictures. It shows the Queen in full length dress sitting on the stairs on board 'Britannia' following a banquet. Knees drawn up, she is engrossed in reading a letter from Prince Charles and has taken off her diamond tiara and laid it at her side on the stairs.

The wedding of the Prince and Princess of Wales in July 1982 provided a bonanza for photographers − and their honeymoon, as far as sections of Fleet Street were concerned, proved one of the most expensive fiascos of all time.

Speed was essential when it came to despatching still pictures of the wedding ceremony to a world that, as far as 700 million of its inhabitants were concerned, was already watching live coverage on television. The privileged photographers actually inside St Paul's Cathedral were positioned on tiered scaffolding, high up in the south transept. As they finished each roll of film it was collected, put in a small purple velvet bag and lowered by cord to messengers who were waiting below ready to whisk it off for processing.

Sygma, one of the most successful picture agencies, with headquarters in Paris, assigned ten top photographers to cover the wedding for clients − magazines and newspapers − around the world. One of the photographers had a pass for inside St Paul's Cathedral. Of the others, two were positioned outside Buckingham Palace, three were outside St Paul's, and the other four were on roving commissions along the processional route

Everyone had familiarised himself with what was going to happen on the day itself, so that the elaborate plans would succeed without a hitch.

Within five minutes of the newly married Prince and Princess stepping into the open landau that was to carry them through cheering crowds back to the Palace, the ten men of Sygma had rendezvoused at a pre-arranged spot at the rear of the Cathedral. All their film − some forty rolls − was handed over to one photographer who swung himself on to the pillion of a motocycle for a hair-raising six mile ride to Battersea where a helicopter was standing by. A fifteen minute flight, and the helicopter landed at the small Biggin Hill airport, miles from central London where, with fast Customs clearance pre-arranged, a Lear jet was standing by on the tarmac, engines running. Minutes later the pilot was landing at the airport nearest to the centre of Paris, and a dispatch rider was revving up ready to speed the package of film to the laboratories for processing. Total time taken from St Paul's Cathedral to inside the French laboratories: fifty-nine minutes. Largely because of the speed of their highly organised operation, Sygma probably grossed five times more than any other agency with their pictures of the wedding. The ten men of Sygma − the photographers − each received between one and two thousand pounds for their morning's work, plus repeat fees.

Coverage of the Royal couple's honeymoon was not such a successful operation however. Prince Charles had very nearly achieved his ambition of keeping his engagement to Lady Diana Spencer an absolute secret, as far as the Press was concerned, right up until the release of the official announcement.* He had been annoyed that there had been a leak, but pleased that it was *The Times* rather than its sister paper *The Sun* (both owned by the Australian magnate, Rupert Murdoch) that had managed the coup. However he was determined that his honeymoon should not be spoiled by prying eyes and hounding reporters.

The Press soon learned that the Prince and Princess of Wales were to spend the first night of their married life at Broadlands, the home of the late Earl Mountbatten, in Hampshire, where the Queen and Prince Philip had spent part of their honeymoon in 1947. After a few days of well guarded privacy they would be prepared to face up to the crowds and cameras once more when they flew to Gibraltar to board the Royal Yacht 'Britannia' for the main part of their honeymoon – a twelve day cruise of the Mediterranean ending up at Port Said in Egypt and a meeting with President Anwar Sadat and his wife Jihan.

It was what lay between Gibraltar and Port Said that occupied journalists' minds. Once it left port, was 'Britannia' going to head towards the north African coast, the Cote d'Azur, the Aegean Sea, or the eastern end of the Mediterranean? Everyone had a theory, but no-one really had a clue. No-one even knew for sure about Egypt – there was no official word. But someone had been tipped off that 'Britannia' had been booked to pass through the Suez Canal en route for Australia and the Queen's Pacific tour later in the year.

The complete answer, in fact, lay locked away aboard 'Britannia' – in an envelope containing the carefully worked out itinerary, along with a mass of information about tides, water temperatures, secluded coves and beaches, historical landmarks and names of interesting (or otherwise) local residents, along the way.

Long before the Royal Wedding day, the staffs of British embassies and consulates in countries bordering the Mediterranean had been secretly preparing dossiers – rather like travel brochures – to help Charles and Diana decide where they would like to go on their honeymoon.

---

* One of photographer Steve Wood's greatest regrets is that he never managed to get a picture of Charles and Diana together before their engagement. On the day of the announcement he was out fox-hunting with the South Dorset and couldn't get back to London in time to go to the Palace for the official photo-call. Prince Charles sent him a telegram, ''Nice to catch you out, Mr Wood.''

The Prince of Wales' Assistant Private Secretary, Francis Cornish, who was to be one of the very few Household members on board 'Britannia' throughout the cruise, had flown on secret missions a number of times to liaise with officials in the countries whose coastal waters 'Britannia' might use. The Royal Yacht can be a totally self-sufficient floating hotel, but protocol, courtesy and security arrangements required that a number of people be let into the secret of the route the honeymoon cruise would take. But that number did *not* incude the Press.

Some thirty photographers and reporters had flown out to Gibraltar to report on the ecstatic reception given by the Gibraltarians to the newly-wed Prince and Princess of Wales. Tim Graham and Terry Fincher, through quick thinking and foresight, had obtained probably the best pictures – a back view of the Prince and Princess, standing at the taffrail of 'Britannia', holding hands and looking out across what seemed a deserted sea. (In fact Charles and Diana were acknowledging the cheering coming from a score of small boats bobbing about below them.) But once the handsome ship, with its shiny royal blue hull and gleaming white superstructure, had eased away from the quayside and made for the open sea, the British and foreign Press had repaired to the Holiday Inn to plan their next move.

There was talk of combining forces – and credit cards – to hire a large boat to trail 'Britannia'. But the cost was probably going to be an astronomical £10,000, and once it was rumoured that the Royal Yacht was capable of scudding along at something like 23 knots, enthusiasm dwindled. Maps were pored over, and quite suddenly the Mediterranean Sea assumed the proportions of the Pacific Ocean, and the 412 foot yacht the size of a rowing boat. Under cover of darkness – another clever ruse, to set sail at night – 'Britannia' could give the slip to any ship plodding in its wake. Not too reluctantly, the majority of reporters and photographers, after telephoning their offices, abandoned the chase before it had even begun and booked their flights home. James Whitaker, with the voice that carries from one end of a bar to the other, announced that he would be taking advantage of the honeymoon respite to holiday in Portugal.

There were a few, however, who were not prepared to give up the chase so easily. One French picture agency hired a light aircraft and with two photographers aboard criss-crossed the sea for ten whole days without once sighting 'Britannia'. The British search parties at least began less recklessly. In deciding where to begin looking they quickly ruled out the coasts of Spain and France as being too well dotted with holiday resorts – the appearance of 'Britannia' would be spotted and reported within minutes. Tunisia and Algeria were possibilities. There were excellent stretches of deserted beach along the African coastline. The Greek islands – now *there* was a thought. But how to track down a ship threading its way through a maze of channels among a scatter of tiny rocky outcrops?

In the event, a few reporters flew to Tangier, drew a blank, and were summoned back to London before they spent any more money. Another search party, having reached Rome on its way to Athens, was told by its newsdesk to proceed forthwith to Sardinia, on the strength of a tip that Charles and Diana intended dropping in on the Aga Khan. The only way of getting to northern Sardinia in a hurry was by chartering a jet. This the two photographers and one reporter did, found the Aga Khan's yacht in harbour and deserted, had a meal, stayed the night, and flew back to Rome the next day. The price of a ticket by scheduled flight was £17.00. The price of the charter: £1500!

After Rome, on to Athens; and because there was no aircraft available, a drive across the width of Greece to reach Patras at five in the morning. This time there was word that 'Britannia' had anchored off the island of Ithaka. A boat was needed, but none was available. Finally they hired a private pleasure boat for £300, the owner insisting he and his family come along too – once he had found and installed new batteries in the boat, which took three hours. Arrival in Ithaka coincided with the sight of 'Britannia' slipping over the horizon. They returned to Athens. Then flew to Crete. Then to Port Said. And ended up driving 500 miles along the edge of the Suez Canal to Hurghada in time to witness a relaxed and sunburned Prince and Princess of Wales elegantly taking leave of President and Mrs Sadat.

In the 11 days between leaving Gibraltar and arriving in Egypt, one of the photographers had taken exactly 15 pictures – none of them of the Prince and Princess of Wales, and just six of them of a very distant Royal Yacht. The cost of the whole operation: approximately £3000. The total estimated expense of despatching some thirty newsmen, photographers, and T.V. crews on a mad search of the Mediterannean: at least £40,000. It could only make Prince Charles smile.

But, to be fair, the pursuing Press had not been all that far out in their calculations. 'Britannia' had sailed first to the Algerian coast, and along the coast of Tunisia before heading northeast to Sicily and through the Straits of Messina to Ithaka. There Charles and Diana had swum and soaked up sun, and in the evenings dined under a canopy of stars. They had cruised around the northwest point of Crete, stopped briefly at the tiny island of Thira, and passed close to Rhodes. Late in the afternoon of August 12th, the anchor chain ran out from the bow of 'Britannia' as the ship slipped into the harbour of Port Said and an armada of sightseers' boats came out to greet the Prince and his young and beautiful bride. The world's attention was on them once more, but at least they had managed to give the world's Press the slip for a few precious private days at the start of a very public married life.

7. ROYALTY AND TELEVISION

"Above all this our royalty is to be reverenced, and if you begin to poke about it you cannot reverence it . . . In its mystery is its life. We must not let daylight in upon magic"
Walter Bagehot, author of 'English Constitution' 1867

"When people heard privately that I was making a documentary film about the life of the Royal Family they said 'how on earth are you going to get the access that you'll need?'"
Richard Cawston, producer of 'Royal Family'

"Mark Phillips is the only registered failure of Television Interviewing Training Consultancy, a company which trains people to put themselves over well on television. 'He was bloody hopeless' said his tutor in 1982. 'Eventually I told him just to keep quiet and keep smiling.'"
Craig Brown and Lesley Cunliffe, 'The Book of Royal Lists'

If newspapermen and photographers are the "baddies", then television producers and cameramen are the "goodies" in the Royal Family's eyes. There are exceptions to this general rule of course, but not many. The reason for the favouritism, as Fleet Street would have it, is partly to do with the fact that television rarely pries into the Royal Family's private life, except to report on what newspapers are getting up to. All four television channel news services are careful to be respectful in their coverage of Royal events. Gossip, if reported at all, is identified as gossip put about by others − usually the newspapers. Lapses in the broadcasting services' own sense of good taste are infrequent − showing a picture of a bare-breasted Koo Stark, Prince Andrew's current girlfriend, at the end of a B.B.C. nine o'clock news bulletin was, for many viewers, particularly offensive for being unexpected.

Light entertainment programmes can sometimes give offence with jokes about individual members of the Royal Family, but complaints come from viewers rather than from anyone inside Buckingham Palace. Queen Victoria might not have been amused at some of the antics shown on television, but Queen Eliabeth II very often is. The Palace Press Officer never divulges which television programmes are the Queen's favourites but at one time they were said to include "anything that has Dudley Moore in it". "Crossroads", one of the least demanding of Britain's soap-operas, was said to be a favourite of both Queen Elizabeth the Queen Mother and of the twenty-two-year old Princess of Wales.

When they are not giving a banquet, attending a charity film première, or simply catching up with a mountain of paper work, members of the Royal Family watch television as indiscriminately as most people, though probably they are more critical of programmes than many. Prince Philip, watching the News, is quite likely to thump his armchair and shout at whoever is being interviewed that he is talking a load of arrant nonsense − quite possibly it will be the trade union leader or Cabinet Minister who recently met the Prince at an official function.

The Queen keeps a notepad handy and jots down any point she would like followed up by one of her staff. In the days when the B.B.C. ran a show called "The Black and White Minstrels" her quick eye and ear spotted that when the singers snapped their fingers during one particular song and dance routine, the sound was of fingers uncovered whereas, in fact, the singers were wearing white gloves! A Member of The Household arriving at his desk the following morning found a note from Her Majesty asking him to discover the reason for this inconsistency. He 'phoned the B.B.C and the producer, tickled pink that he could count the Queen amongst his audience and even more pleased that he had such an attentive viewer, explained the process of post-sound synchronisation. The Queen's curiosity was thus satisfied.

Nowadays the importance of television in the reporting of Royal events is firmly established. Very early on in the planning of any major occasion the question will be asked, 'Where do we put the cameras?' meaning television cameras and not Press photographers − *they* tend to come later.* Route plans with camera positions

---

* One reason the colour photographs of the historic baptism of Prince William at Buckingham Palace were below the usual high standard was generally thought to be because the two photographers present, representing the world's Press, had to work with lighting that had been rigged to suit television cameras.

pencilled-in are shown to the Queen and sometimes come back with suggestions about where a camera might be better placed. Having travelled many well-televised routes many times she is adept at knowing the best camera sites. This is one of the reasons television often gets excellent close-ups of members of the Royal Family looking straight into the camera. Another reason, of course, is that the director — seeing the pictures different cameras are getting — can cut to the best picture. Those who had a close up view of the Royal Wedding from inside St Paul's Cathedral rarely saw Prince Philip converse with the Queen, whereas those watching on television at home gained the impression they were laughing and talking most of the time while waiting for the bride to arrive. Quick cutting caught the happy faces that everyone — well, almost everyone — wanted to see. ("Televising that damned wedding added years to the life of the monarchy in Britain," grumbled a Republican in a pub afterwards.)

The wedding of the Prince of Wales and Lady Diana Spencer in July 1981, watched by a total estimated audience around the world of over 700 million, was probably the most spectacularly happy event ever seen on television — though a hidden sign of the changing times was demonstrated by the number of camera positions (duplicating those used to televise the thanksgiving service for the Queen Mother's 70th birthday) that had to be changed "for security reasons". The B.B.C. gave instructions to its television and radio teams commentating on the procession to and from St Paul's Cathedral that, in the case of terrorist bombs or lunatic attacks, they were to continue concentrating on the wedding if the "disturbances" happened over half a mile away, but to show them if they occurred on or near the actual route.*

Television has not always been the Royal Family's favoured friend however. Until the Queen's coronation, in 1953, it was Press and cinema newsreels that were given special treatment, and television that was regarded with grave suspicion. Newsreels could be edited, still pictures could be seen before publication. But live television went out — well, *live!* There was no chance of editing, or censoring, what people saw. When it came to covering major Royal events, even cinema newsreels had their problems, not all of them emanating from the Palace. At the coronation of King George VI in 1937, they were allowed, for the first time, to string microphones across the nave of Westminster Abbey. But the *Daily Mirror,* apparently without irony,

---

* There had been some uncertainty about what to show when, in June 1981, shots (blank, as it turned out) were fired at the Queen as she rode along the Mall on the way to the Trooping the Colour ceremony. In the event, picture and commentary stayed with the Royal parade.

reported that the Archbishop of Canterbury, "ever vigilant of public interest and good taste" would view the news film before it was shown to cinema audiences and "cut out anything which may be considered unsuitable for the public at large to see."

The religious part of the ceremony was broadcast 'live' on the wireless and relayed by loudspeaker to those lining the processional route. However, on the words "His Majesty King George VI is acclaimed" there was, "some uncertainty among those sitting in the stands whether or not to stand up, whether in the case of men, hats should be removed, and whether cigarettes should be extinguished." Television cameras were forbidden entry to the Abbey, so the B.B.C. was only able to show the procession. An audience of 60,000 watched on tiny screens, up to a range of sixty-three miles from the point of transmission. Ipswich was the limit.

Opinions about television, among the Establishment at any rate, hardly changed in the years immediately after World War II. Black and white sets, with nine inch screens, began appearing in the shops and television aerials started sprouting alongside suburban chimneys. But not in the houses of the great and the influential. And not in the Palace. (The first television set – with a 14 inch screen – was installed at Buckingham Palace by the B.B.C. not long before the Queen's accession. A video machine, also a present from the B.B.C., was sent round in plenty of time for her son's wedding some 30 years later.)

It was not that the Royal Family weren't as intrigued by the new form of entertainment as anyone else. It was just that they, and more especially the Sovereign's advisers, saw it as no more than that: a piece of entertainment for the masses; a peep show. The B.B.C., of course, did its best to prove it was something slightly more uplifting, and wasn't above involving royalty to further its case, as and when it could. There was the occasion when it took its cameras, and Richard Dimbleby, to St. James's Palace to televise a needlework exhibition. Queen Elizabeth, today the Queen Mother, was to tour the exhibition and – provided the camera stayed the requisite thirty feet distant (there were no zoom lenses in those days) – Their Majesties raised no objection to the B.B.C. Television Service being present. As it happened, the Queen arrived almost too late to be included in any of the live programme, which was especially unfortunate since one of the prize exhibits was a needlework rug made by Queen Mary, the mother of the King. Relaxing over a drink after the programme and asked by the Queen if he thought the programme had gone well, the producer said yes, though it was such a pity that Her Majesty had been delayed at the Palace. "Oh yes," replied the Queen, "but you see the King and I were watching your programme and we couldn't tear ourselves away from mother's rug!"

The producer of that particular programme was Peter Dimmock, then thirty-two years old, a tiger newly unleashed from Fleet Street, and today, over thirty years later, a distinguished senior executive with the American Broadcasting Service. Dimmock and his boss at the B.B.C., the legendary S.J. de Lotbinière, were the men primed with the responsibility of televising the Queen's coronation in 1953, and at the outset they ran into resolute opposition from Establishment figures within the Church of England, the Palace and the Government.

Hitherto secret Cabinet papers, released early in 1983 under the 30 year rule,* reveal that the Queen was in favour of a May rather than a June coronation (a May date was ruled out because it would have clashed with local government elections) and nervous about allowing television cameras into Westminster Abbey. Only 26 years old, and still grieving the death of her father, King George VI, she was fearful of the extra strain that would be imposed if she knew cameras would be watching every move she made during a complicated ceremony lasting two hours.

Both the Archbishop of Canterbury, Dr Geoffrey Fisher, and the Duke of Norfolk who as Earl Marshall was in charge of the coronation arrangements, had serious misgivings. Indeed, almost a year previously, within two months of the King's death, a coronation Joint Committee, chaired by the Duke of Norfolk, had decided to ban live television from the proceedings inside the Abbey.

The Prime Minister, Winston Churchill, had received a note from his Private Secretary summing up the Joint Committee's views: 'Whereas the filming of the ceremony could be cut where appropriate, live television would not only add to the strain on the Queen (who does not herself want television) but would mean that any mistakes, unintentional incidents or undignified behaviour by the spectators would be seen by millions of people without any possibility of cutting or censorship.'

Churchill and his Cabinet generally agreed with the ban, but once this became known there was such a public outcry that some Ministers began having second thoughts. The Secretary of the Cabinet, Sir Norman Brook, produced a paper setting down the arguments for and against televising the coronation.

Arguing the case against, he wrote of the 'awkward precedent' that would be created. "What arguments will remain for refusing T.V. facilities of e.g. Royal funerals or weddings, religious services, or even proceedings in the House of Commons?" On the other hand, he

---

* The Public Records Act frees government papers after an interval of 30 years, though any department originating a report can request it to be held back, subject to the approval of the Lord Chancellor. Some files relating to the Royal Family are marked 'closed for 100 years'.

conceded: "Television has come to stay and unless it is fully used on an occasion like this it will be said that we are not moving with the times."

The outcome was a compromise. Cameras were to be allowed inside the Abbey after all, but they wouldn't be permitted to show close-ups or shots of the annointing of the Queen, the Prayer of Consecration, and the Sacrament itself. Furthermore the B.B.C. was to be given 'guidance' before being given the go-ahead to do anything.

Dimmock and de Lotbinière were delighted to learn that they were to be actually allowed inside Westminster Abbey, but their battles with officialdom were far from over. As part of the pre-planning, they requested to be allowed to position cameras on the altar side of the choir screen. The Committee solemnly shook its collective head. Out of the question. Since this part of the Church was where a large part of the ceremony — including the actual crowning — was to take place, it did seem rather important to Dimmock and his boss that viewers should have the opportunity of witnessing the historic event. The Committee was adamant. Those watching their television sets at home would be allowed to see as much as the majority of the eight hundred guests sitting in the nave of the Abbey — effectively, Dimmock argued, next to nothing! Stolid silence from the Committee.

The underlying fear was that this new fangled form of broadcasting couldn't be altogether trusted. What was to stop it showing a picture of a scowling Princess, or an ermine-cloaked peer picking his nose? It did not altogether help the B.B.C.'s cause perhaps, that the person who would be responsible for directing the cameras and selecting the pictures inside the Abbey, the young and enthusiastic Mr Dimmock, was best known at the time as a commentator on horseracing.

His boss, on the other hand, the elegant Mr de Lotbinière, must have seemed to Establishment figures quite a reasonable sort of chap, the kind who would be willing to listen. In fact the lean Lotbinière, six feet seven tall, and the dashing, sparkly-eyed Dimmock made an excellent team. Dimmock pushed, and Lotbinière pacified, while the seventeen stones of Richard Dimbleby prepared to deliver a commentary, the subdued brilliance of which would go down in broadcasting history.

The breakthrough finally came when, after much lobbying, the B.B.C. was invited to demonstrate how it would operate with one of its cameras on the *other* side of the Choir Screen. The positioning of this camera — the key to the success of the whole operation — was vitally important. Dimmock wanted to place it on the right hand side of the choir stalls, but he was told he couldn't do that because the orchestra would be there.

119

However, by dint of persuasion and with much murmuring and misgiving on the part of some, he was eventually given permission to hide a camera in the midst of the orchestra on the day of the coronation itself. It meant using the smallest cameraman in the team, a Mr Flanagan, and making sure he was clad – even though he was hardly visible among the musicians – in full morning dress. He still had to wear earphones in order to receive directions from the control centre, but in case his voice was overheard by the assembled congregation he wasn't permitted to speak. Asked a question, he scratched his head to indicate 'yes', and pulled his ear when he meant 'no'.

By the time the day of the coronation arrived – June 2nd 1953 – Peter Dimmock and his band of extremely hard working cameramen and crews had been almost accepted by Palace and Clergy alike. Dimmock was still denied permission to show a close-up of the Queen during the ceremony – though, typically, he took a chance and did it anyway. He, alone, was tipped off by the Palace that the 4-year-old Prince Charles would be slipped into the Abbey and would stand between the Queen Mother and Princess Margaret. But he wasn't allowed to tell anyone, not even his cameramen, until the actual moment arrived. In the event, the picture of the small boy fishing in his grandmother's handbag for a sweetie while his mother went through the process of being crowned Queen was, for the twenty million viewers huddled round television sets, one of the highlights of the whole exciting day. An interesting side issue is contained in a survey carried out soon afterwards. A cross section of viewers were asked to name what, for them, had been the most stirring moment of all. Many mentioned the actual moment of crowning, but the majority spoke with pride of the conquest of Mount Everest – announced on the same day but now, 30 years on, seldom recalled.

Peter Dimmock maintains that the worldwide success of the televising of the Queen's Coronation was a watershed in the relationship between the Palace and those at the B.B.C. who had striven to show that television could transmit pictures of great events that were "in good taste". Overnight, it seemed, television had become almost respectable.

The young Queen and her (for the most part) middle-aged advisers were certainly gratified by the response from all quarters to the live coverage. They were aware – though, again, they would be loath to speak in such terms – of the PR value, which was, without question, tremendous. However, the Palace could foresee dangers. The monarchy had survived as long as it had despite its remoteness from ordinary people. As far back as Roman days, the man in the street had been able to familiarise himself with the face of the head of state by looking at the coins of his realm. Postage stamps also served a dual purpose. Line drawings and newspaper cartoons sometimes cruelly distorted images, but the arrival of photography extended the possibility for millions of not only knowing what individual members of the Royal Family actually looked like but of how they behaved. Even so, only a very small proportion of the population ever had an opportunity of actually seeing these mysterious people close-to; and even fewer had any idea of what their voices sounded like. When King George V made the first Christmas Day broadcast in 1932 "to my people throughout the Empire", wireless listeners discovered, as did the King's biographer, Harold Nicolson, that "his was a wonderful voice, strong, emphatic, vibrant, with undertones of sentiment, devoid of all artifice or prose".

Cinema newsreels showed members of the Royal Family launching ships, opening world fairs, laying foundation stones. But only in short, carefully edited bursts with flag waving commentary that reached its zenith in wartime.* B.B.C. Television News also covered Royal events. But, again, usually with cumbersome film cameras. Not that the television cameras used on outside broadcasts weren't even more cumbersome. But these could put out live pictures, and this was what in particular gave concern to the Queen's advisers. They were also very wary — as was the Queen herself — of being seen too often, of becoming too well known. Familiarity might not breed contempt in this case, but just possibly might lead to boredom.

In 1957, with serious misgivings about the outcome, the Queen finally gave way to pressure and agreed to deliver her traditional Christmas Day message on television. Her father, George VI, had always found speaking into a microphone an ordeal — "I don't begin to enjoy Christmas until it is over" — and the Queen was just as nervous about appearing in front of cameras. She could make those around her relax — the small army of technicians and advisers, up to 90 in all, that sweated under the lights — but the moment the actual broadcast began, her own face seemed to freeze into near immobility. Peter Dimmock, who directed the early Christmas broadcasts, and the Duke of Edinburgh who, as always, was a tower of strength to his wife, tried telling jokes, making faces, *anything* to help the Queen enter the living rooms of millions of her subjects, as it were, and reflect the Christmas sentiment of family unity. All to very little avail. The maddening thing, Dimmock remembers, was that the moment the picture faded from the screens, the 'live' transmission over for another year, a radiant smile of relief spread across the Queen's face. "While viewers were being shown a still-picture and hearing the National Anthem being played, the Queen was at last

---

* A Mass Observation survey of the time noted that in 38 newsreels screened between the outbreak of war and January 1940, members of the Royal Family appeared 36 times and were applauded 13 times.

looking the way we all wanted her to look."

As it happened, the year which ended with the Queen making her first Christmas Day television broadcast had not been a particularly comfortable one for the monarchy nor for Court officials at the Palace.

In the August edition of the *National and English Review,* the owner and editor, a young peer named Altrincham, had criticised the Queen's advisers − "almost without exception the 'tweedy' sort" − for failing lamentably to live with the times. It was their fault, he felt, that the Queen made such poor speeches. "The personality conveyed by the utterances which are put into her mouth is that of a priggish schoolgirl, captain of the hockey team, a prefect and a recent candidate for confirmation."

John Osborne, at one time the generally acclaimed spokesman for the radical young, came out with an article in the magazine *Encounter* attacking the Royal symbol as "a gold filling in a mouth full of decay." To cap it all, Malcolm Muggeridge, in a lengthy and well thought out examination, for the American *Saturday Evening Post,* wrote of "the royal soap opera . . . a sort of substitute or ersatz religion." Even the Queen's Press Relations Officer, he wrote, must be out of the top drawer − "a circumstance which makes them quite exceptionally incompetent."

Commander Richard Colville was the Palace Press Secretary at the time and it did seem to several people, including one or two members of the Royal Family, that he was too rigidly conformist. Sections of the Press, and not just the gossip columnists, thought he was an unutterable snob who dismissed them as he would tradesmen.

Someone who has always held a quite different view is Sir William Heseltine, now Deputy Private Secretary to the Queen. Bill Heseltine first came over from Australia in 1960, where he had been Private Secretary to the Prime Minister, to work on attachment as Colville's assistant. Heseltine thought him "one of the best organised men I have ever known, a marvellously tidy administrator."

Colville's charge, as laid down by the Queen, was to protect the private life of the Royal Family and to see that the younger members, Prince Charles and Princess Anne in particular, were left alone by the media to lead lives as normal as possible. He introduced the system of 'Royal Rotas' whereby, even at official Royal events, only a limited number of journalists are allowed access to report on the occasion.

However, when Colville retired in 1968 − after 21 years of Royal Service − and the Queen asked his Assistant to take over, the time had come for a re-examination of Palace-Press relations. Colville had managed to fob-off all newspaper enquiries that he considered to be of too trivial a nature, and at the same time had made tidy arrangements for coverage of all official duties undertaken by the Royal Family. But this near starvation diet had in turn led Fleet Street to grub around for itself, picking up morsels of information where and how it could, without being too fastidious about its source or accuracy.

It struck Bill Heseltine that perhaps there was at least some substance to the critics' complaints. Perhaps there *was* something slightly "fuddy-duddy" about the way the Queen was advised in the area of public relations. What concerned him particularly was the fact that the public had ceased to know almost anything about the Royal Family except what they gleaned from often highly inventive gossip columns or in the unadorned reports of official events. He felt perhaps the time had come to round-out the picture a little more. So very cautiously he approached the problem.

Prince Philip, who had already pioneered several changes in Palace behaviour over the years since the Queen had come to the Throne, was aware of where at least part of the problem lay. Just a month after the Queen's new Press Secretary took up his appointment, Prince Philip was saying on Tyne-Tees Television's *Face the Press:* "I think the thing, the Monarchy, is part of the fabric of the country. And, as the fabric alters, so the Monarchy and its people's relation to it alters. In 1953" (the year of the Queen's coronation) "the situation in this country was totally different. And I think young people, a young Queen, and a young family was infinitely more newsworthy and amusing. You know, we're getting on for middle-age, and I dare say when we're really ancient, there might be a bit more reverence again. I don't know, but I would have thought we were entering probably the least interesting period of the kind of glamorous existence. And I think this follows. This is the way it works. I think there *is* a change. I think people have got more accustomed to us – they take us much more naturally. There used to be much more interest. Now people take it as a matter of course. Either they can't stand us, or they think we're all right."

The Duke of Edinburgh had probably got it about right. Especially among the young, attitudes towards the Royal Family in the 1960s were decidedly apathetic. What did they *do?* Apart from Lord Snowdon, who had helped make photography a cult among school-leavers, which of them had the talent to survive for more than a week on their own outside the Palace gates? Prince Charles, with his capers as an undergraduate comedian at Cambridge, might turn out in the end to be an okay guy. But his jokes so far were pretty puerile, and his favourite sport was polo – not something the plebs played.

In the summer of 1968, the Prince of Wales was still not twenty and was generally regarded as young for his age, with a degree of innocence that was at the same time both attractive and slightly worrying for those charged with helping to plan his future. Looming up in just over a year's time was his Investiture as Prince of Wales by the Queen at Carnaervon Castle. This piece of ritual pageantry, last performed in 1911 for an even younger Prince (Edward, later Edward VIII, and then Duke of Windsor) was already drawing the attention of television producers who saw the opportunity of a good "peg" on which to hang a programme – quite apart, that is, from the televising of the actual ceremony itself.

Requests began arriving on Bill Heseltine's desk at the Palace for facilities to make documentary films about a-day-in-the-life of, a-week-in-the-life of, a-*year*-in-the-life of Prince Charles. All were given due consideration, but very early on the conclusion reached inside the Palace was that the idea of making a biographical film about someone not yet in his twenties would be pointless, not to say absurd.*

At the same time, ever since returning from Australia in 1965, Heseltine had been looking for a better way to project the Royal Family than through the newspapers and women's magazines. He wanted the public to see them as *people* doing a *useful* job of work. Television with its vast audience and ever-growing influence, might prove the medium to show the Royal Family in a new light.

There was another factor to be considered. Whatever the official line might be, it was by no means certain that the Investiture of the Heir to the Throne was going to prove an overwhelming success in the eyes of the public. There had already been murmurings about the cost, and suggestions that such a ceremony was an archaic irrelevance that was likely to diminish the role of the monarchy in a modern society, rather than give it a much needed boost. Perhaps, just perhaps, if a film was made that centred on the Queen and was shown just before the Investiture, it might alter people's minds, or at least give them a new slant on what a modern monarchy was all about.

Informal discussion began between Prince Philip, Bill Heseltine, and Lord Brabourne, Lord Mountbatten's son-in-law and a professional film-maker himself. The Queen's views, obviously, were of paramount importance. When asked, her immediate reaction to the idea of such a film was not over-enthusiastic. She did not relish the idea of being filmed at practically every turn over a period of several months – "It's no good, I'm not a film star" – and she needed to be convinced that lifting the veil that had protected the mystique of monarchy for centuries, by even a fraction, would not prove to be a

---

* Thirteen years later the Palace view on print biographies about the Princess of Wales was almost identical – though it did not prevent at least a dozen books being published.

mistake in the long run. Another risk she modestly foresaw was that the end result might turn out to be just *too* boring to watch! However, with some apprehension, she finally gave her consent to the project, and to his complete surprise Richard Cawston, at the time Head of Documentary Programmes at the B.B.C., was asked to the Palace "to discuss a certain project".

Cawston, mild mannered and pedantic, had already earned himself a distinguished career. A product of Westminster School, Oriel College, Oxford, and the Royal Corps of Signals (1941-46), he had been one of the B.B.C.'s earliest post-war film editors and then producer of its original Television Newsreel. He had won several television awards for documentaries on such diverse subjects as the legal profession in Britain, and the way other countries ran their television services. As he was later keen to stress, it was because of his work as a director and producer that he was approached by the Palace, and not because of his executive position at the B.B.C.

Initially it was Prince Philip's idea that a Trust should be set up to make the film, with any profits going to charity. Whichever way it was to be done, Cawston was apprehensive from the outset about retaining the same amount of editorial freedom that he would have had with any other programme. At his first meeting at the Palace he was told he could, of course, make the film any way he liked — provided there was an editorial committee overseeing his work. Wouldn't an *advisory* committee be better, he suggested. "Right" Prince Philip promptly agreed. "We'll have an advisory committee to help you. I'll be chairman and the four of us will be the committee."

Initially, the other three members were Lord Brabourne (who already knew Cawston from council work for the British Film Academy), Cawston himself, and Bill Heseltine. When Cawston pointed out that he would want to work with the same team of technicians that he'd used on other films it became apparent that the film would have to be largely a B.B.C. affair and the idea of forming a Trust was abandoned. But the newly formed committee also realised that it couldn't possibly offer facilities to make the first major film about the Royal Family to just one television channel. The abrasive Independent Television Channel (abrasive was a much-used word at the time) that had been strenuously competing with 'Aunty' B.B.C. since 1955 would have to be given a look-in somewhere.

It was suggested, and agreed, that commercial television could look after the sales and promotion side of the operation, leaving the organisational effort to the B.B.C. The job of actually making the film was to be left entirely in the hands of Richard Cawston, however. Arrangements would have to be made for him to be taken off the B.B.C.'s payroll temporarily and if any of his crew were asked for whom they were working they were to reply rather grandly: "A B.B.C./I.T.V. consortium."

Huw Wheldon, Welsh wizard and managing director of the B.B.C. at the time, was delighted with what his erstwhile Head of Documentary Programmes had already achieved. The eyes lit up and the hands were rubbed together as he exclaimed: "Marvellous, you've driven this bus into our own garage." In his enthusiasm, he may even have added "boy-o".

Robin Gill, on the other hand, I.T.V.'s nominee who joined the committee, appeared distinctly miffed. At their first meeting he told Cawston: "We can produce things as well, you know. We don't just sell them." But in this case he had to be content with selling, for Cawston had no intention of being co-producer. It was just not the way he worked. Or, he might have added, the way things had already been arranged before I.T.V. was brought in.

The first meeting of the committee took place in April 1968. Filming was planned to start in July, and the finished product was to be ready for showing, on a world-wide basis, the following summer. The total cost was budgeted at £99,000, the B.B.C. and I.T.V. "lending" the consortium half each. A notional fee of £15,000 was charged to each channel for the rights to show the film in the United Kingdom in perpetuity. Half the profits would go to the consortium – i.e. be divided eventually between the B.B.C. and I.T.V. equally – and the other half would be set aside for charity.*

Once these important logistics had been sorted out, Cawston was in a position to go ahead with his plans to film throughout the summer, autumn and winter, and into the following spring. It was essential to his scheme that he should accompany the Queen on her State visits to Brazil and Chile in November 1968. Equally, it was essential to show Her Majesty carrying out her normal round of duties at home. But most important of all – for this was where the film was to be different from anything that had been done previously – he had to build up enough trust with the Royal Family for them to allow his cameras to film their off-duty moments.

This objective was never likely to be easy to achieve. Despite the fact that Cawston had tacit approval to film, more or less, wherever

---

* 'Royal Family' was sold in 140 countries outside Britain. The total profits amounted to about £120,000. Long after the film was made Cawston approached the Queen to see if she would donate her half share as a founding donation to build new premises at 195 Piccadilly for the Society of Film and Television Arts, of which Lord Mountbatten was President. Her ready agreement meant that the rest of the £500,000 needed to get the project off the ground became more easily available than it might otherwise have done.

he wished, relationships during the first few months between him and the Royal Family were sometimes very strained indeed. Unlike others he had filmed in the past, the Queen and Prince Philip had years of experience of appearing in front of cameras of one sort or another. But the film cameras they were accustomed to used 35mm film, weighed nearly two hundredweight, and required two men to hoist them onto a tripod. They were operated from fixed positions, and so intruded hardly at all on the events being filmed. Furthermore, they rarely filmed with synchronised sound because the extra equipment needed was so bulky. However, during the early part of the sixties, new methods had been tried out by documentary and current affairs film makers, involving the use of 16mm film, and much lighter cameras which could be operated from the shoulder. The cameraman and his sound assistant no longer needed to be stuck in one position. They could move around, adjusting focus, or stand in one position for several minutes at a time, "zooming-in" for a close-up on a subject thirty feet away and picking up the person's dialogue with a rifle microphone. *Cinema-verité* was the plaything of the up-and-coming young film directors in the nineteen sixties, and by the end of the decade their elders mastered and refined the new techniques. Trade union protectiveness still meant that a television film crew was normally made up of at least eight people, but this number of bodies getting in each other's way was still fewer than the crew needed to make a feature film.

At first the *ciné verité* technique met with opposition from the Palace. They had assumed that "informal moments", if not actually scripted, would at least be rehearsed. And the Queen did *not* expect that everything she and others said would be clearly overheard. Early on, when Cawston was filming the Queen's presence at an official public event, he suffered the indignity of seeing his sound recordist bodily removed from the scene by a police officer. The Press, too, objected strongly to Cawston's camera being allowed to roam almost at will while they were severely restricted in their movements. In order to smooth ruffled feathers he eventually agreed that on those occasions when the Press and newsreels had also been invited to attend and report, his B.B.C./I.T.V. consortium would operate under the same rules as the others. The ban on sound, however, presented a much more serious problem.

At a time when his colleagues, especially the young ones, were thrusting microphones in almost every conceivable place and even wobbly-walking their cameramen into bedrooms in order to make true-life documentaries for the small screen, it would be ridiculously old fashioned, Cawston and his colleagues argued, to make a film about the life of the Royal Family that relied on commentary and distant, indecipherable sound.

The contra-argument of Prince Philip, supported by others at the Palace, was that the use of long range microphones meant that those being filmed ran a very high risk at times of sounding downright silly. When the Queen and Prince Philip talked to a great many people individually in one afternoon, it was pointed out, it was almost inevitable that they employed the same question several times and repeated the same comments. Strung together in a film, their efforts to please everyone could be made to look stupid. Similarly the tapes could be edited to give a totally inappropriate impression, and sequences could be shot that caught the Queen, or other members of the Royal Family, completely off-guard.

Cawston, a most upright man, was quick to point out that he was not a journalist. Prince Philip had complained that all newspapers seemed to want was a picture of him picking his nose. Again Cawston insisted that that might be the way some popular newspapers operated, but it wasn't his way. His intention was to show people as they actually were, but not as they were in their off-moments. At the same time he obviously felt it was his duty to put it quite plainly to Prince Philip that dialogue must be recorded along with the film — and from the beginning, if the final outcome was to stand any chance of being a success. It would be too late at the end of a year's shooting to regret that sound hadn't been used in some early sequences. If it would help, Cawston was prepared to give an undertaking that he wouldn't record any dialogue without first obtaining the Queen's permission, and that all the tapes and film would be locked away each night until the final, edited film was seen and approved by the Queen. (It was a concession no documentary director would want to make, but there was probably no alternative if filming was to go ahead.) The bargain was finally struck as the result of a crucial interview between Prince Philip and Cawston at the Palace of Holyrood in Edinburgh in the summer of 1968. From that point on, with both sides agreeing to the rules, relationships improved and trust began to be built up.

It was not long afterwards, while the Royal Family were on their traditional summer holiday at Balmoral, that Cawston shot the famous barbecue sequence — the scene still recalled most clearly by millions of viewers around the world — in which Prince Philip and Princess Anne behaved like hundreds of fathers and daughters given the task of barbecuing sausages for a family picnic.*

---

* Of the several rumours circulating in Fleet Street to this day is one that alleges that once the camera had stopped turning the Queen and Prince Philip went inside to sit down to a full knife-and-fork meal, leaving the film crew outside to eat the barbecue. In fact, rain forced everyone to take cover, and everyone had his share of well-turned sausages.

Prince William creates as much interest today as did Princess Elizabeth and Princess Margaret fifty years ago, when being perambulated in the park. But the disapproval of the nannies was unmistakable and, in 1983, the presence of a police officer essential.

Unlike the Princess of Wales, Prince Charles has had to run the gauntlet of photographers since childhood. The first Heir to the Throne to attend school, the early days were bound to attract Press attention.

The unscheduled appearance of the four-year-old Prince Charles during the Queen's Coronation in 1953 came as a delightful surprise for television viewers.

Just detectable is the broken cello string which flew up and stung Prince Edward's cheek during the making of 'Royal Family' in 1969. One or two television viewers complained that the producer had deliberately planned the string to snap!

Harry Arnold and James Whitaker, two of the best-known 'Royal Watchers' in Fleet Street. They reported the Bikini incident, but have also been responsible for more popular 'scoops'.

Michael Shea, the Queen's Press Secretary, who shares Her Majesty's distaste for invasion of privacy.

Above: Queen Elizabeth the Queen Mother, probably the most popular Member of all the Royal Family with both Press and public alike. Two adoring grandsons give presents on her 75th birthday.

Below: In the 30 years since her Coronation, the Queen has travelled more miles and met more Heads of State than any other Monarch. Here, she is with President Nyerere of Tanzania, in London, 1975.

Hat and shoe sizes are sent ahead to organisers when, as here in Calgary, Canada, in 1977, it is known that the Royal visitors are willing to "dress up".

Princess Anne's public "image" vastly improved after Fleet Street reported her hard work on a tour of Africa for the Save the Children Fund in 1982. Some newsmen had been sent out initially to report on rumours of a marriage breakdown!

The picture that surprised the world, and made the 19-year-old Lady Diana Spencer wary of the Press. Taken at the kindergarten where she worked, it was a rare occasion before her engagement when she posed to please.

The front page of *The Sun*, September 8, 1980 which started everyone guessing - again - about whom Prince Charles would eventually marry.

A photographer takes a picture of a television crew filming a hurrying Lady Diana - illustrating that media attention can sometimes make news in itself.

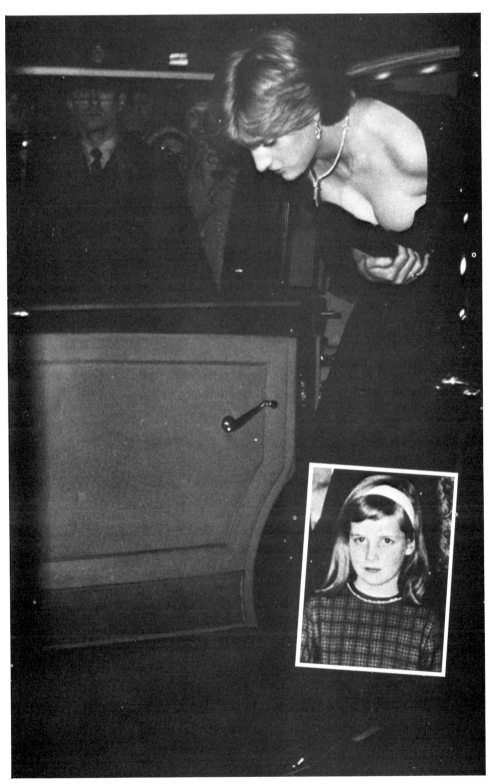

"Wait till you see what's coming next?" Prince Charles told photographers as he stepped out of the limousine ahead of his fiancée, at their first joint public engagement. Inset: the Princess of Wales, aged seven.

Above: It needed a skilled, and lucky, photographer to catch the fleeting kiss, on the balcony of Buckingham Palace after the Royal wedding.

Below: On her first Royal tour, to Wales in the autumn of 1981, the new Princess of Wales occasionally showed signs of nerves and inexperience. But the tour as a whole was a triumph.

X

Time magazine ran a cover-story, in February, 1983 about Palace-Press relations. "Diana is in the acutely uncomfortable position of being the world's most gawked-at celebrity."

The *News of the World's* 'Sunday' magazine had fun imagining a pantomime line-up "that would be the envy of the showbiz world."

Actress Koo Stark, whose friendship with Prince Andrew made her a focus for both Press and public interest alike.

"I don't think mother feels 'A bit of all right' becomes a lady who after all could be on the short list for the throne"

'Please, Charles! Lots of babies throw their breakfasts on the floor . . .'

Unlike their counterparts of 100 years ago, who often viciously attacked Members of the Royal Family, today's cartoonists tend to raise a smile first, and make a point second.

A pop music fan, the Princess of Wales was in her element - and the elements - when she toured London's Capital Radio station in November 1982.

Presumably to emphasise its remarkable scoop, and to make an additional point, the *Daily Express* placed an advertisement in the *U.K. Press Gazette*.

The Times, too, included a comment on the publicity resulting from the Queen's ordeal, with this cartoon by Lurie.

This historic picture, made slightly dismal by the atrocious weather, was posed at President Reagan's California ranch, in March 1983. But it would not have been taken at all if reporters had not pressed for access.

The Prince and Princess of Wales' tour of Canada in June, 1983 was not only a success with the public but may also have heralded improved relationships between Palace and Press.

After viewing "rushes" of the holiday scenes at Balmoral which included shots of the Queen going into a local shop to buy her youngest son, the four-year-old Prince Edward, an ice cream, Cawston realised he already had shot hundreds of feet of quite unique material. But what gave him many sleepless nights was not knowing whether the Queen would agree to any of it being shown!

There was a particularly anxious moment when, through her Press Secretary, Cawston was informed that the Queen would welcome an opportunity of viewing some of the material. Cawston replied that he had always made it a firm rule never to show people their "rushes". (He didn't add, though he might have, that he had once told the subject of another of his films: "Even if I was filming the Queen of England I wouldn't allow her to see the rushes.") Informed of her producer's reaction, the Queen sent a message saying she respected his decision. Clearly, she was prepared to repress her natural curiosity and rely, as is her natural inclination, on the advice of someone with long professional experience. In fact as filming progressed, the Queen, who had started out sceptical of the whole project, became more and more interested, involving herself in almost every aspect. She instructed that Cawston should be placed next to her at table when the family were dining informally so that the two of them could discuss forthcoming "scenes". She even specially arranged one particular sequence – the meeting between President Nixon and Prince Charles and Princess Anne in the George III room at Buckingham Palace. "We must have something special for our film," she told Cawston. Before she was to give an audience to distinguished politicians – especially those from overseas – she would have a private word with them to explain what was required by the camera. It was typical of her character that once she had agreed to do something, she would make sure that it was carried out properly.

The more he was given access to film the Queen's private life, the more conscious Cawston became of his responsibility as a film producer. He saw it as no part of his job to try to analyse, even less criticise, the monarchy as an institution. His brief was to show the Queen on- and off-duty. But the more time he spent doing just this, the nearer he came to the conclusion that the monarchy was a job inherited by a family and not carried out by a single individual. The Queen was Head of State, but she was also a wife and mother. This he saw as one of the major differences between the role of a President and the role of the British monarch. It was one of the main reasons he called his film Royal Family and not *The* Royal Family, the title most people still remember. He was particularly careful, however, not to mix or even overlap the two elements of the Queen's life so when it came to editing he didn't switch straight from a sequence showing the monarch as Head of State to one showing her in a family situation but always placed other material in between. Even so, there were those who felt the need to issue a warning. Cawston recalls David Attenborough, anthropologist and at the time Controller of B.B.C.2 saying to him: "You're killing the monarchy, you know, with this film you're making. The whole institution depends on mystique and the tribal chief in his hut. If any member of the tribe ever sees inside the hut then the whole system of tribal chiefdom is damaged and the tribe eventually disintegrates."

Altogether, over a period of several months, Cawston and his crew shot twenty-five hours of film which had to be edited down to a programme lasting one hour and forty-five minutes. Even that was longer than most programmes being shown on any of the three channels. But when Cawston proposed for the viewers' sake, that there should be an interval in the middle he was howled down by Paul Fox, then the controller of B.B.C.1, and now the head of the commercial station, Yorkshire Television. "I'm *not* having an interval on my channel." Fox insisted. The idea of anything resembling a commercial break on the B.B.C. was anathema. Fox eventually conceded, however, provided Cawston thought of an acceptable way of filling a two minute gap. The solution finally chosen was simply a slide showing Buckingham Palace, over which Cawston ran a caption letting viewers know that there was one minute to go, 30 seconds to go, etc. On the night, *go* the twenty-seven million viewers certainly did! The Metropolitan Water Board later reported that its resources were strained to the point of collapse as a result of the number of chains being pulled almost simultaneously!

Prince Philip was the first member of the Royal Family to be given a preview of the finished work. After months of almost unbearable strain and effort, the day finally arrived when Cawston walked into Buckingham Palace carrying two large circular cans containing what he already knew to be an epoch-making film.

Prince Philip, accompanied by his advisers, watched the film in the ground floor Palace viewing theatre, without a word being said by anyone. Then as the lights went up he turned to Cawston and, smiling broadly, congratulated him on a remarkably fine piece of work. There was only one passage, he said, that he was slightly worried about. This was the sequence in which Prince Charles was demonstrating to his youngest brother, Prince Edward, the intricacies of tightening the strings of his cello. One of the strings had snapped and an end whiplashed against Edward's cheek, causing him to flush and then to cry. The moment after it had happened, Cawston had stopped filming, but the sequence up to this point remained in the finished film. Prince Philip said he wasn't sure if Prince Edward should be shown bursting into tears. It was his only worry. Cawston suggested that a child trying to hold back his tears, and failing, was a very human reaction which most parents would identify with. Even so, Prince Philip said he would ask the boy's mother for her opinion before making a final decision. The message subsequently relayed to Cawston was that the Queen had seen the film privately and approved of it in total, and saw no objection to the sequence of Prince Edward's unfortunate accident being retained.*

Initial public reaction to the showing of the film on B.B.C. television a few weeks later was everything the Palace, and the television companies, could have hoped for. Robin Gill, managing director of the I.T.V. company that was to sell the film overseas, declared that it was "electrifying, the most exciting film ever made for television." "Richard Cawston's film, *Royal Family,* could not have had a better critical reception had it been the combined work of Eisenstein, Hitchcock and Fellini," wrote Milton Shulman in the *Evening Standard.*

On its first showing the film drew an audience of twenty-three million — very high, but not as high as the number that watched the World Cup football final in 1966 (almost thirty million). However, when *Royal Family* was repeated a week later, nearly a third of the fifteen million viewers were watching goggle-eyed for the second time.

Andrew Duncan, a freelance journalist who, in the same year, had been given almost as much facility by Buckingham Palace to write about the Royal Family as Cawston had been to make a film about it, looked back in print a year later** and wrote that *"Royal Family* showed the women's magazine view of royalty in a reasonably chatty, but over-long way, and cleverly entwined nostalgia, patriotism, modernity and humour to give an appearance of reality, but the main impact was achieved by showing the Queen as a fairly unremarkable sort of woman."

In Cawston's eyes the chief effect his film achieved was to create a totally different image of the Royal Family from the one held by many people at the time. "They suddenly became people, not just remote figures, and the importance of having a Royal Family like them struck home." (Largely because of the film, the ceremony of investiture of the Prince of Wales took on a fascination of its own and, to most people, did not appear as a piece of antiquated pageantry.)

Cawston was not being conceited about his own work, but he was

---

* Some viewers complained to Cawston afterwards that it was very cruel of him to arrange for the cello string to break!
** The Reality of Monarchy by Andrew Duncan, published by William Heinemann Ltd. in 1970.

pointing to what he believed was the most vital ingredient in the film's success: the use of natural dialogue. "The great break-through in that film was the sound-track. People actually heard the Queen's voice, other than when she was making a formal speech. For the first time audiences all over the world heard her making jokes and laughing with her family."

Even the B.B.C.'s own Audience Research Department seemed taken aback by its findings. Its slightly convoluted report concluded: "The norm is for broadcasts to reinforce existingly held opinions. The fact that changes *did* occur" (after the film was shown) "suggests that some of those who chose to view the film had attitudes towards Her Majesty which . . . were seen to be so 'incorrect' (in the light of the information that the film provided) that a new and different image was adopted."

Though the great majority of people who saw the film in Britain (it was sold to 140 television stations overseas also) thoroughly approved there were a few, more far sighted than others perhaps, who raised some interesting questions.

Milton Shulman, of the London *Evening Standard,* after giving credit to the undoubted popularity of the film, pondered on whether such a film, made with the Monarch's cooperation, might have constitutional and historical consequences which went well beyond its current interest as a piece of TV entertainment.

"What has actually happened is that an old image has been replaced by a fresh one. The emphasis on authority and remoteness which was the essence of the previous image has, ever since George VI, been giving way to a friendlier image of homeliness, industry and relaxation.

"But just as it was untrue that the royal family sat down to break-fast wearing coronets as they munched their cornflakes, so is it untrue that they now behave in their private moments like a middle-class family in Surbiton or Croydon.

"Judging from Cawston's film, it is fortunate that at this moment of time we have a royal family that fits in so splendidly with a public relations man's dream.

"Yet is it, in the long run, wise for the Queen's advisers to set as a precedent this right of the TV camera to act as an image-making apparatus for the Monarchy? Every institution that has so far attempted to use TV to popularize or aggrandize itself has been diminished and trivialized by it."

In an article in the *Listener* after the film's first showing, the late-lamented editor and broadcaster William Hardcastle commented on the fact that *Royal Family* was being quickly followed by a television appearance by Prince Charles, subjecting himself to an unscripted interview. Would the next step be an interview with the Queen? "I doubt it" wrote Hardcastle. "The refurbishing of the royal image that has been going on for some time now has been managed with some skill, and skill in this field involves judgement of when enough is enough. My guess is that *Royal Family* is the completion of a process rather than a herald of further revelations to come."

As it transpired, Hardcastle's prophecy was to turn out to be almost totally accurate. Though one or two programmes about the Royal Family were made, and the Prince of Wales and Prince Philip appeared on television several times, there was no extension or even repetition of the insight offered to Cawston in *Royal Family*. He himself was invited to take charge of the Queen's Christmas broadcast – an annual event he still enjoys producing, and into which he inserts filmed family scenes as a sort of review of the Royal Family year. He was also responsible for *Royal Heritage,* a marvellous historical series, transmitted in the year of the Queen's Silver Jubilee, in which several members of the Royal Family acted as 'guides', outlining to viewers the stories behind some of the nation's priceless treasures. (The most notable appearance was that of Queen Elizabeth, the Queen Mother, showing herself to be a wonderful television raconteur and interviewee.) But, on the whole, Palace reaction to *Royal Family* was a belief that while the final outcome justified all the effort, enough *was* enough. Even today, some fourteen years after the event, there are those among the senior Members of the Queen's Household who wonder if doors normally closed tight shut were not opened just a fraction too much.

Interestingly, only once since 1969 has a proposal for a television film, parallel in scope and importance to *Royal Family,* been seriously considered, and approved, by Buckingham Palace. Yet in that case not a foot of film was shot, and not a word about the project ever found its way into the columns of the Press, even though the project was being actively planned and discussed over a period totalling twelve months.*

The story of 'the Royal Film that never was' has remained one of the best kept secrets of Palace-media relations for almost five years, and the main reason for revealing it now is because it demonstrates very well the special problems encountered when writing about, or making a film about, a group of people as sensitive to 'image-making' as the Royal Family. Recounting the tale may even, with

* The only hint appeared in an edition of *Time Out* magazine (19-25 January 1979) where, in an article not complimentary to the then Chairman of *Thames Televsion,* Mr Howard Thomas, the author, David Clark, asked: "Could it be that a secret project to make a fawning documentary about the Royal Family is part of his search for final royal recognition?"

luck, lead to the solving of a mystery.

In July 1978 the present author, who moved from newspapers and magazines to television and was at one time a producer with Granada Television's 'World in Action' current affairs programme, wrote to Jeremy Isaacs, then Director of Programmes at Thames Television, now Chief Executive of Channel 4. The idea I put to him was to make a documentary film, at least an hour long, about the work and life of the Prince of Wales. It was envisaged that Prince Charles would participate wholeheartedly in a film which would mark the tenth anniversary of his Investiture.

To the delight of the few people involved at that stage, when Thames Television formally put the proposal forward for consideration the response from Buckingham Palace was positively encouraging. The executive producer of the film was to be Mike Wooller, then Head of Documentaries at Thames, now Managing Director of Goldcrest Television. At a meeting at Buckingham Palace on November 10th 1978, Wooller and I, together with a brilliant young director, Tim King (who was to co-produce with me) were informed that both the Queen and Prince Charles had given the go-ahead to the making of the film. There were two provisos: approval of a detailed outline, still to be drawn up, and the right, if they thought it necessary, to stop certain parts of the finished film being shown. This final editorial control was not something that any television producer would normally agree to, but it had applied in the making of *Royal Family,* without any apparent harm being done, and so no real objection was raised.

Usually the initial response to any major proposal put by the media to the Palace is swift. But even when the answer is 'yes, in principle' there is sometimes a long gap, with much further discussion, before action replaces words. Other unavoidable and necessary events and considerations – such as State visits, overseas tours, and more mundane duties of the Sovereign and her officials – tend to intervene. As autumn dragged towards winter none of these other priorities helped the producers of the film who were impatient to make a start. A treatment had been written, tentative plans had been made to travel to Balmoral to discuss the film with the Prince of Wales. Contracts had been drawn up and initialled, and several expense account lunches had been enjoyed during which, at a Palace official's suggestion, Prince Charles was referred to throughout as 'George' in case those at adjoining tables eavesdropped on conversation.

Security was an important element in the planning. One of the suggestions made, but not acted upon, was that *Thames* should be allowed to install an editing machine and store its film in a room at the Palace. A stipulation made by the Palace was that all material not used in the finished film should be handed over at the end for placing in the Royal Archives. The Palace also made it clear that any Press announcement about the forthcoming project was to be jointly agreed, and any leak to the newspapers beforehand, however unintentional, would almost certainly result in the withdrawal of all facilities.

By the end of three months, preparations were almost complete. Budgets and tentative schedules had been drawn up. A film crew was standing by. At least one person had made arrangements to leave his present job in order to work on the film. An announcement had been prepared for release to the Press, and though security was as tight as ever, rumours buzzing around *Thames'* offices were proving almost uncontainable.

Then, in the last week of January, 1979 the producers received what for them was a shattering piece of news from the Palace: the whole project was to be postponed, probably until the end of the year. "The Prince of Wales' Private Secretary was leaving. His successor, Edward Adeane, would not be taking up his new appointment officially until May and would like a chance to settle in . . ." "The project was postponed, not cancelled . . ." "It was still very clearly in the Prince of Wales' mind to go ahead . . ." "The whole question of making such a film at such a time had been reopened for discussion." . . . By whom? Though no-one was prepared to say, apparently by the Queen herself.*

Thames had planned that the film would take almost a year to complete and would probably be shown in December as its big Christmas attraction. Prince Charles, 32 years of age and still waiting for the right girl to come along, was the cause of a great deal of interest and speculation.**

Also a source of speculation was what his major role would be now that he had left the Royal Navy.

A revised treatment laid more emphasis, at the Palace's firm suggestion, on the Prince's working life, with less scope for showing what he was like as a private individual. This was not entirely in

---

* Much later the author heard, almost by accident, of a conversation between the Queen and someone not employed at Buckingham Palace in which this person recalled Her Majesty mentioning the film and her worry that the treatment did not appear to have a focal point.
** The question of what would happen if Prince Charles became engaged to be married during the making of the film was raised early on at a Palace meeting by one of the producers. Interestingly, the response from one of the Household was that such an event was unlikely to happen during the ensuing twelve months.

keeping with what had been said at earlier meetings when one of the Queen's advisers had assured the producers that what nobody wanted was "a puff for the Prince". The film should be an honest portrait of the Prince of Wales, "warts and all". It seemed that the position had altered somewhat since then, and within the Palace walls, there were strong arguments for and against making the film at all. The Queen and the Prince of Wales were said to be still in favour, but other very influential people were thought to be opposed.

(A slightly influencing factor may have been a biography of Prince Charles by Anthony Holden, which was not due to be published until later in the year, but which had already been read in manuscript form within the Palace and had not been universally approved of – partly, it was suspected, because it got too near the truth in some areas.)

The final blow, as far as *Thames* was concerned, came in the second week of July 1979 when Bryan Cowgill, the company's managing director was officially informed by the Palace that His Royal Highness had decided that he did not wish to pursue the proposal for the making of the documentary. It was made plain, at the same time, that no-one was at fault, that the professionalism of all concerned was of the highest standards, and that, of course, there was no question of facilities similar to those that had been offered being made available to any other organisation in the foreseeable future. Indeed the Palace said that if *Thames* still wished to make a film about the Prince of Wales' planned visit to India in November (which the producers had hoped to cover as part of their original documentary) then this could still be arranged.

Quite naturally, there was regret on all sides at this final outcome of several months' work, but no-one was able (or prepared) to say why the project had been cancelled and who finally made the decision not to go ahead with a plan that initially, indeed for nearly a year, had apparently had the Queen's blessing.

The answer to the second question must surely have been the Monarch herself. The Prince of Wales would never have proceeded with such an important exercise without the Queen's full knowledge and agreement. And the Duke of Edinburgh's influence on the making of such decisions should never be underestimated. But a wholly satisfactory answer to the first question – why was the project cancelled? – was never obtained by the producers of the film. Did insurmountable problems arise over the legal contract, the memorandum of conditions, drafted between the Palace and Thames Television (a substantial part of any profits on the film were to have been made over to charities connected with the Prince of Wales); or was cooperation from certain departments within the Palace lacking? These are riddles that go unsolved. The mystery remains.

Despite the severe blow to their original plans, *Thames* producers investigated the feasibility of making a film about Prince Charles' visit to India — "at least we'll get pictures of him on an elephant," someone observed laconically — but the problems of setting up such an operation in the space of a few weeks, and the cost of flying a crew half-way round the world were immense. In the event, the whole debate about whether or not to proceed became, once again, purely academic. At least it was not Buckingham Palace that finally squashed all hopes, but the government of India. It did so by the simple expedient of falling from the grace of the people. A general election was called, and in consequence the Prince of Wales' visit to the sub-continent was called off. Thus ended a frustrating episode, from the points of view of both sides, in Palace-media relations.*

However, all did not end entirely in gloom. For some time Buckingham Palace had been considering a request by a freelance ex-B.B.C. journalist to make a documentary film about Princess Anne. Permission was now given for this project to go ahead, and *Thames* was offered the opportunity of making the film. It grasped the chance somewhat gingerly, in the light of its recent experience, and signed up Tim King — who had been going to direct the Prince Charles film — as director/producer.

The prospect of working closely for any length of time with Princess Anne must have seemed a somewhat daunting challenge. Of all the members of the Royal Family, the Princess has long had the reputation, with the media at least, of being the most difficult to deal with, on almost any level.** "Bossy," "aloof," "bad tempered," were just some of the adjectives used to describe her. On the eve of her marriage to Captain Mark Phillips in November 1973, a joint interview given to both B.B.C. and I.T.V. had drawn acid comment from Alan Coren, humorist and editor of *Punch,* writing as television critic for *The Times:*

"Who, watching Princess Anne and her fiancé muttering awkwardly, unoriginal, unglamorous, unexciting, could have felt for one moment that there was anything magical or mysterious left in the institution of royalty? And who watching these very simple, very

---

* It was thought by the producers of the film that Prince Philip might not have been enthusiastic about the project when it was first mooted, but when I took the opportunity during an interview marking the Prince's sixtieth birthday, in 1981, to touch upon the subject of the film His Royal Highness merely shook his head and said he knew nothing about the matter.

** It was not until November 1982, when she undertook an exhausting tour of Africa in her capacity as President of the Save the Children Fund, that Fleet Street's regard for her increased dramatically.

ordinary people squirming beneath unanswerable questions, exposed before gawping millions in a dreary trailer for tomorrow's yet mightier gawp, could ever again withhold sympathy from those who have greatness thrust upon them, yet are totally inadequate to the demands thus made?

"Everyone lost. Andrew Gardner and Alastair Burnet sat in their best ties and matching hankies and asked excruciatingly embarrassing questions: 'Can you cook?' 'Can you sew?' 'Was it love at first sight?' The couple fixed glazed looks upon the simpering professionals and mumbled from the backs of their throats."

Poor Princess Anne. Not for the first or last time, having agreed to do something she did not particularly want to do in order to "improve her image" (a term and an ambition that leave her cold anyway), she was simply torn to shreds for her efforts.

At least in Tim King she had a director who was not known for his preference for formal interviews. He was of the "fly-on-the-wall" school. The latest novel method was several stages on from that used by Richard Cawston in *Royal Family,* but again it relied on the cooperation of the subject. In this case, King wanted to install a radio microphone 'about the person' of the Princess so that he could catch the dialogue between her and whoever she was with, while the sound engineer stood, or sat, some way off.

He plumped for the idea of secreting a microphone in the handle of her handbag, and at some considerable expense to *Thames,* purchased what he imagined would be the sort of black leather handbag Princess Anne might use, and presented it for approval. The *Sunday People* somehow heard about the story and got it, partly wrong. *Thames* did not pay £250 for the bag, as the paper claimed (the actual amount was nearer £100) and Princess Anne did not disapprove of Mr King's choice, as the paper also stated − though she did strongly object to the publicity and made plain she was inclined to stop all filming as a result. Furthermore, what she did insist on (and no paper ever got hold of this fact) was that there should be an on/off switch on the concealed microphone. This in turn led, on more than one occasion, to the expression on the face of an eavesdropping sound engineer changing from avid interest to disgruntled despair as Princess Anne abruptly cut him off.

There were other problems − there is almost always tension and moments of frustration in the making of any documentary film − but someone described by the *People* as "one of the *Thames* team who asked to remain anonymous" was quoted as saying: "It's almost as if the Princess is playing cat and mouse with the film crew − just to prove she has the power . . . Nobody dares to talk about this, but privately a lot are saying that she should be shown up. The trouble is that, unlike her, we all have our jobs to worry about."

Part of the problem lay in the fact that it had been stipulated from the outset that the film was to be about the way Princess Anne carried out her public duties as the daughter of the Queen (the title that eventually went up on millions of television screens was 'Princess Anne — Her Working Life') and she was not prepared to diverge in the slightest from that. Tim King, on the other hand, would like to have shown at least some scenes of the Princess moving into and out of her public life, in order to demonstrate the extraordinary capacity for sheer physical effort that practically every member of the Royal Family possesses.

On one occasion, when Princess Anne was due to travel over 100 miles to spend a whole day carrying out public engagements, she was up before seven and out horse riding in the fields round her home in Gloucestershire. King and his crew arrived later, in order to film her leaving the house, but asked if they could also film her out riding, or at any rate leading her horse back to the stables. The answer was a firm 'No', as it so often was to their suggestions. There was to be no filming of her family or any aspect of her home life. She was sticking to what had been agreed: a film about her working life, and to almost all requests for anything else her response was invariably "That's all been done before."

Presumably this was in reference to another very different documentary, agreed to by Captain Mark Phillips without reference to Buckingham Palace's Press Office, which was made by *London Weekend Television* and shown while Tim King was still in the throes of making his film. Called "Brian Moore Meets Captain Mark Phillips", it was intended to be mainly about the Captain's love of horses and his prowess as a competitor in international eventing. But largely because of his wife's participation, especially when sports commentator Moore interviewed them both, viewers and newspapers alike were treated to some fascinating remarks from Princess Anne. On pregnancy (she was carrying baby Zara at the time): "It's a very boring time. I am not particularly maternal — it's an occupational hazard of being a wife." On working with her husband on their farm: "I am the slave-labour around the place, an extra tractor driver or whatever. There is a limit to how interesting a 40 acre field can be, in my opinion."

These opinions — thrown out lightly during an interview — point up the risks taken by anyone who agrees to talk publicly about themselves, but which particularly affects those who rarely give interviews and are usually too honest to be artful.

Television is the medium of the age, for the Royal Family like everyone else. In its recording of sparkling and stately events over the years, from the Queen's coronation thirty years ago to the wedding of the Prince and Princess of Wales in 1981, it has helped to portray and sustain the existence of the monarchy more than any other medium. Its bosses have nurtured close and good relations with the Palace so that, for instance, the first cameras to be favoured with a view of the inside of Highgrove, Prince Charles and Princess Diana's country home, were from B.B.C. television's 'Nationwide' programme. And the first to see inside Kensington Palace only a week after the Prince and Princess took up residence, were from B.B.C. television's children's programme 'Blue Peter'.* In both cases the producers, interviewers and crews were asked not to divulge where the interviews actually took place − and they didn't.

In the thirty years since the Queen's coronation, the doubts about television that were only too apparent then in royal circles have almost entirely disappeared. Television − more or less − is to be trusted. The Press − more rather than less − is not. The fact that this may have more to do with different requirements than with different moralities is thought hardly worth considering. Yet the fact is that while television mostly confines itself to recording what the Royal Family does, the popular Press considers that part of its job is to find out what the Royal Family is up to. The Press makes comment. Television does not. Both approaches, to judge by viewing figures and newspaper sales, are popular with the public; and both have value in allowing a balanced view to be taken.

At the same time it does seem highly unlikely that some of the newspapermen who have reported on royal activities over the years would ever receive the compliment paid by Princess Anne to Tim King and his production team after they had completed their film. The Princess invited all of them to one of the Queen's garden parties at Buckingham Palace − and made a point of extending the invitation to include wives and husbands. She also made a point of seeking them out among the swarm of national and local dignitaries that attend these annual jamborees to have a word and make sure they were being looked after. It was one of the kind actions of a Princess that went unreported.

---

* An equerry's room at Kensington Palace was 'stage-dressed', and re-dressed, for the interview with Prince Charles − on the subject of the raising from the seabed of the wreck of Henry VIII's flagship 'Mary Rose'. But the filming was interrupted on a number of occasions by the sound, 'off-stage', of the programme's pet labrador, Goldie, slurping water from an especially provided drinking bowl!

8. THE VIEW FROM ABROAD

"The Royal Family represents all the integrity, and yet the Press spends half its life looking for all the dirt."
James Goldstone, American film director of 'Charles and Diana — A Royal Love Story'

"Hassle in the Castle — Charles Fears Marriage on Skids after Blazing Showdown with Di"
Headline in American newspaper, barely 13 months after the wedding of the Prince and Princess of Wales

"He's not the one who married Diana, and he's not the one who took Koo Stark to the Caribbean. He's the one who married the Queen."
A Texas television interviewer introducing Prince Philip, November 1982

The Queen stood at the door of a caravan outside the entrance to one of England's most stately houses. She was wearing a full length silk evening gown, brown slippers, and was smoking a cigarette . . .

It was not really the Queen, of course, but the distinguished actress Margaret Tyzack, who was playing the part of the Queen in a two hour drama (100 minutes without the commercials) for showing on A.B.C. Television in America. The caravan was her dressing room, and the stately home was Mentmore Towers in Buckinghamshire — once the home of the Rothschilds and the Earls of Rosebery and now the British seat of the World Government of the Age of Enlightenment and followers of His Holiness Maharishi Mahesh Yogi, at one time guru to the Beatles.

Inside the massive, gloomy building a room has been decked out to resemble one of the Queen's private apartments at Buckingham

Palace − a sofa either side of a high, wide and roaring fireplace, with ancestors looking down from oil paintings on the walls.

The director of the film, James Goldstone, is asking for 'a royal tight-two-shot' and suggesting the extras in the scene 'rhubarb' with hub-bub − "low, slow, polite hub-bub, if you please."

Mona Washbourne, playing the part of Queen Elizabeth the Queen Mother, sips colourless liquid from a champagne glass and jokes, "I hope they drink something better than this. This stuff is filthy." Christopher Lee (Prince Philip) suggests his next line, which refers to Lady Diana Spencer, should read "I'm quite taken with her" not "by her". Goldstone says "'I enjoy her' is what we took out!" and later claims that the only historical inaccuracy in the draft script was that Prince Philip's name was spelt with two 'l's. There are no fewer than nine parts for reporters on the cast list, for this is a film, 'Charles and Diana − A Royal Love Story', that depicts the harassment as well as the happiness of a royal courtship. The story starts with the Investiture of Prince Charles − 'the placing of the mantle of history on his shoulders' − and ends − 'as all love stories should' − with 'the kiss on the balcony' (of Buckingham Palace) after the wedding.

As any travel agent will tell you, Americans are "just crazy about the Royals". Along with the Japanese they make up the bulk of overseas visitors to be seen at any one time on the pavement outside Buckingham Palace. Millions of them crawled out of their beds to watch the wedding of Prince Charles and Lady Diana on satellite television. Thousands stood in lashing rain in Los Angeles and San Francisco to catch a glimpse of the Queen and Prince Philip during their tour of California in February and March 1983. (See Chapter 10.)

It is often said that the explanation for American 'royalomania' lies in the fact that so many of them are descended from European stock and that many of them quietly regret that their ancestors threw off the shackles of the English king, George III, in 1776. It seems much more likely that they may feel temporarily part of a tradition more worthwhile than their own simply because it is longer. "We have less of a sacrosanct historical perspective because we have only 200 years of history," is how one American put it.

Americans tend to show a greater degree of awe in the near-presence of Royalty than most British people do. The British show a chummy respect. The Americans, some of them, almost genuflect on occasion. Coming from a society without Lords and Dukes and a class structure based largely on wealth rather than inheritance alone, some Americans might see in the British Royal Family mostly a colourful relic of a quaint old England. The women who read magazines like *Good Housekeeping* lap up feature articles about the private lives of

Royalty — and not just British Royalty either; the Rainiers of Monaco are just as popular, mainly because the late Princess Grace was a Kelly and an American film star before she married.

The element of fairy tale has strong appeal, and when that fades the editors of mass-selling tabloids, unconstrained by dreams of knighthoods, tickle the fancy of their readers with gossipy stories that allege, with much alliteration, 'his stuffiness and her spending sprees spark a spate of spats between Charles and Di'.

Buckingham Palace, while never forgetting the importance of good Anglo-American relations, has always maintained a dignified and, some would say, slightly superior stance where American journalists — and movie makers in particular — are concerned. The New York born editor of a prestigious magazine who persistently requested an interview with the Queen, or failing that, "at least something worthwhile and exclusive — like spending a day with her" finally had it pointed out that Her Majesty, unlike some Heads of State, was *not* up for re-election every four years.

Clyde Phillips, the producer of the A.B.C. network docu-drama about Charles and Diana, made absolutely no approach to the Palace before setting up his film but found that, at least in one instance, permission to use a certain location for a polo scene was mysteriously withdrawn. When, by prior arrangement he thought, the unit went to film outside the Young England kindergarten, where Princess Diana once worked, there was a noticeable frostiness once they arrived.

Two films were made for American television about the courtship of Charles and Diana. Until now neither has been shown on any of Britain's four television channels, and Buckingham Palace will not say whether or not the Prince and Princess viewed video tapes of either production.*

One version — 'Charles and Diana: a Royal Romance' — was made for CBS of America and, apart from a few exteriors, was shot entirely in that country, some of it at the Sacred Heart Academy on East 91st Street, New York. The part of Prince Charles was played by a then hardly known English actor, Christopher Barnes — after some argument with the American Screen Actors Guild who wanted to know why an American couldn't be cast in the role. Catherine Oxenberg, daughter of Princess Elizabeth of Yugoslavia, so herself a distant relative of the Royal Family, was cast as Diana. (She had been a guest at the eve of wedding ball of the real Lady Diana). And

---

* A high grade British TV drama series, Edward and Mrs Simpson, made by *Thames Television* was avidly watched, and for the most part enjoyed, by several members of the Royal Family, including the Queen, and the Queen Mother whose life, as the young Duchess of York, was portrayed in the film.

Queen Elizabeth the Queen Mother was played by Olivia de Havilland whom, one TV critic cuttingly remarked, "three or four decades and 40 or 50 extra pounds have not made any easier to take."

The second version — 'Charles and Diana — a Royal Love Story' — was made for A.B.C. and filmed entirely in Britain over a period of 26 days. No attempt was made to gain permission to film in or near some of the actual buildings that figure in the film. Mentmore was used for the interior shots of Buckingham Palace. The gardens at Pinewood Film Studios doubled as Palace gardens, and the river at Denham, Bucks. (with a few granite stones added) became the stretch of the Dee, near Balmoral Castle, where Charles fished for salmon and Diana looked on. Scenes of Prince Charles conferring in his study with his Private Secretary (played by Rod Taylor) were shot at Brocket Hall, near Welwyn, Hertfordshire, described in the brochure sent out to potential clients as "the finest conference, seminar and meeting facility in the country". Brocket Hall is the seat of the 3rd Baron Brocket, and as the scenes shot in his house coincided with news of an intruder reaching the Queen's bedroom at Buckingham Palace it was perhaps appropriate that the house — where Elizabeth I heard news of her elder sister Mary's death — could boast that "a complex intruder alarm and flood-lighting system is permanently in use and full screening is available for top level discussions".

Casting the film proved difficult, partly because of a nervousness about appearing in a film which might not meet with Royal approval. Both James Mason (mooted for the part of either Prince Philip or the Hon. Edward Adeane) and Billie Whitelaw (the Queen) were approached through their respective agents and turned down the parts.

The excellent young actor David Robb ('Flame Trees of Thika') was cast as the Prince of Wales — he was "ramrod straight and had a wonderful wooden quality which was just right for the Prince" according to the film's producer. He was also someone "on whom we could place the burden of history".

Over 100 aspiring young actresses were auditioned for the role of Diana. Clyde Phillips, the producer, was looking for someone who had not so much the appearance of the Princess but more the essence of her personality — "someone who could do the business with the eyes — the coyness". The choice eventually fell to Caroline Bliss, a twenty-one year old student of the Bristol Old Vic Theatre School. It was her film debut.

Both giant TV organisations — C.B.S. and A.B.C. — raced to get their finished film onto the small screens in millions of homes across America. Each had invested something like three million dollars in their projects. Schedules were torn apart as each network leapfrogged its rival to be first on the air. In the end A.B.C. won the race and came out on September 17, 1982, a Friday night, competing with an episode of 'Dallas'. C.B.S. followed on the Monday.

Major TV critics were not kind in their reviews, but, as Howard Rosenberg pointed out in the *Los Angeles Times:* "The handy thing about having two TV movies on the courtship of Prince Charles and the former Lady Diana Spencer is that it provides a choice of history. Pick the fable you like best." Rosenberg thought the A.B.C. movie, with David Robb and Caroline Bliss, was "a royal snore", leaving you to wonder how these stuffy monotonous people keep themselves awake . . . The trouble with Charles and Diana, as subjects of a drama, is that they seem to have done nothing more interesting than marry publicly before a TV audience of millions."

The alternative version – C.B.S.'s "The Royal Romance of Charles and Diana" – was, according to Rosenberg, "one of those rare trashers, a superbly asinine presentation that was at once exquisitely bad and highly watchable, a sort of a tribute to 'Gidget Fits Married'." He also pointed out that in the A.B.C. film Prince Charles' Private Secretary was identified as Mr Adeane, and in the C.B.S. offering as Mr Griffiths.

Meanwhile, across on the other side of the continent, writing in the *Washington Post,* Tom Shales decided that A.B.C.'s offering was 48 times better than the C.B.S. movie. Mona Washbourne was "huggably regal" as the Queen Mother, and Christopher Lee played Prince Philip with "debonair gusto". But Ray Milland, playing "Mr Griffiths" for C.B.S., looked like a collaboration of Charles Adams and Edward Gorey "sneering as though he smelled cabbage in the next room".

The actors who had played the part of Prince Charles neither looked nor particularly acted the part, but the actresses in the role of Diana were "quite fine". However the C.B.S. film unfortunately made Diana out to be something of a Pollyanna, or a Cinderella – a sweet innocent sprite upon whom a fairy godmother bestowed a few crucial wishes. "In the A.B.C. version, more believably, Lady Di rather cunningly contrives to bump into the Prince and thus make his acquaintance, giving dear old fate something of a kick in the arse."

Rosenberg, in the *Los Angeles Times,* wanted to know why, as long as they were fantasies, both movies weren't "really juicy". "I wanted to see the real dirt about the reported tiff between Diana and the Queen Mother," (sic), "hear some more gossip about Diana not being (gasp) pure before her betrothal to Charles. And how about those stories of coolness between the Queen and Philip? Maybe next time, maybe on N.B.C."

Tom Shales probably drew the most sensible conclusion when, in his critique, he wrote that neither film was as impressive or affecting as TV news coverage of the actual wedding of Charles and Diana the previous July – "which only goes to prove something that didn't need proving in the first place."

Part-fantasies like 'Royal Romance' and 'Royal Love Story' are tolerated, though not much liked, by Buckingham Palace partly because they tend to be respectful, if coy, – fiction built on fact like rich cream in a layered cake – and partly because, after all, there's precious little that can be done to stop them being made or being shown, even in Britain. It might be very different if a British television company ever attempted to make a dramatised documentary of its own about, say, Prince Andrew, his heroics and his hideaways.

The Royal Family prefers, on the whole, to do its own role-playing rather than see actors dress up like Princes and Princesses. Mike Yarwood's clever mimicry of Prince Charles on television is said to have palled somewhat with the original ("it doesn't seem quite as clever as it was") though Prince Andrew evidently still rolls about at the sight of himself being impersonated, especially when he's depicted as being "a lad with the girls".

The Lord Chamberlain's Office has a set of guidelines to discourage any advertiser from using any image of the Royal Family to help sell products. Soon after Prince William was born an advertisement began appearing in British newspapers for an "aluminium frame kiddy carrier with stand and wipeable clean adjustable inner seat". The pen-and-ink illustration that went with the advertisement showed a baby hoisted on the back of a very proud father who bore a quite uncanny resemblance to Prince Charles. The advertising agency said this was purely coincidental. The drawing was of "an ordinary wholesome-looking bloke". However, soon after the Palace got to hear of it, the face was replaced with "another ordinary wholesome-looking bloke".

The Palace has less chance of monitoring advertisements in foreign newspapers and, as with films, no way of putting a stop to them. In Brazil, a picture of the Princess of Wales' face was blatantly used on hoardings to advertise toothpaste, and on the continent a company director's wife who looks and dresses like the Queen has made a steady income over the years from public appearances.

Europeans – the French, German and Italians in particular – revel in stories about Britain's Royal Family and often seem little concerned about whether the reports are true or not. An Italian magazine, in March 1982, voiced the fear, based on no evidence whatsoever, that Princess Diana – who was expecting her first baby – might find that her child was prey to the blood disease haemophilia, which afflicted the heir to the last Czar of Russia. "Poor Diana," ran the story that accompanied the picture of a radiant

Princess, "she smiles happily, but she is not aware of the terrible truth in her womb."*

A French magazine, at about the same time, published a backview picture of Diana bending over, with a supportive husband placing his hand on the small of her back. The caption to the picture explained that the Princess had suddenly succumbed to early pregnancy sickness. What she was in fact doing was plunging a spade into a pile of earth in order to plant a commemorative tree in Hyde Park, and Prince Charles, much experienced in these matters, was showing her how! But *that,* of course, would not have made nearly such an arresting caption!

Before they were even engaged, the German magazine *Seven Days* put a bogus colour picture on its cover showing Charles and Diana standing together, with Diana apparently cradling a baby in her arms − three pictures had been pasted together to achieve the effect. Inside the magazine, Diana was quoted as saying: "Naturally I will give my future man a lot of babies. To have a large number of children is normal in my family." She had never said any such thing! Another German magazine, in December 1981, carried a faked picture of the Princess of Wales holding a puppy while the Queen Mother benignly looked on. "She gave Diana a little dog so the baby would have a playmate," read the caption underneath.

Over the years the Royal Family have grown accustomed to such deceptions. The Queen is said to be even amused by some of the more outrageous inventions and her Embassy staff in one or two of the European capitals send over copies of papers from time to time. But to the editors who publish such magazines and newspapers, the British Royal Family is almost always a circulation booster.

For a period in 1982, Buckingham Palace Press Office kept a file of untrue stories published in British newspapers − known in the business as 'fliers', and none of them quite as unfounded as those appearing in Europe. But after a short time the practice was dropped because "it took up too much time!"

For several weeks newspapers, including the prestigious *Sunday Times,* published tales about "the sauciest bed in France" − an ornate, canopied four-poster bed, originally fashioned in the sixteenth century for Diane de Poitiers, mistress of Henry II, which Prince Charles was supposed to have bought for over £100,000 as a

---

* In 1972 the Paris publication *France Dimanche* calculated from its cuttings files that over a period of 14 years French journals had published 63 reports of the Queen's imminent abdication, 73 reports of her divorce from Prince Philip, 115 reports of quarrels with Lord Snowdon, and 92 reports of the Queen being pregnant. In the case of the latter, two of the speculations turned out to be true.

present for his wife when their first child was born. Bureaucratic red tape was said to have delayed its export from France, and there was a suggestion that it was not Prince Charles but another admirer of his wife who had purchased the bed. Mystery continued to surround the whole matter until, quietly, the story just slid away . . .

Even the more upmarket magazines such as *Bunte,* which has a circulation approaching one and a half million copies a week, and concentrates heavily on undoctored pictures of the Royal Family find that paying up to £1000 for a cover picture can practically ensure an increase in sales. But not always. One German magazine group has learned that a picture of Princess Anne or Princess Margaret on the cover actually *reduces* sales. But when *Bunte* came out with a 12 page colour picture story of the Royal Wedding on the evening of the day after it happened (the art editor did the 'page layouts' on board the 'plane as it flew from London to Offenberg) the circulation of the magazine increased by half a million copies. According to the magazine's London editor, Johannes Gewiess, a picture of the Princess of Wales on the cover practically guarantees the sales of the magazine will go up by between ten and fifteen per cent. As photographers working for continental magazines discovered (freelances are commissioned for between £150 and £200 a day, plus expenses, to cover a Royal story) the chances of selling a picture of Prince Charles on his own were practically nil for a period of several months after his marriage. "The only way for him to get his picture into a foreign paper or magazine was to stand so close to Princess Diana that it was impossible to get the scissors between them."

Through long and disillusioning experience the majority of the Royal Family have become resigned to the treatment they receive from certain elements of the overseas Press. Princess Margaret who (largely through her own actions, some would argue) has endured the attentions of the media as much if not more than other members of the Royal Family, concluded many years ago that the best precaution against being hurt was never to read a word that was written about her.

Group Captain Peter Townsend, whose romance with Princess Margaret caused a furore in 1953, was also plagued by the Press. But on occasion, he went out of his way to help reporters. Terry Fincher, a veteran photographer, recalls being one of a pack of Fleet Street journalists pursuing Townsend's car as he sped from Lydd airport through the narrow roads of Kent to an unknown destination in London after flying in from voluntary 'exile' in Brussels. "Suddenly, to our great surprise, he drew up at the side of the road and got out of his car. The Fleet Street cars − there must have been 30 of us − screeched to a halt behind him. 'Look,' said the Group Captain, 'if you go on chasing me like this, there's going to be a most frightful accident. If you're that anxious to know, this is the address I shall be staying at in London, and where I'm going now.' He gave out the address, then everyone got back into their cars and drove on at a more sensible speed."

Princess Alexandra once confessed to the author that she enjoyed reading gossip columns but hated figuring in them. "If I want to lose my temper or shout about something, I want it contained in the privacy of my home. I don't want it written about."

Her husband, the Honourable Angus Ogilvy, shares much the same opinion. There was an occasion, however, when he almost literally made his own headlines. It happened on the eve of his marriage to Princess Alexandra when his every move was being shadowed by the Press – this was 20 years ago, in 1963, so nothing much has changed. Driving a spanking new Jaguar he collided with the rear of a taxi outside the Albert Hall while on his way to a stag party. By an extraordinary double stroke of ill luck, as far as Mr Ogilvy was concerned, it turned out that the passenger in the taxi was a Fleet Street photographer. He jumped out of the cab and met a penitent bridegroom-to-be inspecting the damage to both vehicles and holding his hands up as if to say "All my fault". The picture the photographer took was on the front page of three million copies of the *Daily Express* the following morning.

There are occasions, though, when it is impossible to ignore what is being reported – when even to consider a passive stance could have serious political repercussions, to say nothing of imperilling close family relationships. The Royal Family rarely resorts to the Law to protect its good name, but if it decides it has excellent reason for so doing then it does not hesitate long.

Simon Regan, a British freelance journalist, has told of falling into conversation with a group of four men in the hotel where he was staying in the rundown King's Cross area of Sydney, Australia on April 13, 1981. Prince Charles was on a visit to Australia at the time and discussion centred round the topic of republicanism which, as anti-Royalists, the four men favoured. Regan had no particularly strong views on the matter, though he was the author of two fairly unflattering books about Royalty – one about Prince Charles and the other about Princess Margaret. He had also written a biography of Rupert Murdoch, the Australian newspaper tycoon, and it was in order to add new material to this book that he had flown out from Britain.

Over the course of the next few evenings, Regan had lengthy conversations with the four men over rounds of beer in the hotel bar. He declined to reveal their identities to the Press later, but the group included an employee of Australian Telecom, the national telephone company, a well-known newspaperman, an industrialist, and a youth named 'Beachboy'. Much of the talk was about whether or not Prince Charles would be invited to become Governor-General of Australia, and the likelihood that an official announcement was imminent.

The four men, calling themselves 'Militant Action', wanted Regan to write an article about them and each time they met produced items of what sounded like privileged inside information about government thinking at the highest level. They told him that the Prince of Wales was not, after all, to be offered the Governor-Generalship because – despite Prime Minister Malcolm Fraser's efforts to win over certain people – opposition to the idea, especially from young people in Australia, was too strong.

Regan asked for proof of all this, and the men said they would bring along some tape-recordings for him to hear. These were the tapes that were to cause such fascination around the world. They were also to lead to Prince Charles taking legal action preventing their publication. The tapes purported to be recordings of four conversations between Prince Charles and his fiancée, monitored while the Prince was staying at the house of Mr Sinclair Hill some 275 miles from Sydney. A fifth tape was alleged to contain a conversation between the Queen and Prince Charles. Regan was convinced the tapes were genuine, partly because he thought Charles' voice was instantly recognisable, but he was not allowed to have copies and had to rely on taking down transcripts of the conversations.

To anyone with knowledge of the manner in which the Prince of Wales actually speaks, some of the dialogue must have aroused suspicion from the start. The intention of the men who had approached Regan, or so it seems, was to cause political embarrassment; in fact most of the material he brought back with him to London was more likely to make the reader laugh, or cringe. In one exchange, Lady Diana was supposed to have told Prince Charles: *"Yesterday at lunch I told her,"* (Queen Elizabeth the Queen Mother) *"that I could cry for happiness and she said 'Then come and cry your eyes out, my darling, but be careful that the servants don't see you.'"* In one of the very few references to the Governor-Generalship, Prince Charles was purported to have said: *"I'll have to speak to the Queen, of course. But I suspect that it would suit her if I had a sensible job for a while. But are you"* (Diana) *"really so sure? They are a fairly rough lot out here."* Regan maintained that he never intended his transcripts of the tapes to be published – at least not without more careful consideration and checking – but his agent in Munich "jumped the gun" and *Die Aktuelle* bought the rights to publish. (The asking price was said to have been about £4,250.)

The Prince of Wales, now back in Britain, was "appalled" by reports that his telephone calls to Lady Diana had been tapped.

While the couple relaxed in seclusion at Balmoral, a Palace spokesman expressed the hope that should it turn out that 'phone tapping of private conversations had taken place, then "it will be universally condemned by responsible British newspapers. It is a contemptible act, quite apart from being illegal."

Even while this comment was being made – a comment, incidentally, which almost certainly reflected the views of most people in Britain* – moves were being made for the Palace to get hold of at least some of the transcripts. The Prince of Wales and Lady Diana had already been granted a temporary injunction restraining Simon Regan from "disclosing, divulging, or making use of the content" of the alleged conversations but until Charles and Diana had had an opportunity to read the transcripts themselves they could not be certain they were bogus. "If the royal 'phone was on the old fashioned open-wire system," said a senior Australian telephone union executive, "it could have been tapped by simply clambering up the telegraph pole."

Prince Charles must have been worried for he had only to cast his mind back to the beginning of February when it had been Lady Diana who was in Australia and he had been in England trying to ring her.** He told a television interviewer later: "I rang up on one occasion, and they said, 'No, we're not taking any calls.' So I said 'It's the Prince of Wales speaking.' 'How do I know it's the Prince of Wales?' came back the reply. I said: 'You don't, but I am" in a rage . . . They said the phones were tapped or something – which I found highly unlikely . . ."

On the day after the temporary injunction had been granted, and the Prince and Lady Diana had been shown a copy of a transcript of two conversations they were supposed to have had, the London

---

* The *Daily Mirror* in its Comment column on May 5th 1981 described the bugging as outrageous, squalid – and unforgiveable. *"The Royals don't have much privacy and they shouldn't expect too much. Being in the public eye is part of their job.*

"But one privilege at least they should have. The privilege which belongs to any couple about to marry. The privilege of a man to talk to his girl in private."
** The night after Prince Charles had proposed to Lady Diana Spencer at Buckingham Palace she had secretly flown to Australia with her mother and step-father and gone to stay at the Shand Kydd's sheep station at Yass because Prince Charles had wanted her to have time "to think things over". But the Australian Press had discovered her and she had been spirited away to a friend's beach house on the coast of New South Wales – where Prince Charles' 'phone calls eventually found her.

solicitor acting for them both was able to announce that "we are quite satisfied that the telephone conversations did not take place."

But this did not stop *Die Aktuelle* publishing extracts from the alleged conversations. Less than 24 hours after three Nuremburg judges agreed that publication would be an illegal invasion of the couple's privacy, the magazine began appearing in newsstands in various parts of Germany, with a print run 350,000 copies in excess of the norm. It had been printed ahead of schedule and by the time the injunction arrived, explained the magazine editor, copies had already been distributed. "Because of the interest and because of the competition we wanted to be the first and not one of the last."

In London, the Secretary of State, Mr John Biffen, immediately banned imports of the magazine under the 1954 Import of Goods Control Order and Article 36 of the Treaty of Rome — used in the past to restrict the import of shoes. Customs officials were instructed to seize any copies landed at British ports or airports — penalty for knowingly defying the ban: up to a £1000 fine and six months imprisonment. As newspaper editors only had to ask their correspondents in Germany to telex to London translations of the article in *Die Aktuelle* the import ban appeared to be a case of over-reacting, but it demonstrated the determination of the authorities — and the Palace — to stamp on what were, after all, fakes.

The *Irish Independent* ran the *Die Aktuelle* feature — though not in editions sold in Northern Ireland or in Britain — and its sister paper, the *Sunday World,* also printed in Dublin, published extracts in Northern Ireland the following day. However the newspaper's distributors stepped in to stop the paper circulating in mainland Britain.

Only one Australian newspaper, Melbourne's racy *Sunday Observer,* published the story even though, in an editorial, it said the tapes "if indeed they are genuine, were obtained by illegal and despicable means which are to be condemned." Its own somewhat dubious decision to publish was "to clear the air by presenting the fullest possible information. This is a duty we as journalists owe to our readers." The paper had paid no money for the alleged extracts (though presumably they helped sell copies of the paper) "nor would it ever dream of doing so."

Simon Regan, whose meeting with four men in a bar in Sydney had sparked off the whole train of events, issued a statement saying that at no time had he given *Die Aktuelle* or any other publication authority to publish the material he had gathered, and had received no payment through sales.

After a fortnight's investigation, Australian police and government officials reached the conclusion that it would have been impossible to monitor conversations between Prince Charles and Lady Diana in London and that no bugging occurred. Neither were any tapes placed in a Sydney bank for safekeeping, as the four men claimed.

The whole thing, apparently, had been an elaborate hoax.

9. "YOUR MAJESTY – MR PRESIDENT"

"I have to tell you, Queen Elizabeth is a most charming down-to-earth person . . . Incidentally, she's a very good rider."
President Ronald Reagan, in an interview for Time magazine, August 1982

"I think in some ways the Queen and Prince Philip embody the best of what we would like, but we don't want to lead their kind of lives ourselves. So we designate people to live it for us. They're ambulatory deities in a sense."
Enid Goldstein on a 'phone-in programme on K.C.B.S. Radio, San Francisco

"British people of every age and kind and class dream about the Queen because she represents the soothing, the reassuring, the stabilising influence in life. Nobody dreams about Mr Reagan."
Robert Lacey, in a filmed interview for American television

Monday, June 7 1982, turned out to be one of the warmest days in London for years. The pairs of policemen pacing slowly round the fountains of Trafalgar Square were in short-sleeve order, the drivers of the old red buses had slid open their cab doors. It was a day for smiling.

A few hundred yards to the west, in the street that runs up from St. James's Palace to Piccadilly, the manager of a snack bar had optimistically placed tables and chairs on the pavement and by ten o'clock every seat was taken.

Across the road, and down a narrow street in Little St. James's, a steady trickle of perspiring men and dishevelled women could be seen either entering or leaving a grey stone building. It was once a gentleman's club but now functioned as a government briefing centre for the world's Press when it comes to London for an event of international interest. In this case the event was a visit by the President of the United States and his First Lady.

According to a White House aide all Presidents recognised the need, sooner rather than later, to break into their concentration on domestic issues and make the trip across the Atlantic, "visit the major allies and the cornerstone of our foreign policy, i.e. Europe." A major difference between this visit and those by previous U.S. Heads of State, however, was that President and Mrs Reagan would not only be calling on the Queen but would actually be staying overnight as her guests at Windsor Castle. No other American President had ever been so honoured.* Hence the increased interest by public and Press alike; and hence the culture shock that had reverberated through Buckingham Palace and Whitehall in the months of preparation leading up to the actual arrival . . .

As the Queen was to rediscover when she and the Duke of Edinburgh toured the west coast of the United States for 10 days in February and March 1983, the British and the Americans tend to approach certain matters — such as events of interest to the media — in very different styles. A Buckingham Palace aide was to comment ruefully, and with only slight exaggeration, at the time of President and Mrs Reagan's visit to Britain: "We tend to have an organisation first, and then slot-in the press arrangements, whereas the White House, it would seem, tend to make its press arrangements first and then fit the event around them."

Right from the start, White House advance parties were concerned to learn if timings of major events in the President's programme would tie in with prime-time television news bulletins back home in the States. In the event no change in planned timings proved necessary. The President's arrival at Windsor, scheduled for 6.30 p.m., would make the mid-day news in mid-America. His historic speech to the assembled Houses of Parliament the following morning would catch breakfast T.V. in New York, and the glittering banquet given by the Queen in his honour at Windsor Castle would be nicely captured by the evening bulletins. The only event that wouldn't be seen live was the planned ride-out from Windsor Castle with the Queen and the President side by side on horseback. No-one suggested the time of that should be changed in order to suit the satellite. However one T.V. journalist did say to a Member of the Household: "Will you please tell the Queen to ride so that she's

---

* Ronald Reagan was the sixth American President to make an official visit to London, but the first accorded the honour of staying at Windsor since Woodrow Wilson was the guest of King George V in 1919.

facing this direction. It's better from our point of view.'' He was informed that ''one does not *tell* the Queen to do anything.''

Civil servants and Buckingham Palace officials worked frantically long hours in the weeks leading up to the visit in an effort to meet all requirements – "perhaps the logistical schedules were over-maximised," conceded a White House counterpart. The sort of questions asked were: What arrangements have been made for alternate airports? Where are the nearest hospitals to Windsor Castle and the Houses of Parliament? Has anyone checked out the blood supply situation yet?

Not car-loads but *bus*-loads of T.V. personnel turned up in advance to plan coverage. C.I.A. men went over every inch of ground, even, it is said, testing the light bulbs in the Lancaster Tower of Windsor Castle, where the President and Nancy Reagan were to sleep, for bugging devices or explosive devices or both.

In Washington, the President's Press Office has a staff of fifty-five. Even allowing for the fact that the Queen does not hold political office, the Palace Press Office, numbering seven in all, seemed woefuly small to have to cope with the hoards of journalists, something like 600 in number, who were about to descend on London from the United States and the continent. But with the help of counterparts at the Foreign and Commonwealth Office and the Central Office of Information, they somehow managed to handle most queries.

It had to be pointed out, however, that unlike the President and Mrs Reagan, the Queen does not have her own official photographer. And so it would not be very much appreciated if a White House photographer were to be allowed to snap away during informal moments, out of the public eye, even if these pictures – which are the kind taken wherever Mr and Mrs Reagan travel – were to be kept for private albums only.* And no, it would not be possible for hand-

---

* When the Queen received the Pope at Buckingham Palace during his six day visit to Britain in May 1982, his two Italian official photographers had to be politely but firmly restrained from accompanying him when he entered the 1844 room for a private conversation with the Queen. The Queen, incidentally, had hoped that the Pontiff would join her for a private lunch. No official invitation was extended, however, when it was learned from the Vatican that His Holiness makes it a practice not to sit down to a meal with other Heads of State. But his charismatic popularity was demonstrated not only in towns up and down the country but in the Palace too where, most unusually, cordons were erected in the Quadrangle so that staff, normally fairly blasé about visits by foreign Heads of State, could witness and applaud the arrival and departure of this much-loved man.

held television cameras to roam through the corridors of Windsor Castle and tape the President and Mrs Reagan taking breakfast in the Lancaster Tower. "You do understand, don't you?" The media readily complied but, one suspects, did not always completely comprehend. A White House aide observed: "In the United States, the Press plays a much stronger role in political life than it does in Britain where there is a much more controlled environment. Over here it's like a bureaucrat's *dream*."

Journalists the world over have a way of impingeing on bureaucrats' dreams, and disrupting the best laid plans. On the morning of the day President and Mrs Reagan were due to fly into London – that warm sunny day in June 1982 – scores of them besieged the Press Centre in Little St. James's Street and bombarded a much-harassed clerical staff for accreditation to report, in words or pictures, the historic meeting of Queen and President. Looking like so many package-deal holidaymakers they cajoled, they blustered, they sweet-talked the totally bemused civil servants into handing out car stickers and yellow tickets. They already had, most of them, laminated cards bearing their name and a picture overstamped by the Foreign and Commonwealth Office. Those who were told they must supply two photographs of themselves disappeared and miraculously reappeared within minutes triumphantly clutching passport-size photos. Others, always prepared for impending disaster, dug into the recesses of their wallets to spill out dog-eared 'spares' which had been taken, by the look of them, when their owners were much younger and slimmer.

But what the majority had come to collect was the set of cards which would get them past the police cordons and into the 'Press positions'. Altogether there were some fourteen cards – no-one had a chance of being handed the full pack – to allow coverage of the President's two day visit. 'Position Two' was near the first tee on the Queen's private golf course at Windsor where the President and Mrs Reagan would arrive by helicopter from Heathrow airport, less than five miles away.* Positions Five and Six overlooked the East Terrace rose gardens, and Seven and Eight were in the Castle quadrangle where the President would be invited to inspect a Guard of Honour.

But it was Position Twelve that was most in demand: a chance to see the Queen and the President go riding together. Even though it

---

* Probably distraught by pressure of work, a Ministry official had written in the official Press briefing that "The President accompanied by the Duke of Windsor, arrives at Windsor in a helicopter close to Stand 2." It was, of course, the Duke of Edinburgh who had greeted the distinguished visitor. The Duke of Windsor had been dead some ten years.

meant an early call − 8.00 a.m. for a 9.30 'off' − a good deal of horse-trading was attempted. "I'll give you a Nine and a Ten for your Twelve." But few were willing to relinquish a coveted Twelve position.

When the President of the United States travels, the government of the United States goes with him. No-one, not even the Vice-President, is left wholly in charge back in Washington D.C. On a major overseas tour, like this one, the President is not only accompanied by his Secretary of State but also by practically the whole of the White House telephone exchange (one man followed Mr Reagan around everywhere, carrying a small suitcase containing the 'hot line'; another with another case was his personal physician). Also in tow was a small army of secret servicemen, food tasters (known as 'food co-ordinators') and between 225 and 275 accredited media men and women, a large proportion of whom are technicians of one sort or another.

The President and his wife and their immediate staff fly in Air Force One, accompanied by a dozen or so agency reporters and television crews who are officially known as 'The Protective Pool', and unofficially as 'The Death Watch'. The theory is that there should always be journalists in the immediate vicinity of the Presidential party to record any tragedy or emergency that may occur. When the President travels in a helicopter they shadow him in another helicopter. Only when he's on the ground do they merge with the other media people, and to prevent them getting ideas above their station none of them is attached to the Protective Pool on a permanent basis.

A back-up 'plane to the President's carries fifty more White House staff. A third large jet is at the disposal of the media, and a fourth is crammed with communication equipment and the people who rig and operate it.

Normally, the minimum requirement for a Presidential trip to Europe calls for stop-offs at London, Paris, Bonn, Rome and NATO headquarters. On this occasion Paris was slotted in with the summit economic conference at Versailles, and the NATO summit took place in Bonn instead of Brussels. West Berlin was near enough to Bonn and Rome and could be done on a flying visit, which, as one State Department official frankly admitted, "just left London to do."

Staying two nights at Windsor Castle, as far as Reagan's political aides were concerned, was a pleasant interlude in a hectic programme, a piece of PR providing a distraction from the hard-nosed meetings with politicians and military men on the continent. Doubts had been raised about how the great American public would react to seeing its President photographed in an ancient Castle against a historical backcloth of Kings and Queens, privilege and position.

Given his Hollywood image, would the President be seen to be over-acting, a would-be knight in armour at the court of Elizabeth II? Might the Press try to send him up? Would they pounce on any incident suggesting that Mrs Nancy Reagan was 'queening' it? What-ever the answers, it was decided to take the risk – a small risk, as it turned out.* The overall outcome of the President's tour, it was hoped, would be to show Europeans that he was not – as his critics suggested – a President with little grasp of foreign affairs and demonstrate to Americans back home that he was the finest ambass-ador their country could have. It meant a lot of hard work for everyone.

By the time the Presidential helicopter finally landed on the golf course outside Windsor Castle on the evening of June 7, the Reagans had already had a busy day. Up at 6.30 a.m. in Paris, leave Orly Airport at eight. Fly to Rome, meet the Pope, *and* the President *and* the Prime Minister of Italy before flying on to London for the historic meeting with "the Queen of England".

In London, the media men and women had been busy too. After picking up their passes they had sped along the motorway, stickers – GP – on their windscreens proclaiming the greatest privilege of all: a place to park. Each had photostat maps of the Castle and its environs issued by the Foreign Office – perhaps rashly, considering the effect on security – to show where the President's helicopter would land and the route he and Mrs Reagan, the Queen, and other welcoming members of the Royal Family would take as they walked through the rose garden and entered the massive Chester Tower on their way to the Quadrangle.

As always on such occasions, the Press was required to turn up early and hang around for hours. But there were diversions. Photo-grapher Tim Graham, anxious to secure the best position possible in advance of the President's arrival, made his way to St. George's Gateway, hoping for permission to enter the Quadrangle. As he waited for official approval (predictably, not granted) a large Mercedes drew up, two long tapering aerials outside, and two large unmistakably American Secret Servicemen inside. Said one of them to the portly police constable who barred his way: "Say, could you oblige me by radio-ing your superior and asking him where our command post is situated?" The policeman, not to be hurried, approached the Mercedes slowly, stooped down and peered into the

---

* A rumour circulating both in Washington and London at the time strongly hinted that President and Mrs Reagan had let it be known early on in the preparations that they would welcome any invitation the Queen might wish to extend to them to stay at Buckingham Palace or Windsor Castle.

159

interior before countering with: "You've got your own radio, why don't you ask?" "Because," confessed the CIA man with a sheepish grin, "we don't like letting them know we're lost." It was a warm moment in a hot, sticky afternoon.

At 5.15 a policeman unlocked the handsome wrought iron gates that give entry to the Long Walk leading up to the George IV gateway, and a raggle-taggle of some 150 news and television men, with a nosegay of women, queued up to be body-searched by uniformed policemen and women. (One policeman, checking that a reporter's pipe wasn't in fact a gun disguised, singed his finger by sticking it in the burning bowl.) Then, with tripods looking from a distance like machine-guns, and 600mm lenses like bazookas, the column advanced up the slope towards the grand stone face of the Castle walls, the windows of the Queen's private apartments gleaming in the slanting evening sun. "From up there we must look like the Peasants' Revolt," said the man from the *Guardian.*

Passing under the Royal Apartments, through the George IV archway, the Press party arrived in the Quadrangle and crunched to a halt on the gravelled road that runs round a rectangle of grass. Approximately the size of a football pitch, it is as sacrosanct as the Wembley turf. A reporter, crossing it diagonally in order to reach a Press stand on the other side, was severely reprimanded for so doing. A few moments later the Lord Chamberlain, Lord Maclean — a former Chief Scout — not yet changed from summer linen jacket into something more sombre, nearly suffered a similar fate but veered off just in time. Later still, Michael Shea, resplendent in black tail coat and striped trousers, several times trod the sacred turf with impunity as he paced backwards and forwards between the tiered stands, making sure members of the Press were as contented as ever they can be. "He looks like the White Rabbit in Alice in Wonderland, forever looking at his watch," remarked one jaded reporter.

Clouds loomed thunderous dark and nearly another hour passed before Grenadier Guards, magnificent in scarlet and bearskin, marched onto the green quadrangle and stamped boot imprints all over the grass. The accompanying band entertained with part of Beethoven's Ninth, and then a helicopter appeared over the battlements, only to disappear a moment later as it came in to land on the other side of the Castle.

More music, more straightening-up of military lines, and then, as silently as mourners emerging from church, there appeared from a door on the left the people for whom everyone had been waiting. Strangely, there being no general public present there was none of the usual cheering and flag waving that normally greets popular Heads of State. Perhaps that was why the Queen appeared even more solemn than usual, and the President of the United States, a smile applied to his face, looked decidedly nervous.

Mrs Reagan walked side by side with the Queen, followed by President Reagan and the Duke of Edinburgh, with Prince Charles two steps behind them.* Halfway across the Quadrangle they came to a rug, spread out on the stone paving, turned, and stood still as the band played the national anthems of their respective countries.

President Reagan, no doubt weary and possibly overawed by the setting and occasion, was not a study of self-assurance. The Duke of Edinburgh came to his aid, with courtesy and good sense cueing his actions. What precisely to do when the commander of the Guard of Honour advanced upon the President with news that the Guard was ready for his inspection? When to move? Which direction to take? The President must have inspected a hundred Guards of Honour in his time, but there are nuances in such matters, no doubt differing from country to country. With television cameras aimed at him, he must have been grateful for guidance.

If any gaffe at all was committed that first day, it was down to Mrs Reagan. She had entered walking side by side with the Queen. Surely that was wrong? Surely protocol dictated that the visiting Head of State, the President, should walk with the Queen?

It says something for them, and to an extent counters the accusations of inaccurate reporting often levelled against them, that the representatives of *The Sun* and the *Daily Star* were among the most assiduous in attempts to check the facts. After the Queen and her guests had exited, stage left, coveys of newsmen clustered together with their notebooks, looking for all the world like punters after the big race. Michael Shea and Larry Speakes, President Reagan's acting Press Secretary, were consulted. Why did Mrs Reagan walk with the Queen when surely it should have been the President who did so? Mr Speakes, unflustered, spoke with a soft, reassuring smile: "In our country, ladies always go first. It's a Reagan family tradition." What diplomacy! What a small, but oh-so-useful quote. The reporters repaired happily to the local hostelry to file their stories.

That night, on the ten o'clock Independent Television news, coverage of President and Mrs Reagan's arrival figured almost at the very end of the running order, following after news of fighting in

---

* Everyone had wondered whether the Princess of Wales, who was over eight months pregnant at the time, would be in the welcoming party. When it was learned that she would not be, reporters scanned the first floor windows of the private apartment, hoping that one of the shadowy figures that flitted from casement to casement — like a scene from a film about Henry VIII — would turn out to be the Princess. But they were not to be rewarded. She was, in fact, at Buckingham Palace.

Lebanon, the latest from the Falklands crisis, and a purely domestic story. Anthony Carthew, ITN's Court Correspondent, wrote one of his usual pithy commentaries to accompany the film, describing President Reagan as looking "a bit like John Wayne on a bad day". The 71-year-old President retired to his bed in the Lancaster Tower, sleepy but not hurt.

The next morning, after a breakfast of bacon and eggs, Mr Reagan, comfortable in riding breeches, high boots and open necked cream shirt, talked over the latest situation in Lebanon with the Secretary of State Alexander Haig. If either man chose to, they could have pulled aside the yellow curtains and seen – quite apart from an English summer morning shining its best – a trail of media folk once again wending their way up the slope. This time they were being coralled in a large enclosure outside the Castle walls, some of them directly below the President's bedroom window.

This time the number – in the region of 100 at least – had come to record a President riding out with a Queen. Included in the party were those who had been too weary to make it out to Windsor the night before. They were impressed, as well they might have been, at the splendour of the setting. But first sight of the 900-year-old Castle did not constrain one American reporter from asking the hoary old question: "Tell me, with a place as beautiful as this, why did they have to go and build it so close to the airport?", or another asking, quite seriously: "Just so I get it right, is Prince Philip the Queen's husband?"

Shortly before 9.30, all idle chatter was silenced by the clip-clop of horses' hooves and the appearance of the Queen and the President riding gently up the road from the Royal Mews. The Queen was wearing hacking jacket, jodhpurs, and a silk scarf over her hair (much to the annoyance of safety addicts who thought she should have been wearing a hard hat). She was riding Burmese, the 20-year-old horse which had been her mount at the Trooping the Colour ceremony a year previously, when a youth in the crowd had pointed a gun at her and fired six blanks.

The President, a tweed jacket over his open neck shirt, was riding Centennial, an eight-year-old gelding presented to the Queen by the Canadian Mounted Police in her Silver Jubilee Year. He had been offered the choice of a western or an English style saddle and had chosen the latter. But he looked comfortable enough, and much more relaxed than he had the previous evening. When he and the Queen drew level with the centre of the Press pack he turned to face them and pose for pictures, just as he must have done for fan magazines so many years ago. The Queen seemed less than willing to follow his example, though she smiled pleasantly enough. But then a bit like tracers, questions began shooting out from the penned-up reporters, and the Queen's expression stiffened.

"How are you feeling on the horse, Mr President?"

"Great." Said with an incline of the head and a Reagan smile.

"Does the horse ride well?"

"Fine. Fine horse."

Though his replies (and the questions) up to this point could not be said to have been scintillating, the President, looking down on the reporters appeared willing to field a few more lobs. But out of the corner of his eye he must have noticed that the Queen or her horse, or perhaps both, were becoming slightly agitated and were beginning to move away. It had certainly never been suggested that this part of the President's programme, which was purely for the benefit of photographers and television audiences, should turn into an impromptu Press conference!

"The Queen couldn't believe people shouting questions at the President" wrote John Edwards in the *Daily Mail* the next morning. "She looked furious enough to call out the Guards." But at the State Banquet that evening the Queen informed at least one guest that the problem had been her horse. Burmese, she explained, was not used to stopping at this point on a ride and was keen to be on his way.

After a moment's more banter, the President tugged on his horse's rein and the two Heads of State rode off into the East together, followed by two mounted American bodyguards, Lieutenant-Colonel Sir John Miller, the Queen's Crown Equerry, and Mr Roger Oliver, the Windsor Castle stud groom, followed by the Duke of Edinburgh at the reins of a carriage and four, with Mrs Reagan up there beside him, followed by a Land Rover with security and communications men aboard, followed by . . .

The pictures in the newspapers that evening showed an idyllic scene of a handsome couple chatting to one another as they rode down an apparently deserted avenue between spreading oak and cedar trees. As David Hewson described it in *The Times* "The retreating figures on horseback might have been the closing shot of a John Ford western were it not for the distraction of the ensuing train of security men, some on horseback, some in Land Rovers, and the dimly visible figures with walkie-talkies hiding in surrounding bushes."*

But once clear of the media, and the Duke of Edinburgh and Mrs Reagan who, by pre-arrangement, went off on a different circuit, the Queen and the President were able, through long practice, to blind themselves almost to the bodyguards behind, and the boatloads of police on the river. They went past the home farm, and a little further on the Queen pointed out the Royal mausoleum where Queen

---

* The Secret Service codename for the President is Rawhide — or was until too many people discovered the fact.

Victoria and Prince Albert are buried. It was a gentle, pleasant ride. But after about forty-five minutes it was time to be getting back. In a couple of hours President Reagan was due to make a historic speech to representatives of both Houses of Parliament calling for a 'campaign for democracy' and a 'crusade for freedom'. And after lunch with Prime Minister Margaret Thatcher he was due back at Windsor Castle with Mrs Reagan to prepare for the sumptuous State Banquet in his honour that evening.

By all accounts the President and the Queen got along famously. His easy charm and the Queen's noted ability to put distinguished visitors at ease ensured that both enjoyed themselves hugely. At the end of a memorable but exhausting day the Queen personally conducted the Reagans to their suite in the Lancaster Tower shortly before midnight and then, to the surprise and delight of her other guests, returned to chat and laugh some more for another half-hour.

A couple of months later, reminiscing to *Time* magazine's Hugh Sidey, the President recalled in his folksey fashion how "at this magnificent banquet at which you had close to 200 people at a single table, you sit in the middle, the Queen and I on one side and Nancy and Prince Philip on the other. When the toasts are over, the two of us exit down that table. The footmen pull the chairs back, and the Lord Chamberlain precedes us walking backward. I suddenly saw this tiny figure beside me walking, waving her hand. She's steering him. She said to me, 'You know, we don't get those chairs even, and he could fall over and hurt himself'."

When, the morning after the banquet, the President and First Lady, along with their vast entourage, flew off on the next stage of their European tour, they left behind a somewhat frazzled Palace staff and a public who felt slightly cheated that they had been given scant opportunity to catch even a glimpse of a President whom some still remembered from 1940s movies.* Serious consideration had, in fact, been given early on in the planning to the idea that the President might 'spontaneously' decide to stop his armour-plated limousine at some point along his route (at a pub, or a greengrocers were two suggestions) in order to meet the locals. But those responsible for his security shuddered at the thought, "and anyway, there just wouldn't be the time."

Mrs Reagan was scheduled to make an afternoon visit to a children's ward at St Bartholomew's hospital but this was called off because of 'a logistical nightmare'. "It was generally believed that

---

* One enterprising local cinema manager booked a re-showing of 'The Hasty Heart' in the week the Reagans were at Windsor. This was the 1948 film that Ronald Reagan made with Patricia Neal and Richard Todd on his first visit to Britain.

the cancellation was both unkind and unwise," wrote Enid Nemy in *The New York Times,* "particularly in a country where she had received scathing criticism of her clothes, entourage and life style during the Royal Wedding last year."*

The British Press might have been surprised to learn that its American colleagues thought its coverage had been 'scathing' (wry observation, like wine, doesn't always travel well) but certainly on this visit the *Daily Mirror* at least paid Nancy Reagan a compliment (and the Queen's couturiers none at all) by switching heads on a picture of the two ladies walking side by side so that it appeared that the Queen was wearing Mrs Reagan's smart hat and elegant two-piece. "The Queen could look twenty years younger in Nancy Reagan's clothes," enthused the writer of the article, Mary Malone, but failed to point out that America's First Lady was three years *older* than the Queen. "Who could feel relaxed and comfortable inside that armour the Queen has made her own . . ." Scathing criticism?

Though the general public may not have had much of a look-in, the media — after all the hectic kerfuffle at the start — ended up fairly happy with the arrangements made for them to report on the President's visit. Even the omnipresent secret servicemen, micro-phones on lapels and gun holsters invisible under finely tailored jackets, were civil at all times, and even smiled occasionally. They also had a way of popping up in unexpected places.

On the afternoon of the second day three of the most senior members of the Queen's Household were standing on the wide garden terrace behind Buckingham Palace watching President Reagan fly in by helicopter from Windsor *en route* to the Houses of Parliament. Suddenly one of them thought he heard a 'phone ringing. Then the others did too. But they were baffled as to where the sound was coming from — it wasn't coming from inside the Palace. Eventually one of them moved inquisitively towards one of the giant urns that line the terrace. Cautiously peering inside, he saw a peach coloured telephone, and lifting the receiver he spoke: "Buckingham Palace." The voice at the other end was unmistakably American. It was a secret serviceman asking for a colleague.

---

* However, Ms Nemy added in her report, "Mrs Reagan did invite the teenaged cancer victim who was to have escorted her on her tour" (of the hospital) "to visit Windsor the next morning, where she presented the youngster with White House books and a pen."

10. YOUR MAJESTY – MR PRESIDENT

"The coming of Queen Elizabeth has been met by a disgusting display of monarchy adulation – all over the United States. It well illustrates that many Americans, leaders as well as some of the general public, have forgotten what this country is all about."
A reader's letter in a Seattle newspaper, March 1983

"The Queen is the high-wire artist, constantly defying the gravity of a world that largely has no place left for Kings and Queens."
Peter McKay, Daily Mail, March 12, 1983

"The Queen's appearances abroad do more in days to gain goodwill for Britain than all the politicians and diplomats lumped together could achieve in years."
Lord Home, former Prime Minister and Foreign Secretary

On Saturday February 26 1983 the Royal Yacht 'Britannia' sailed into San Diego harbour, California, in vile windy-wet weather, and berthed at Broadway Pier. There was little or no time for those of the media who had been invited to meet the Queen and the Duke of Edinburgh at a reception aboard the Royal Yacht to return to their hotel and change clothes after standing in rain to witness the ship's arrival, and then tour after her on a trip round the harbour. So it was a motley crew of bedraggled reporters and photographers, British and American, who clambered up the gangway and onto the shelter deck shortly after midday.

Typically, the Royal Navy ('Britannia' is manned by 22 officers and 254 men) had arranged for a cheval mirror to be lashed to a stairway so that the ladies especially could attempt a rescue on their rain-flattened hair. At the top of the stairs, ready to receive her guests, the Queen, wearing a remarkable blue and white dress and polka dot peaked hat, removed a white glove in order to catch hold of a wisp of hair caught on her tongue. When the last of the journalists had shaken hands, she and Prince Philip moved among the media, exchanging pleasantries and generally putting everyone at ease in the manner that they have honed to perfection over the years.

Conversations on these occasions, reporters are informed beforehand, are off the record, but an American television commentator, perhaps inadvertently, broke the rules when he chummily told his viewers the same evening how "the Queen was standing there and nobody didn't seem to be doing much, and nobody offered, so I just asked her if she'd be riding horses at the President's ranch," (where she was due to go later on in the tour) "and she said of course she would because that was the whole idea of the trip wasn't it. Laugh. Also asked her what she'd be doing at Yosemite," (the Queen and Prince Philip would be staying the weekend at a hotel in the beautiful national park north of San Francisco) "and she said: 'Well, it'll give me a chance to put my feet up a bit,' which I thought was a rather common touch."

This 'no-big-deal' attitude was fairly typical of American journalists' attitudes at the start of the first-ever visit of a reigning British monarch to California. However, it did not reflect the response to the Queen's arrival as shown in the streets by the thousands of flag waving well-wishers and before long the newsmen's respect was won over as well.

They continued to be puzzled, however, by the appearance ("Was it really a *monocle* that guy was wearing?"), by the behaviour ("Have you ever *seen* so much alcohol consumed in such a short space of time?"), and most of all by some of the incidents that the British media thought good stories.

The acting Mayor of San Diego, informal and natural, placed his palm briefly and lightly on the Queen's back as she found her footing during the course of the harbour tour. "The Queen was visibly bothered, and frowned her disapproval," reported the *Daily Express*. Again, when asked if she had seen the film 'The Prince and the Pauper', and then, if she would like to change places with a pauper, the Queen evidently replied that she would not like to be a pauper and on the whole she found it pleasurable to be the Queen.

Harmless enough stuff, thought most Americans. Most unusual, pointed out the 'Brits' who could not remember ever seeing *anyone* place a hand on the Queen's back, nor hear the monarch express a personal opinion in public about her rôle in life.

Throughout the tour, the British pounced on the minutiae while the Americans – on the whole – seemed to roll out reams of verbiage. Perhaps the fact that they were writing for multi-paged local papers and the Brits were filing for less ample national papers accounted for the difference.

An amazingly large number of men and women — some 3000 came and went — were accredited to the tour, and when some 750 of them crowded into the 'media room' at the San Diego Holiday Inn for the first briefing of the American tour, the Queen's Press Secretary, Michael Shea, gripped the edges of the lectern and stared into the glare of the television lights with the evangelical zeal of a minister who has never seen such a vast congregation.

After saying how much Her Majesty the Queen and His Royal Highness the Duke of Edinburgh were looking forward to their visit, he expressed the hope that everyone was suitably "accredited, accommodated, and know what your transport arrangements are." Wearing a tie purchased from Bancroft of New York, a Daks suit from Simpson of Piccadilly, and shoes that had come apart at the sole, Mr Shea himself was that afternoon — his one free day in three weeks — going in search of new shirts.

He announced that he had appointed — like church elders — three distinguished men, Terry Fincher (freelance photographer), John Osman (B.B.C. Diplomatic and Court Correspondent), and Brian Vine (Head of the *Daily Express* Washington Bureau) to liaise on British pooling arrangements, adding *"Nemme contra Dicente"*, the meaning of which must have floated way above the heads of most of his listeners and into the air-conditioning. Then, in the manner of all fine preachers, Shea delivered a timely warning. "Beware differences between fact and fiction when it comes to what the Queen likes and dislikes," he intoned. "Quite often she's said to favour this particular performer or that particular singer." (A clear reference, this, to the forthcoming Royal night out in Hollywood.) "Very frequently, this is no more than the wishful thinking of P.F. men."

The Queen's Press Secretary wished also to draw attention to the fact that, while the Royal Yacht was quite a sizeable vessel, 'there is no swimming pool, there is no cinema, no ballroom, no chapel, no helicopter landing pad, and there isn't even a kid leather lavatory seat." As *Time* magazine had reported there was.*)

"Equally," he continued, "a fair amount of nonsense is talked about bowing and curtseying, and wearing gloves, and how one addresses the Queen. Basically what you do is what is set down by the host organisation for the particular occasion and what you feel comfortable with."

Following on after Mr Shea (protocol dictated he should come first as representative of the host nation, but he was unavoidably delayed)

---

* The Queen's Press Secretary, however, is also capable of getting his facts wrong. On a number of occasions at Press briefings during the American tour he spoke of the ceremony of 'Beating the Retreat' when, to be punctilious, the correct description is 'Beat Retreat'.

was Mr Eric Rosenberger, a somewhat lugubrious looking gentleman from Massachusetts who got off to a good start in a lazy voice not unlike that of Humphrey Bogart. "I'm Eric Rosenberger, I'm here on behalf of Mike Deaver, trying to work this trip."*

Their styles were different, but in the arduous days that followed both Mr Shea and Mr Rosenberger were to serve the media well. If the names of Whitaker and Arnold (who were not 'working the trip', though Whitaker was, literally, to make a guest appearance later) sounded like a firm of solicitors, then Shea-Rosenberger had the ring of a Hatton Garden jewellers.

The man who bore the brunt of handling the media, as far as the British media was concerned, was Mr Charles Anson, a career diplomat who had been sent out to the West Coast by the British Embassy in Washington, coupled with John Houlton, the British Vice-Consul in Los Angeles, who did valuable work behind the scenes.

On a working level, the highlight of the tour was undoubtedly to be the meeting between the Queen and the President of the United States, and the visit to the Reagan ranch up in the hills behind the town of Santa Barbara, which would match up nicely, everyone agreed, with the horse ride at Windsor Castle the previous year.

However a calamity intervened. The worst storms and flooding in years hit the west coast of America, California in particular, at the end of February, calling for a rapid change in the itinerary.

Following a day and a night in San Diego, the 'Britannia' was due to sail on to Long Beach, California, and from there to Santa Barbara at midnight on February 28, after the Queen and Prince Philip had spent a hectic one and a half days in Los Angeles visiting a space centre, a music centre, a city hall, and enjoying a night out with film stars at the Twentieth Century Fox Studios.

The seas were so rough, however, that it was decided that the Queen, who is not the best of sailors, and Prince Philip should fly down to Santa Barbara (where storms had silted-up the harbour anyway) and meet up with President and Mrs Reagan in (of all places) an aircraft hangar.

But even this did not prove to be such a simple operation. A tornado had hit the Los Angeles area on March 1st, flooding the roads to such a depth that the Royal limousines would not be able to make it from the yacht to the airport.

Mr E.H. Martin drives a U.S. Navy bus that ferries personnel in fine weather or foul. When, on the morning of the 1st, he received a call to report to Pier 9, Long Beach Naval Station, he imagined his

---

* Michael K. Deaver, Deputy Chief of Staff and Assistant to President Reagan.

job would be to transport Royal Navy ratings. Instead, he found that the Queen of England was to be his chief passenger, sitting there, right next to him, as he splashed his bus through the blinding rain to the airport. "The police in Los Angeles gave up about seven o'clock this morning," Michael K. Deaver told reporters later, "but we just kept pushing, telling them we had to get through the water because the Queen didn't want to disappoint anybody."

Neither did the President of the United States. So anxious was he not to be late in arriving to greet the Queen that he was far too early. For 19 minutes he and Mrs Reagan sat in their bomb-proof limousine under a flyover by the side of a freeway exit. Even when they and their entourage finally arrived at Santa Barbara airport there was still a while to wait. Inside the huge aircraft hangar, once the home of the giant 'Guppy' airplane, the President was spirited into a shed hardly more than twelve feet square, with a sign TRACER AVIATION painted over the door. Tracer Aviation could never have dreamed it would get such totally unexpected and free publicity as television cameras from worldwide networks trained in on the door from a tier of packed Press stands on the other side of the hangar.

The 15th Air Force band played catchy tunes, and the small crowd of arms-vetted spectators waited in a pen. After a few minutes the restless President ducked out of his hut and came over to them to "press the flesh". It was, American reporters told their British colleagues, the first time since the attempt on his life that he had gone among people shaking hands like this. As if to emphasise the point his limousine kept pace with him, the passenger door on his side held wide open. Secret Servicemen surrounded the President. One of them, a machine gun in his attaché case, was almost bowled over as photographers raced across the white polished linoleum hangar floor from their 'fixed position' in order to take pictures. As they did so, a bandsman with a sense of humour tootled the opening bars of the Posthorn Gallop . . .

Eventually the 'plane carrying the Royal party landed on the shiny-wet runway and taxied up to and into the hangar. It was one of the most impressive entrances ever made by a monarch. As the forward door of the aircraft opened and the Queen came down the stairs a great cheer went up from the crowd. At the end of the strip of red carpet, the President of the United States and his First Lady smiled warmly as they greeted their distinguished guests, Queen Elizabeth II and the Duke of Edinburgh.

The next stage was to get the Royal party up to the President's Rancho del Cielo, 2400 feet above sea-level and 30 miles west of Santa Barbara over roads that, it was already known, were awash with overflowing mountain streams.

Every reporter and photographer on the trip was rarin' to make the journey up to the ranch, despite the atrocious weather, because few opportunities had been offered in the past to visit the President in his hideaway. A chance to photograph both the President and the Queen at his home was rightly regarded as something not to be missed.

However, at a Press briefing the previous day, the patient Mr Rosenberger had indicated that the only Press people who would be allowed near the ranch would be the President's White House Protective Pool. This example of favouritism, as he saw it, so enraged Mr Paul Callan of the *Daily Mirror,* a writer of some repute, that he fired off several rounds of hurtful words at Mr Rosenberger, though their encounter began peacefully.

"Are writers, both of the American and the British Press," enquired Mr Callan, "allowed to go to the President's ranch in order to see the Queen and the President together?"

"No, there's no coverage at all at the ranch," replied Mr Rosenberger. "But let me add one thing to avoid rumours. The President has a protective pool that's going to take him up to the ranch and come right down again. They'll be gone before the Queen arrives."

"That's ridiculous," exploded Mr Callan, a round faced man with round spectacles, who frequently wears a bow tie. "Why can't the Queen have a protective pool! Why do you have these double standards?"

"No double standards," replied the laconic Rosenberger.

"Of course there are double standards," shouted Callan, from the body of the hall. "Why are you giving extra facilities to the American Press which we allowed you to have when the White House Press visited Windsor Castle, but not the British? The British Press are not getting a fair crack of the whip in this. We wish to go up to the ranch and report what the Queen is doing with President Reagan."

"The White House Press goes to the President's ranch every time the President's there on arrival and departure," explained Rosenberger, speaking from his lectern.

"Some of us have come all the way from London to do this, but not to be told by the White House we can't do it." Reminiscent of the House of Commons, rumblings of agreement came from the sixty or so journalists assembled, some of whom approved of Callan's outburst, while others were embarrassed by it.

"Excuse me. The White House Press is *not* going up to the ranch to cover the Queen. And you're here to cover the Queen, so I think it's a moot point."

"Don't give us that baloney. Do you think they're not going to write about the Queen being there? Are they going to ask the President only political questions?"

"They don't even *get* to the ranch. They only get to the entrance, then turn round and come right down again. It's a very boring trip

171

for those guys. They don't get to see a thing."

"If it's so boring, why do they bother to go?"

Applause, applause. Victory for the British over their old American enemies, it seemed, on a technical knock-out. But it was all fairly childish stuff.

"Can we move on?" suggested a tired-sounding Rosenberger.

"No," insisted Callan. "You've got to organise something for tomorrow."

At this point Mr Charles Anson, the British Press Attaché from Washington, intervened in a still, quiet voice.

"Eric, could you clarify exactly what this Protective Pool does. Does it actually go inside the ranch?"

"The Protective Pool does *not* go inside the ranch."

"Yes, but those guys will get much closer than we'll ever get." Alex Brummer of the *Guardian* pointed out.

"This is a question of privilege," spluttered Callan, his fire still not extinguished.

"Can I make a suggestion," volunteered the silver-haired John Osman, suitably the Diplomatic and Court Correspondent of B.B.C. radio, who had been until recently the B.B.C. man in Moscow. "That at least the British Press get precisely the same facilities as the Protective Pool. In that way we'll know we've not missed anything."

Mr Rosenberger and Mr Anson exchanged glances which seemed to indicate that the suggestion might offer a way out. Mr Callan was in favour, though he still eyed both men warily.

Altercations between media and those organising Press facilities are infrequent — though there is usually at least one "bust-up' on every Royal tour.* The public seldom learns of the confrontations that take place behind the scenes, though if the outcome is successful from the journalists' point of view the proof is often visible in the next morning's newspaper and television reports.

In the case of the Reagan ranch wrangle, it is very unlikely that the historic pictures would have been taken of the Reagans standing with the Queen and Prince Philip outside the one storey building, had not Paul Callan forcefully pleaded for himself and his colleagues.

Having carried the day, it was just rotten bad luck that he was not included among the small band of British journalists who bucketed up to the Rancho de Cielo the following morning. Names had been put in a hat and Callan's unfortunately was not one of those drawn

---

* In April 1983, photographers and reporters covering the Prince and Princess of Wales' tour of New Zealand boycotted almost a whole day's programme of events in protest at the way media arrangements had been organised, apparently to the detriment of the overseas Press.

out. Among those who did make the journey were Peter McKay *(Daily Mail)*, Brian Vine *(Daily Express)* and Alex Brummer, Washington correspondent of the *Guardian*. When they returned to Press H.Q. at the Holiday Inn, Santa Barbara, they were greeted almost like explorers who had reached the North Pole. They had a tale to tell.

The standard practice on these occasions is for reporters to 'pool' their report for the benefit of others who were required to stay behind. Accordingly, Peter McKay – one of the highest paid journalists in Fleet Street – sat behind a portable typewriter and rapidly tapped out an account, urged on by Vine and Brummer who kept up a flow of anecdotal material.

"Prewide-nt Reagan 's invitadbion to the Queen to
join him in a barbecue and ride at his sunny
Californian ranchx home ended in ax chaos yesterday."

The standard of typing would not have been acceptable at Pitman's college, and McKay's writing is usually more stylish ("This is absolute drivel," he exclaimed at one point) but the three page report furnished some of the facts at least.

Due to the flooding, which made the road up to the mountain ranch almost impassable, the Queen had transferred from a limousine to a four-wheel-drive vehicle shortly after setting out from Santa Barbara airport. She had pulled on boots, donned a raincoat, and tied a scarf over her hat to protect its feather trimmings.

For almost an hour the Royal motorcade bounced and bumped up the hill – followed at some distance by the Press – splashing its way through small ravines and sending clouds of spray fifteen feet high. Steers roamed about blindly in the driving rain. Uprooted trees lay on the hillside, broken off branches littered the roadside. At journey's end, Michael Shea who tends to beam even more than usual in adverse conditions – perhaps it's the Gordonstoun influence – informed reporters that "the Queen had found the trip delightful and terribly exciting."

Brian Vine of the *Daily Express* thought she looked rather more as if she was at Newmarket races and had just seen her horse come in last. In fact it was the Queen's determination not to disappoint the President, coupled perhaps with a curiosity to see what Nancy Reagan's home was really like, that had got everyone up there on the mountain top. And, more likely than not, she felt almost at home herself in swirling mists and practically zero visibility so like Balmoral.

The President, who had gone ahead to make sure everything was ready, came to the door with Mrs Reagan to greet his Royal guests. To the delight of the British Press, he was all got up in denim jacket, string tie, and trousers held up by a belt with a large silver buckle. As he and the First Lady posed for pictures with the Queen and Prince Philip, Mr Reagan was unable to resist the temptation to speak to journalists − just as he had been unable to resist at Windsor the previous year. "You've seen this before, when we signed the tax bill" were his mortal words on this occasion. Outwardly at least, the Queen did not appear to wish to be as friendly. Maybe she'd had enough of both the weather and the media for the time being. At any rate, after 30 seconds and with another downpour threatening, she turned to go inside the house. Not, however, before Michael Shea had got a snap for his own family album − causing Prince Philip to comment: "Et tu Brute".

The appalling weather had ruled out any chance of a horseback ride over some of the 600 acres surrounding the ranch-house, but the Reagan staff had prepared lunch for their guests who included the Foreign Secretary and his wife, Mr and Mrs Francis Pym, and the President's Chief of Staff, Mr James Baker and his wife.*

In homely surroundings that owed more to plastic than fine old mahogany, they sat down to a meal of refried beans, enchiladas, tacos and other delicacies. Johnnie Carson made a crack on his NBC television show a few nights later when the Queen and Prince Philip were entertaining the President and Mrs Reagan to dinner aboard 'Britannia' − by now safely tied up at Pier 50 in San Francisco harbour. "I understand," quipped the irrepressible Mr Carson, "that Queen Elizabeth is getting even for the Mexican dinner that they had at the Reagan ranch. They're serving boiled beef and warm beer."

Invariably, dinner on 'Britannia' is a moderately grand occasion in a most romantic setting. However seedy and run-down the surrounding dock area may be, guests arrive at the quayside and step out of their cars opposite a gleaming floodlit ship, 412 feet in length, with a hull of royal blue, decorated with a gold band below the upper deck, and a superstructure of white with buff coloured funnel and masts. At the bow is the Royal Coat of Arms, at the stern the Royal Cipher. A huge, illuminated Royal Standard bends to the wind on the

---

* On the way back down the hill to their own late-lunch refreshments, the British Press suddenly came across a large dog rising out of the mists. Naturally they immediately identified it as the Hound of the Baskervilles, but on closer inspection they found a name tag on its collar which read: "P. Reagan, Rancho del Cielo" and even gave a telephone number. They tried to get through after they'd returned to their hotel, but the number appeared to be permanently engaged. Maybe the storms had brought down the lines, or perhaps it was just that ever changing security arrangements had rendered the number out of date.

midships mast. Royal Naval officers in full dress uniform, courteous, helpful and never over-formal, escort guests to the drawing room where aperitifs are served before dinner.

At one end of the room doors − closed at this stage − give access across a passageway to the dining room itself. Three 20 feet long mahogany tables − two of them parallel to the ship's side, the other, the top table, at right angles − have places laid for a maximum of fifty-six. The position of every knife, fork, spoon and glass is measured by ruler; the average time required to lay the tables is three hours.

There is a selection of centre-pieces available in the ship's strong room, but two favourite items used are the huge old Nelson and Collingwood trophies − one presented by a grateful nation to Lord Nelson's widow and the other to Lord Collingwood, after the Battle of Trafalgar. To the right of the Queen's place, at the top table, is a handy notepad encased in silver with an etching of 'Britannia' on the cover.

All the chairs are Hepplewhite, the china is Minton − white bordered in gold, with the Royal Cipher. For dessert and coffee a green and gold service − Spode Copeland − is used. The glasses − two for wine, one for port, one for water and one for champagne − are Brierley crystal. On the night President Reagan and Mrs Reagan came to dinner, the champagne was Bollinger '75.

At a pre-arranged signal the communicating doors are folded open and guests process into the dining room, a lady on each gentleman's arm. Sometimes, as tonight, the principle guests and their hosts stay behind in the drawing room for a few more minutes to allow formal photographs to be taken. As the door opens once more and (in this instance) the Queen and the President enter, followed by Prince Philip and Mrs Reagan, the guests remain standing until the Royal couple and their honoured guests have taken their seats. (Perhaps surprisingly, since the Queen is Governor of the Church of England, grace is not said.)

Johnnie Carson was mistaken. The main course was not boiled beef but veal, brought out from England on 'Britannia'. The wines were Californian, but the selection was made in London. Normally the flowers − nine arrangements in the dining room, twenty in the drawing room − come from the gardens at Windsor; but on this occasion they were purchased locally.* Thirteen stewards serve the fifty-six diners while a Royal Marine band plays light music in the adjacent drawing room. Ashtrays are brought to the table only after

---

* Flower arrangements on 'Britannia' − considered by experts to be easily of prize-winning standard − are the responsibility of Petty Officer Ian Maudsley, an ex-Royal Marine Commando.

the toasts have been proposed when cigars and cigarettes are offered to guests.

By 9.30, as the Queen knows from long experience, everyone is expected to have finished the meal and be ready to retire for coffee and liqueurs in the drawing room.* Otherwise crew under the command of Lieutenant Commander Nick Carter, Keeper of the Royal Apartments, have insufficient time to "clear the covers, dismantle the tables, vacuum the carpet and rig the bars". At 10.00 p.m. those invited to the Reception begin arriving − 158 of them on this occasion. They usually include diplomats, politicians, entertainers, TV personalities, high ranking officers.

Because this was an extra special occasion for the Reagans − they were celebrating their 31st wedding anniversary − the Queen had arranged a small, very private, party after the Reception and following the Beat Retreat ceremony, at which an iced fruit cake, candle burning, was carried into the room.

The President and Mrs Reagan retired to the guest suite, comprising a sitting room, bedroom, and bathroom, which is directly below the dining room. Directly over the dining room are the Queen and the Duke of Edinburgh's Staterooms.

It is not unusual for foreign leaders and Heads of State to stay on board 'Britannia' overnight. A week after the President and Mrs Reagan, Premier Trudeau of Canada would be occupying the guest room. The ship, with its chintzy furniture and pastel shaded carpets and walls, was once described as a floating country house and it is easy to see why the Queen enjoys making it her base on overseas tours. It is very near to being a home away from home.

A much more unusual and unexpected base for the Queen and Prince Philip was the Westin St Francis hotel in Union Square, San Francisco. Frantic rearranging had been done two days earlier when, again due to weather, the Royal party had flown up to San Francisco instead of coming by what *should* have been the more leisurely way, a coastal cruise on board 'Britannia', with Mrs Reagan as a special passenger.

'Britannia' was left to buffet her own way northwards from Los Angeles, catching up a day later, while the Queen and the Duke of Edinburgh and their entourage occupied the 29th, 30th and 31st floors of the St Francis, and Mrs Reagan the London Suite. The President, who was arriving the next day, had been booked in on the 10th to 12th floors months before, but the Queen's arrival was totally

---

* Souvenir hunters among dinner guests are not totally unknown on 'Britannia', nor are inebriates. The latter are quietly 'taken away' if they prove troublesome, while the former usually choose the small, solid silver menu-holders to slip into their pockets or handbags.

unexpected. However the management remained superbly unruffled. "The St Francis has been receiving guests since 1904. We've had half a dozen presidents, and emperors and empresses, so the hotel staff are accustomed to handling things" a spokesman pointed out.

Even so, the Queen evidently thought it would be a nice idea to go out for dinner at a restaurant for a change. (It may have been at Prince Philip's suggestion.) A private room was booked at Trader Vic's, just off Sutter Street, for *fifty-five* – nobody likes to omit friends. For several minutes before the Royal party set off from the St Francis all the elevators, except theirs, were shut down for security reasons, causing considerable irritation to the hundreds of others staying at the hotel. ("What happens if someone has a heart attack on the 25th floor and doctors need to get to him fast?")

Although no announcement had been made, news of the party had leaked out and the hotel foyer was crammed with sightseers. A businessman from Detroit who had arranged with a prospective client to meet 'down in the lobby' found himself unexpectedly confronted by a veritable sea of unknown faces. Clients of the San Raku Japanese restaurant on Sutter Street looked out on a wet empty street one moment and the next were enthralled by the arrival of squads of motorcycle cops and helmeted police with batons held menacingly at port arms.

Presently a cavalcade of at least a dozen motorcycles and limousines, with an ambulance bringing up the rear, drew up outside the back door of Trader Vic's restaurant. So much for any thought of going somewhere for a quiet night out when you are the Queen and the wife of the President of the United States!

On hand by now was James Whitaker of the *Daily Mirror,* flown out first class with his wife from London, with generous expenses paid by a local television station that wanted his expert comment on the Queen's visit.* Mrs Reagan got out of the car on the pavement side. The Queen got out the other side and had to walk round the rear of the limousine. Mr Whitaker shook his head reprovingly. Sometimes his solicitude for his sovereign is very touching.

By all accounts the rest of the evening went well and the Queen and Mrs Reagan were back at their hotel by ten o'clock. The Queen, especially, was deserving of a good night's sleep for the next morning – at 11.20! – she and the Duke of Edinburgh, along with an

---

* He enlightened his viewers on many matters, pointing out, amongst other things, that weights sewn into the hem prevent Royal skirts and kilts blowing heavenwards in a wind, that Ascot is pronounced Ascut, that the Queen is not the Queen of England only, and that her Lady-in-Waiting always carries a spare pair of tights in her handbag in case the Queen's should ladder.

audience of hundreds, were to be subjected to a whirlwind of entertainment at the Symphony Hall by Mary Martin and Tony Bennett who sang, and by a group of beautiful young ladies calling themselves Beach Blanket Babylon who paraded in giant headdresses depicting a variety of city scenes. One had atop her head the San Francisco skyline, and another the landmarks of London, including a model of Big Ben which opened and closed to music, displaying pictures of Prince Charles, Princess Diana and baby Prince William. The Queen was much amused.

Presumably she was less pleased by a well known IRA supporter who had somehow infiltrated security and shouted his protest before being hustled away. "It took me some time to realise it wasn't just someone having a coughing fit," said Michael Shea at a Press briefing that evening. "That was in the balcony. I don't know what it sounded like in the body of the hall."

"But *we* were in the balcony too" said Alex Brummer of the *Guardian,* "and we heard the man very clearly. So how is it the Queen didn't manage to hear?"

"Do you know what he said?"

"Yes. 'Stop the torture.' It was crystal clear, and we were right at the back of the balcony."

"Well, there we are," responded Mr Shea, smiling as he added "Maybe the acoustics were directed towards you."

"Was it a partial hearing problem?" enquired Andrew Morton of the *Daily Star* cheekily.

"Sorry, I can't hear a word you're saying," replied Shea, appearing baffled for a moment as to why his remark should evoke such mirth.

The Queen, for all her innate sense of humour, is nervous of making jokes in public – especially those written into her speeches. At the state dinner in her honour in San Francisco she made reference to British exports to America, adding topically that she hadn't been aware that the weather was included among them. President Reagan, admittedly more used to reacting on cue, roared with laughter and thumped the table with both hands while the Queen stared stolidly at her notes.

As indication of the food consumed (or half-consumed, or hardly touched) on Royal tours it is perhaps worth itemising what was on the menu that night, as created by chef Norbert Brandt.

To begin with there was a lobster terrine, in which scallops, salmon and lobster cooked in spinach leaves mingled under a mosaic of truffles and scallops. Next came double consomme of pheasant with accompanying goose liver quennelles. The main course was loin of veal in balsamic vinegar and shallot sauce. It arrived with truffled potatoes, baby carrots and asparagus tips wrapped in endive leaves, and was followed by a salad of Kentucky limestone lettuce served with Californian goat cheese in walnut oil dressing. The fifth course, an elaborate dessert called "Aurora Pacific", consisted of puff pastry round filled with marinated strawberries and topped with a ginger sabayon, covered with another puff pastry sprinkled with powdered sugar.

The whole of this − all 260 portions of it − had to be transported from the St Francis Hotel to the banquet in trucks, because the de Young Museum where the Queen was entertained only has kitchens large enough to serve the cafeteria − *'No food to be brought in. Please wait in line'* says a notice outside.

As the Royal party moved on from San Francisco to Yosemite, Seattle and then Canada, one of the city's journalists wrote that "the Queen looks like a pleasant lady, somebody's sister, cosy, fun to talk with over a cuppa tea and it was nice of her to drop in. The Prince too."

Alistair Cooke, in a Letter from America for B.B.C. radio spoke of a doughty Republican lady who decided, "along with the rest of us, that whether or not the job is worth doing or ought to be done or should be paid for − all idealogy aside − it is a job of ferocious boredom, and it is done with grace and even temper.

"This revelation alone may have made the Californian visit worthwhile.

"Apart from that, all there is to say is that the mass of ordinary people smiled and clapped. Mean people discovered mean motives, and the trashy press on both sides of the Atlantic wrote trash."

For such a sensible man, and in the light of what they wrote, it seemed a rather harsh verdict to bring against his colleagues, though Clive James, travelling wit-man for the *Observer* − who didn't get to go to the President's ranch either − described Paul Callan as 'a gossip columnist with the literary sensibility of a vampire bat'', which was even harsher.

11. THIRTY YEARS AND MORE

"Sir John Biggs Davison, just back from the Falklands, was impressed that throughout General Menendez's brief governership the portrait of the Queen continued to hang in the Government House dining room, so warm was the Argentine's admiration for the British monarchy."
The Times, November 8, 1982

'Even in 1956, 34% of those questioned still believed the Queen was someone specially chosen by God and in 1964 the figure had only dropped to 30%."
Leonard Harris, 'Long to Reign Over Us'

"Monarchy is an art with very few practitioners and still fewer qualified instructors."
A leader in The Times, August 18, 1982

"The Queen is a Bramley cooking apple . . . clean, long lasting, good for you, reliable, with tartness and an intrepid skin that doesn't show bruising."
Lynda Lee-Potter in the Daily Mail, comparing members of the Royal Family to different kinds of fruit, April 27, 1983

Some thirty years after her coronation − Sovereign of the United Kingdom and Northern Ireland, Canada, Australia, New Zealand, Malta, the Bahamas, Mauritius, Fiji, Barbados, Jamaica, Grenada and Papua New Guinea − Queen Elizabeth II remains essentially the kind of person she was when she acceded to the throne in 1952 at the age of twenty-six. She has matured, of course, and has accumulated a vast amount of knowledge about the world (it is unlikely that any other single international figure has travelled as widely). She has become wise to the ways of politicians, and has won the respect of world statesmen (in Britain, eight Prime Ministers have served under her so far). As a wife, mother and grandmother she has watched with keen and loving interest the fortunes and misfortunes that have befallen members of both her immediate family, and of kinsmen abroad. (At Prince Charles' wedding reception, Prince Andrew announced the name of each guest with the twirl of a rattle: "One King of Norway — King Olaf. One King in exile — King Constantine of Greece.")

Her power of observation, if anything, has become even sharper with the passing of the years — "she only has to give a glance, and we are made aware we've overlooked some detail in the planning," said a courtier — and her sense of purpose and occasion remains as steadfast as ever. Thirty-one years of rule* have invested her with a considerable confidence in her own powers and judgment, which may have been lacking in her days as a very young Queen. But her chief attributes have always been a prodigious sense of dignity and an innate commonsense. "I have never known anyone so commonsensible," enthused one of the Queen's closest advisers. "She has an ability to go straight to the very heart of a matter while the rest of us are still trying to make up our minds. She has learned from years and years of reading official papers and meeting official people to disregard the waffle. Now and again she'll make a decision different from what might have been expected. But afterwards, nine times out of ten, you'll realise she was absolutely right. To some people the Queen may seem to be a fairly ordinary woman doing an extraordinary job, whereas in reality she is an extraordinary woman doing an extremely difficult job. If you doubt that, ask yourself how many times she's put a foot wrong in the past thirty-one years?"

Such fulsome praise would certainly find favour with the majority of the Queen's subjects who in the same thirty-one years have experienced a vicissitude of fortunes, ranging from post war austerity to a period of 'never having had it so good', to present-day uncertainty about whether or not the world will decide to blow itself up. They, along with their children and grandchildren, have never wavered in their respect and admiration for the Queen — love would probably be too intimate a word to describe their feelings. The Queen does not inspire spontaneous affection in the way that her mother does. Small children who dart out from the crowd on a walkabout to present a posy often hesitate at the very last moment, and sometimes even scamper back to their places. Even when a broad smile transforms

---

* The Queen acceded to the Throne on 6th February 1952 and the actual coronation took place on June 2nd, 1953.

the Queen's often sombre appearance, the hand held out to receive the bouquet is encased in a white glove. It is a bit like giving flowers to a headmistress on speech day. After years of experience (the first prescribed walkabout took place in New Zealand in 1969) the Queen still appears uneasy making conversation with strangers – a requirement of Royalty that Prince Charles has forced himself to master, though his quips can sometimes lead him into dangerous territory.* She perceptibly pauses before making a comment. She is a great student of faces and an excellent memoriser of names and places so that when she returns to a town or a country after an absence of several years she is quite likely not to have been prompted when she surprises a local dignitary by not only remembering his name but also some detail about his family – "Wasn't your son about to go into the Army the last time we met?"

It is typical of her character that the Queen does not use her gift of memory to catch out her staff – she is well aware that few would wish to contradict their Monarch! If she is ignorant of a point she will admit that she is. She is equally honest about her personal likes and dislikes where outside interests are concerned. She has never pretended, for instance, that she enjoys the opera or going to watch cricket – though duty requires from time to time her presence at both. Once an England – Australia Test match at Lord's cricket ground ended while the Queen was present, so it was felt necessary to invite both teams back to Buckingham Palace for afternoon tea. As nervousness on all sides grew less one of the Australian team decided to stretch out full length on a damask settee. "I expect you're feeling tired after all your exertions?" smiled one of the Queen's Ladies-in-Waiting. "Know what! I'm fair buggered, Princess," came the reply.

The Queen is extremely cautious about showing whom she likes and whom she doesn't. "In any Court over any period it has been very easy for the Sovereign, by showing likes and dislikes, to have a very unfortunate effect on the courtiers," says a senior member of the Queen's Household. "I think the Queen is as well aware of that as anybody. Nobody around here," (i.e. Buckingham Palace) "feels that he or she is treated any differently from anyone else, and that is achieved by a constant exercise of self control on the part of the Queen herself – it's not that she likes everybody to exactly the same degree but she's determined not to show there's any difference."

---

* Some years ago, while making a short film in Wales, and wired up for sound, Prince Charles was startled by a woman on a walkabout who insisted on telling him that she had had both breasts removed by surgery. "Well, I trust you feel lighter, madam," was his quick, recorded (but untransmitted) response.

The same yardstick applies to Commonwealth Heads of Government who over the years have found the Queen to be a sympathetic and unbiased listener, occasionally prepared to offer advice if asked and sometimes able to act as an unofficial go-between. But whether their meetings take place in the Queen's private apartments at Buckingham Palace or at some more impersonal venue during a Commonwealth Heads of Government conference no-one is allowed to leave the Queen's presence with the feeling that he or she is favoured above others.

Her dealings with British Prime Ministers over the years have been equally circumspect. As a very young Queen she recognised her own inexperience and was not too surprised that her first Prime Minister, Winston Churchill, treated her in a grandfatherly way. But by the time Harold Macmillan arrived at 10 Downing Street she was more self-assured and during the seven years of his office as Prime Minister, up until 1963, she became more and more fascinated by not only the craft of statesmanship but the personalities of politicians as well. "Since Your Majesty showed much interest in the private letter which Mr Kruschev sent me," Harold Macmillan wrote to her in April 1959 "I am arranging for a copy to be sent."

It is said that the Queen got along well with both Sir Harold Wilson and James Callaghan during their terms as Prime Minister, but hard evidence of the relationship between the Queen and Margaret Thatcher is more difficult to obtain.

Ever since taking up office, Britain's first woman Prime Minister, in common with her predecessors, has made the short trip from Downing Street to the Palace for the traditional Tuesday evening meeting with the Sovereign. But as no-one else is ever present at these *tête-à-têtes* (the Private Secretaries of both P.M. and Monarch usually take the opportunity to chat together in another room) very few others, if anyone at all, get to hear of what actually happened. On a purely personal level, however, it is known that during the Falklands conflict Mrs Thatcher showed the Queen deep concern as the mother of a young man caught up in the fighting and always made sure the Palace had the very latest news. Conversely, when Mrs Thatcher's son, Mark, went missing on a car rally in North Africa the Queen telephoned Mr and Mrs Thatcher more than once to offer comfort and reassurance.

In many ways the two women are dissimilar in character – Mrs Thatcher has even been compared to Queen Elizabeth I – but they share an ability to be steely-tough at times, and it would be surprising if during one of their lengthy conversations Mrs Thatcher has not been nearly caught out by the Queen's lightly-spoken but shrewdly-judged questions.

In family matters, Prince Philip is head person – though the

Queen is said to be far less in awe of him than she was at one time. Whereas she used to rely on his support, always generously given, in matters of State as well as domestic affairs, she has come to rely on her own judgment much more and is ready to argue for it if her husband disagrees. Whether or not they quarrel in private, they take care not to spat in public. One of the very few occasions they have appeared to be having a disagreement was in Stockton-on-Tees during a Jubilee Year tour when local dignitaries awaiting their arrival witnessed what looked like a minor ding-dong going in inside the Perspex dome of the Royal Rolls Royce.

Being constantly in the public eye is a facet of their duty to which both the Queen and the Duke have long become reconciled. The public has every sympathy — indeed it is the requirement of Royal life that most people least envy. But, as a former Royal aide points out: "The background to understanding the Royal Family is to appreciate that to them their way of life is totally natural. They don't know any other, and while all of us at some time transplant ourselves and think how we couldn't possibly cope with the life they have to lead, to them it is quite natural. What would be unnatural to them would be to lead *our* sort of life."

There is, however, one aspect of her official life with which the Queen has had difficulty in coming to terms from the very beginning — the attentions of the media. No-one knows better than the Queen where her duty lies, but at the same time no other member of the Royal Family — with the possible exception of Princess Anne and Princess Alexandra — enjoys a harsh spotlight less. In most assessments of the Queen's life, scant attention is paid to the fact that in childhood both she and Princess Margaret were the focus of enormous public interest. "It almost frightens me that the people should love her so much," her father wrote to Queen Mary. The two girls were photographed at every opportunity — partly, one suspects, to underline the virtues of family life and the importance of continuity at a time when the behaviour of their uncle, the Prince of Wales, was giving cause for concern. Journalists were even invited inside their home at 145 Piccadilly to inspect their menagerie of pets.

The Queen is by nature a shy woman who, but for the untimely death of King George VI, might have enjoyed a few more years of unpublicised married life with her Naval husband and two small children. After coming to the Throne, she gave clear instructions to her Press Secretary that he was to do everything possible to defend both her and her family from Press invasion. When her 'second family' was complete — Prince Andrew and Prince Edward are respectively 12 and 16 years younger than Prince Charles — precautions were taken to ensure that the Press was kept well away from both of them for as long as possible.*

It was not until the late nineteen sixties, when relationships between the monarch and her people were showing signs of becoming slightly less hidebound, that the Queen became more tolerant of the media and more aware of its importance as a channel of communication between the monarchy and the people. "The Queen can see as clearly as anybody that the institution which she represents and embodies depends quite heavily on the impact it makes on people through the media," said one of her closest aides, "so to that extent she accepts that certainly the whole of her official life must be adequately covered by the media and that they have a legitimate interest in her private life."

This acceptance, photographers will tell you, does not, however, extend to co-operation. "I've never known the Queen do anything for the Press" says one Royal watcher, "in the way that the Queen Mother does when she deliberately pauses long enough, and even turns, so that everyone has a chance of a decent shot. With the Queen, it all depends on whether you happen to be in the right place at the right time. The Queen doesn't pose − and, quite frankly, because of who she is, most photographers don't think she should, if she doesn't want to."

John Dixon, who successfully combines a career photographing Royalty with illustrating magazine articles on cookery, finds that one of the most difficult things to achieve is a picture of the Queen wearing evening dress in which "her tiara twinkles, her eyes sparkle, and her teeth show well − all at the same time.

"When you're one of a gaggle of photographers she doesn't treat you as a person in your own right, but in the same way as a film star treats a camera. She's doing a job, and you're recording it. She walks towards you fully confident that you'll get out of her way − which of course you do, helped sometimes by one of her security blokes."

In one respect the Queen has not departed one iota from the views expressed to Members of Her Household thirty years ago. She detests Press intrusion. While she appreciates, human nature being as it is, that there is bound to be public interest in the private life of herself and members of her family, she can see no defence whatsoever for noses, and cameras, poking into areas where they have not been invited. Her abhorrence is not limited either to well known incidents involving the Royal Family. Courtiers noted her extreme displeasure,

---

* Prince Andrew carried out his first solo public engagement on December 8 1981 when he addressed the 100th Varsity Rugby Match Dinner. Cliff Morgan, Head of B.B.C. Outside Broadcasts Group, who was down to speak after him, was so bowled over by the Prince's performance − "so impressive, such star quality" − that he altered some of his own speech at the last moment.

for instance, at the way in which widows and other relatives of Falklands war heroes were sought out and interviewed by newspapers. To the Queen, some of these interviews amounted to unwarranted intrusion into private grief.

It is extremely rare for the Queen to express her private opinions publicly – "in a real sense she never demeans herself by evincing exasperation or impatience" – but in 1981, her Deputy Private Secretary, Mr William Heseltine (he was not at the time the holder of a knighthood) wrote to Mrs Doreen Hill, the mother of one of the victims of Peter Sutcliffe, the 'Yorkshire Ripper', informing her that the Queen "certainly shares in the sense of distaste which right-minded people will undoubtedly feel" if it were true that the *Daily Mail* was planning to publish the story of the man accused of her daughter's murder, told by members of his family, and paying them substantial sums of money to do so.

Mrs Hill had written to the Queen, as well as to a number of other public figures, following a report in the magazine *Private Eye* that the *Daily Mail* had done a deal with Sutcliffe's wife, Sonia, under which she would be paid £250,000 for her story. When, in May 1981, Mr Heseltine's reply to Mrs Hill (it began: 'I am commanded by the Queen') was published, the Editor of the *Daily Mail,* Mr David English,* who was in New York, sent a telegram to the Queen's Deputy Private Secretary protesting that one of the Queen's advisers had not shown the courtesy to check the accuracy or otherwise of the allegation before commenting on it. Others had asked if the allegation was true and given him the chance to deny it – "which I did".**

The following day the *Daily Mirror* quoted a Buckingham Palace spokesman as denying that the letter was "specifically" about the *Daily Mail.* "It was simply meant as a condemnation of the practice of cheque-book journalism in general and not a specific condemnation of that one paper."

Notwithstanding, it was the Queen who had made her feelings known.

---

* During the intervening period since then both Mr Heseltine and Mr English have been made the recipients of knighthoods.
** On February 4th, 1983, the Press Council issued a report on Press handling of the Peter Sutcliffe case. It concluded that a fair trial was put gravely to risk by the police and the media, and censured the conduct of a number of newspapers. It accused the *Daily Mail* of gross misconduct and of carrying out "an elaborate and convoluted . . . charade". A draft model contract had been sent to Mrs Sutcliffe, and letters obtained by the Council indicated that offers of up to £90,000 were being made by the *Daily Mail,* the report said.

12. A SUMMER NIGHTMARE

"Whitehall has persistently worked on the 'need to know' principle, which means that sensitive information is kept within the smallest possible group."
Richard Norton-Taylor, the Guardian, July 20 1982

"If it were not for the fact that one or two minor figures had decided to earn a few bob by going to the *Daily Express* and *The Sun*, nobody would have known anything about anything."
Miles Kington, The Times, July 22 1982

"WHERE WERE THE GUARDS?"
Headline to the first leader in The Times, July 13 1982

It was a Saturday in summer and Norman Luck, like countless other husbands in Britain, was spending his day off working in the garden. The date, which held no particular significance for him at the time, was July 10 1982.

Norman, a reporter on the *Daily Express* for 20 years, shares a pleasant detached house in Sanderstead, a leafy Surrey suburb, with his wife, a former airline stewardess. They have no children. Norman's interest, amounting almost to a passion, is Do-It-Yourself home improvement. Indeed he has been supplementing his salary as a general news reporter on the *Express* for the last fifteen years by writing a weekly column for the paper on the subject of D.I.Y. and, like any self-respecting handyman, is proud of the fact that he built an extension to his house at a cost of £4000 after being quoted £10,000 by a professional builder.

On this particular Saturday – July 10th – he had set himself the task of digging a hole in which to make a fishpond, and with typical foresight and attention to detail had judged that, with a friend helping, he would need to push some 400 barrowloads of earth up the one-in-four incline of his front drive to fill the skip that had been deposited at the kerb outside his house. The skip – capacity five yards – was costing him £30 to rent and so he fully intended to fill it in a day.

Norman began digging and filling his wheelbarrow at about eight o'clock in the morning. By half past nine he reckoned he had wheeled some sixteen loads of earth up the drive and dumped them in the skip.

That was when the 'phone rang.

Mrs Luck answered and called her husband in from the garden. Norman recognised immediately the voice of one of his contacts at the other end of the line, someone he had known for several years, someone who had tipped him off on some major stories in the past, someone who – for security reasons – he still takes care to refer to only as 'he-or-she'.

'Heorshe' needed to see Norman to pass on some information. Norman thought of his fishpond, and the skip that was costing him money all the while it stood outside his door. "It's a bit inconvenient," he told Heorshe. "Can't it wait till tomorrow when I'll be in the office?" No, they had to meet today. "Can't you come over here?" No way, said Heorshe. They should meet at a certain crossroads – a point on the border of Kent and Surrey – and when Norman suggested it would make more sense to meet at a pub, Heorshe again baulked at the idea. There was a risk of being followed.

Norman Luck, a newspaperman of long and wide experience, knows that contacts, however reliable their past records, can sometimes have an exaggerated sense of the importance of the information they harbour. Here was a case, he thought, of someone going 'over the top'. However there was something about the tone of the voice, the sense of urgency, that persuaded him to change out of his gardening clothes into something more presentable, and slide behind the wheel of the office Cortina.

He drove to where he'd been told to go. A few moments later a car drew up behind and Heorshe got out. After a brief chat, it now having reached the time when the pubs were open, Heorshe agreed to lead the way to a public house in the area which Norman had not visited before. His friend insisted on entering first, to make sure there was no-one already there whom either might recognise. Norman ordered his usual drink – lager and lime – and a gin and tonic for Heorshe. The drinks were carried to a table away from the bar counter where their conversation would not be overheard.

"Would you believe someone has sat on the Queen's bed last night?" Heorshe asked.

"Yeah, the Duke," Norman replied idly, looking up at the bar and wondering if they had any potato crisps.

"No, someone from outside."

Norman gave Heorshe a look. "Do you mean to say you pulled me out of my house on my day off to tell me that! Even if it was true, how on earth do you think I'd get confirmation?"

"If you try to get confirmation of what I'm telling you you'll probably get a 'D' notice slapped on you."* Heorshe said. Norman took a sip of his lager and looked hard over the rim of his glass at his friend. He must be joking — mustn't he?

The appalling news that someone had indeed broken into Buckingham Palace and actually reached the bedside of the Queen herself without being detected was revealed to the world on the morning of July 12 1982. But the meeting between Norman and his contact took place at lunchtime on July 10.

Over the course of one or two more drinks, Heorshe revealed, bit by bit, more details of his top-secret information. Norman heard about the broken ashtray on which the intruder had cut himself and of how blood from his hand had dripped onto the Queen's bedsheets, of the dialogue that had taken place between the man and the Queen, of how he had climbed into the Palace through a window, apparently completely unchallenged, and had only been arrested after the Queen herself had raised the alarm.

Norman realised that his contact, while giving him potentially sensational information, was being less forthcoming than in the past, almost certainly for fear of inadvertently saying something that, once the story was published, could be traced back to its source.

He decided the best thing all round was to suggest a course of action employed once or twice before: if Heorshe would come clean with everything he knew, then between them they would agree on how much Norman could print without putting his contact at risk. It was an arrangement that had worked in the past, relying as it did on total mutual trust. Heorshe agreed and related the whole sequence of events as he knew it.

Norman went back over every detail, editing in his mind as he went along and working out all the escape routes so that if he were questioned (as he was later, in a roundabout way, by those he suspected were acting for the police) he could fabricate a plausible story as to how he first came to hear about the intruder at the Palace.

Shortly before closing time, Heorshe and Norman left the pub, separately, and went their own ways. When Norman reached home,

---

* A 'D' notice is a 'blackout' on information, publication of which would be deemed to be prejudicial to the national interest. Usually it is only imposed during wartime or grave national emergency.

about three-thirty, his wife's first question was "Why are you so late?", and when Norman told her he'd met a contact who'd told him about an intruder sitting on the Queen's bed in Buckingham Palace her second question, not surprisingly, was "How many have you had?"

In fact, Norman's head was spinning with adrenalin rather than with an excess of lager. If the story were true, he had been offered the biggest scoop of his lifetime. If not true, and he published, he and his editor would almost certainly find themselves in serious trouble.

In addition, there was a further dilemma which was, in some ways, even more worrying. It was Saturday. The soonest that Norman could get his story into the *Daily Express* was breakfast-time, Monday morning — almost 36 hours away. In the meantime all the Sunday papers would be coming out, to say nothing of numerous television and radio news bulletins. What if one of them had also had a tip-off? Even if one of them had got the merest whiff, and published the rumour, then that would leave Fleet Street the whole of Sunday to work on the story and delve for more facts. By Monday morning, he realised, his scoop might turn out to be no more valuable than the time of day to a dead man.

Norman changed back into his overalls and went back into the garden to dig his fishpond and fill the skip.* He would need to give the matter some thought.

Norman Luck is one of Fleet Street's survivors. A professional to the core who has seen editors come and go, and newspapers die painful deaths in the circulation wars that fell competent reporters like front-line soldiers. Luck — despite the aptness of the name — has played only a relatively small part in his career as a reporter. Hard work and hard thinking have been more reliable components. He entered Fleet Street at nineteen, the son of a public relations officer for the Co-op. As a youth he thought he would like to become a vet but as a successful school athlete he grew to like seeing his name in print.

When he began work in the library of the Westminster Press, tapping out paragraphs in the evenings on his mother's typewriter in the hope of selling to Fleet Street, the fashion among young men was to wear smart Italian style suits with narrow lapels and drainpipe trousers. Today Norman Luck still dresses smartly, and carries a briefcase to the office. He could easily be mistaken for a successful executive, in advertising possibly, or a plain-clothes policeman operating out of Savile Row.

On this particular day Norman was simply a worried man. Shortly before eleven, when usually he switched off the television and settled down to write his D.I.Y. column, he picked up the 'phone and rang

* Which, with the help of a friend, he managed to do that same day!

his boss, Mike Steemson, Deputy News Editor of the *Daily Express*. Briefly, he outlined the tip-off he'd been given — mainly as self-protection, in case the Sunday papers did come out with something the following morning but partly to offload a share of his secret.

Steemson in turn alerted the Manchester office of the paper to tackle William Whitelaw, the Home Secretary, the following morning in Carlisle where he was due to address a meeting. He also rang John Warden, the *Express* political editor, so that he could begin attempting to get collaboration of the almost unbelievable story from some of his parliamentary sources.

Fleet Street on a Sunday morning, without most of the traffic trundling to and from Ludgate Circus, is as quiet as most other streets in the City of London on the Sabbath, even though inside the newspaper offices life is turgidly stirring, and outside the bells of St Paul's Cathedral, just down the road, are beckoning the faithful to prayer.

Entering the *Daily Express* building shortly after ten, Norman Luck detected a strange air of urgency. He could recall only one other occasion when the feeling of expectation in the office had been as marked: that had been when the *Daily Express* was on the brink of publishing its exclusive story of Great Train Robber Ronald Biggs' arrest in Argentina.

He went to his desk and began going through the Sunday papers, looking for any sign of *his* story. There was none.*

The *Daily Express* morning editorial conference of department heads usually begins at eleven — on Sundays often a little later. On this Sunday, however, things were different. At eleven o'clock, Norman noticed Mike Steemson, clip-board in hand, already queuing up outside the office of the Editor-of-the-Day, Ted Dickinson.

A few minutes later, when all the senior executives concerned were gathered in his office, Dickinson asked the usual kick-off question

---

* Although Norman Luck didn't know this until later, another newspaper group had come very close to revealing that the Queen's bedroom had been invaded. Under the headline MYSTERY OF THE ROYAL PROWLER, the *Sunday Mail*, Scottish sister paper of the London-printed *Sunday Mirror*, printed a story on July 11, by Brian Cullinan, claiming that, according to the police, a lone intruder had *twice* beaten the Buckingham Palace security net and that there were reports that on the second occasion "he may even have confronted the Queen herself". In London, the *Sunday Mail*'s sister paper, the *Sunday Mirror* had a similar if not identical story by its senior crime reporter, Norman Lucas, but — without cast-iron corroboration — it was decided not to use it.

for these occasions: "Right Mike, what have you got for us today?"

Steemson said the first story on his list was 'The Palace Intruder'. Dickinson knew about the rumours. "Yep. Anything new?"

"Yes," Steemson replied, as calmly as he could. "We've got the full story of the man who sat on the Queen's bed with a broken ashtray spilling blood on the Queen's sheets."

After one or two expressions of disbelief, the conference ended after a shorter time than usual. Nothing else that might make a story that day seemed worthy of much consideration. What *was* needed, and desperately so, was corroboration of Norman Luck's amazing tale.

"How are you so sure about your story?" Norman recalls Dickinson asking him.

"Because I know my contact. I'm so sure I'd resign on this story, and if you're not going to publish it I will resign."* Practically the whole of the rest of the day was taken up with efforts to get Norman's account of what had actually happened either confirmed or denied by the authorities.

On the previous day, at Bow Street Magistrates Court — directly opposite the Royal Opera House in Covent Garden — a thirty-one-year-old unemployed married man, Michael Fagan, of no fixed abode, had been remanded in custody on a charge of entering Buckingham Palace on July 7 — over a month earlier — and stealing a half bottle of wine.

This was the same man, Norman had been assured by Heorshe, who had entered the Queen's bedroom in the early morning of July 9. But the threat of legal action prevented knowledge of any link between the two men being safely printed at this stage. All that could be published with impunity was a bare account of the court appearance. Admittedly — if this account was included among the new revelations about an intruder — readers might reasonably infer that the same man was responsible for both incidents.

But any editor who ran a story about an intruder who had entered the Queen's bedroom, without first obtaining confirmation from at least one official source — either on or off the record — that it had actually happened was running the most appalling risk. If the story was without foundation, then Buckingham Palace would come down

---

* After his hours long conversation with Heorshe, going backwards and forwards over several points, Norman Luck dictated onto tape everything he'd heard, including the dialogue lasting some 10 minutes in all, that took place between the Queen and the intruder in the Queen's bedroom. That tape, which Norman Luck believes he could sell for a great deal of money, but which he never will, remains locked away in a safe.

on him like a ton of bricks – or an executioner's sword! And if he inferred that it was Michael Fagan who had approached the Queen's bed, and it wasn't, then he would be walking into a legal minefield.

Of all the editors in Fleet Street, Christopher Ward, the young editor of the *Daily Express,* might reasonably have been experiencing an additional worry. For it was the *Daily Express,* though not under his editorship, that had come out five years previously with the famous front page headline 'CHARLES TO MARRY ASTRID – OFFICIAL'. Interestingly the story, which was totally untrue, appeared under the by-line of John Warden, the *Express*'s well-informed Political Editor – the same John Warden who was now chasing up his private sources in an effort to back up Norman Luck's unofficial claims.

As afternoon drew into evening and the time to roll the first edition off the presses came even nearer, Christopher Ward wrestled with the decision he knew he had to make. Publish and be damned – or be praised. Or retreat, to fight another day. Go ahead, or spike the biggest news story there had been for years.

On more than one occasion he consulted the paper's lawyer, whose traditional role was to look out for and advise the editor on legal risks. He could find thirty good reasons, Ward remembers, why the laws governing contempt should dissuade him from publishing. "Look," Ward pleaded, almost in desperation, "I don't want you to tell me I *can't* publish the story, I want you to tell me *how* I can publish it."

The argument centred around not only the legal risks but the fact that the *Express*'s lawyer seriously doubted that the story could possibly be true. He had been inside Buckingham Palace himself and he could not believe that any intruder who managed to find his way in could possibly manage to continue unchallenged until he arrived at the Queen's private apartments.

Chris Ward, on the other hand, had 'an uncanny instinct' that the almost unbelievable was true – "that would have been the time to have had a small bet because I did believe what Norman Luck was saying."

Norman himself was almost totally out of all this high-level discussion. He had written his story and he was ready to go home. The weekend duty Press Officer at Buckingham Palace had been telephoned at his home and had said he had absolutely no knowledge of the matter but that, in any case, enquiries of such a nature should be addressed to Scotland Yard – a sure indication, to Norman Luck at any rate, that there was substance to his claim. John Warden and Percy Hoskins, the *Daily Express* crime consultant, were still working on the story when, at about eight o'clock, Norman decided to call it a day.

On his way out of the office he bumped into Ted Dickinson, the Editor-of-the-Day, in the corridor. "Well, are you going to use it?"

Dickinson made a motion with his hands to indicate that the chances were still fifty-fifty. "If we don't, I'm going to have pages 1, 2, 3 and 6 wide open," he said.

"You'll just have to use the Canberra story twice," Norman replied, smiling wearily.*

At 6.30 the next morning he was nudged awake by his wife to listen to what was coming over on the radio. "A report in the *Daily Express* . . ." They'd used it! His story! Strangely, Norman did not show the excitement expected. He was delighted to hear the name of his newspaper broadcast in the headlines, but at the same time he felt a cold sweat breaking out. Why was the *Daily Express* singled out for mention? Surely, after they'd seen the first edition of the *Express* every other newspaper in Fleet Street would have picked up the story? About the only reason they might not have done would be because they had reason to believe it was not true. Obviously, quoting 'a report' in a newspaper meant there had been no official confirmation as yet. But that could be put down to the fact that it was still very early in the day. However, the thought that the rest of Fleet Street hadn't followed up his 'scoop' – *that* was disturbing.**

Driving to the office he had the satisfaction of seeing posters on the news-stand at East Croydon station proclaiming: '*DAILY EXPRESS* EXCLUSIVE! INTRUDER AT QUEEN'S BEDSIDE'. But at the Oval tube station he spotted a *Daily Mail* poster: 'INTRUDER SAT ON QUEEN'S BED'. He stopped the car, about to get out and tell the news-seller he'd put the headline on the wrong poster – it should be on the *Daily Express!* – when he saw that all the other papers displayed were also 'splashing' the story on their front pages. He drove on, a well contented man.

From this point on, the events that Norman Luck had brought to the world's attention became a matter of great concern to those in very high places.

Buckingham spokesmen maintained the line that the whole affair was "entirely a police matter," and later that morning the government Minister responsible for overall charge of the Metro-

---

* On Sunday, July 11, the P. and O. cruiseliner Canberra sailed into Southampton. Aboard were 1500 men of 40 and 42 Royal Marine Commando returning to a heroes' welcome after service in the Falklands conflict with Argentina.
** Christopher Ward, having taken the major risk with Norman Luck's story, and endured a night of uncertainty, also faced a few more agonising hours before the report in the *Daily Express* was confirmed one hundred percent.

politan Police, Home Secretary William Whitelaw, was meeting with Sir David McNee, the Metropolitan Police Commissioner, and the man appointed to examine security breaches, Assistant Commissioner John Dellow.

At a Cabinet meeting, presided over by a justifiably incensed Margaret Thatcher, Whitelaw "spluttered through the bizarre catalogue of blunders and incompetence that led to the Queen finding an intruder pulling back her bedroom curtains and settling down for a chat at 7.15 in the morning".* In the afternoon he reported to the members of the House of Commons that a man had been arrested on the previous Friday morning after entering the bedroom of Her Majesty the Queen, adding gravely: "The House will admire the calm way in which Her Majesty responded to what occurred."

Mr Roy Hattersley, Chief Opposition spokesman on Home Affairs, another portly man, declared that "We in the Opposition are relieved that the incident ended without harm to the Queen." (Cheers from the Members.) But he wanted clarification on whether the man, stated by Mr Whitelaw to have appeared in court on Saturday in connection with a previous incident at the Palace, was related to the occurrence on Friday. More important, indeed, crucially, what steps were taken to improve Palace security after the first incident? (Cheers.) Or was it necessary for the *Daily Express* to enjoy their extraordinary scoop before these matters were taken with the seriousness that the situation warrants?

Mr Whitelaw, no doubt already weary − "No-one is likely to have been more shocked and staggered than I was." − rose slowly to his feet to reply. He had been advised that it would be wrong for him to discuss further whether the two incidents at the Palace were related,** he said, but improvements to security were made immediately on Friday and in no way awaited the *Daily Express* report.***

Over the next few days the whole world was fascinated by the

---

* Ian Waller, The *Sunday Telegraph,* July 18 1982.
** But in the House of Lords, at about the same time as Mr Whitelaw was speaking, Home Under-Secretary Lord Elton, in reply to a question from a former Lord Chancellor, did say: "The man about whom allegations are now being made is the man who was charged for the original offence."
*** The *Daily Express* subsequently ran an advertisement centred around the claim 'If we hadn't told you − nobody would have'. It showed facsimilies of its own front page of July 12: 'INTRUDER AT THE QUEEN'S BEDSIDE' along with those of the first editions of *The Sun* (DI'S HOUSE IN SECURITY SCARE), the *Daily Mirror* (KEEGAN SNUBS SOCCER REBELS), and the *Daily Mail* (WHAT A WELCOME!)

details that emerged in the newspapers, each paper vying with its rivals to match the *Express*'s original scoop. The *Daily Mail,* carrying a front page family snapshot of Michael Fagan with his daughter Samantha, then twelve months old, reported on Thursday the 15th, that the trail of security errors started when an off-duty policeman, passing Buckingham Palace on a motorcycle, saw the intruder and reported the incident. A search was started and then abandoned.

According to *The Times,* Conservative MPs were told privately by Mr Whitelaw that the Queen twice – not once as had been assumed – rang the Palace police for help, but no-one arrived until at least twelve minutes after her first call. The *Daily Mirror* revealed that the footman on duty to the Queen at the time was out walking her Corgi dogs and returned in time to grab Fagan after a chambermaid had raised the alarm.

When the findings of the official enquiry into the quite extraordinary incident were announced, most of what Fleet Street had already reported was corroborated. And what was confirmed was a whole catalogue of security failures. At about a quarter to seven in the morning of July 9 1982, Michael Fagan had climbed the Palace railings, jumping clear of an alarm beam that had been wrongly aligned. He entered a room through an unlocked window. This room contained the priceless Royal stamp collection, but the door to the corridor was locked. So he went back out through the window, shinned up a drainpipe to a flat roof, removed his sandals and socks, got across to a narrow ledge and climbed through another unlocked window – into an office of the Master of the Household, Vice-Admiral Sir Peter Ashmore.

This room had already been opened up for morning dusting by a housemaid, so Fagan was able to step out into the corridor and wander about the Palace at will for the next fifteen minutes. Apparently one of the Palace domestic staff saw him but didn't think his behaviour gave cause for alarm. He found his way to the Queen's private apartments, he later claimed, merely by "following the pictures".* He went first to an ante-room where he broke a glass ashtray into several pieces, then opened the door to the Queen's bedroom and stepped inside in his bare feet onto the thick carpet. His intention, he told police later, was to slash his wrists with a splinter of the glass ashtray in the presence of Her Majesty. He then crossed over to the windows and pulled open the curtains close to the Queen's bed, causing her to wake.

The official report makes note of the fact that the Queen pressed

---

* It has to be remembered that he had been inside the Palace at least once before, and it was claimed by some sources, up to twelve times in all.

the night alarm bell, which rings in the corridor outside and in a nearby pantry, but the police sergeant guarding her door, in accordance with instructions, had gone off duty at 6.00 a.m. (it was now shortly after 7.15) when the domestic staff took over. The footman was exercising the Corgis, and the only other person around, a maid, was vacuuming a nearby room, with the door shut so as not to disturb the Queen. No-one heard the alarm bell.

The Queen used her bedside telephone to instruct the Palace operator to send police to her room. Six minutes later, as no police had arrived, she rang down again. And she must have got out of her bed because "before police officers arrived Her Majesty attracted the attention of the maid and together they ushered Fagan into a nearby pantry on the pretext of supplying him with a cigarette.

"They were joined there by the footman who had returned from exercising the dogs. While Her Majesty kept the dogs away, as the man was getting agitated, the footman helped to keep Fagan in the pantry by supplying him with cigarettes until first one and then another police officer arrived and removed him."

Thus, in sober, straightforward language, the official report of the Home Office describes the course of events. What it does not say, because that was not its purpose, is how the Queen reacted to what must have been a terrifying experience, the outcome of which might so easily have been catastrophic.

The solicitor who appeared on Fagan's behalf in the magistrates court described his client as "naive and unbalanced". The Detective Chief Superintendent who opposed a remand on bail for Fagan said the defendant's actions were "totally unpredictable".*

On January 19, 1983, Fagan was discharged from Park Lane Special Hospital on the decision of a three-member mental health tribunal. Its chairman said that Fagan was 'not yet fully recovered' from a mental illness but it was no longer necessary to detain him. A week later, in a television interview, Fagan said he could not remember sitting on the Queen's bed. "I went into a room, I remember seeing a lady – I can't really say if it was the Queen."

The Queen, roused from sleep and confronted by a man, a total

---

* Fagan has never had to answer charges in connection with his intrusion into the Queen's bedroom – trespass is not a criminal offence in England. On September 23, 1982 a jury at the Central Criminal Court in London took 10 minutes to acquit him of the charge of stealing half a bottle of wine from Buckingham Palace in June. On the basis of medical opinion that he was schizophrenic and potentially dangerous, Fagan was sentenced under Section 60 of the Mental Act 1959 and committed indefinitely to Park Lane Special Hospital, near Liverpool.

stranger, dressed in a T-shirt, jeans and bare feet, had displayed a quite extraordinary degree of self-control. She did not scream, as most other women and men would have done in similar circumstances. She did not panic. On the contrary, she behaved in police textbook style by remaining outwardly calm, by listening patiently to what the man had to say, by discovering what it was he wanted, and by using this information to summon help. She capitalised on Fagan's craving for a smoke to seek out ways of finding both a cigarette and a rescue.

Beset as Fagan was at the time by severe domestic problems that had contributed to mental impairment, he might have done anything. If the Queen had made just one false move or unguarded comment, Fagan's mood might have switched in an instant from morose introspection to furious resentment; from talk to attack. There is no way of knowing from one moment to the next how a man in such a state will react. But it is not being melodramatic to suggest that if the Queen had behaved in any other way it is by no means beyond the realms of possibility that today we would be living in the reign of Charles III and not Elizabeth II.

Interestingly, it was the degree of courage and great presence shown by the Queen that accounted, in part at least, for Heorshe 'leaking' news of the incident to Norman Luck. Apparently, Heorshe's fear was that the whole matter of an intruder at the Palace would be hushed up by the authorities unless the story was 'broken'. And, if that happened, no-one would learn of the Queen's magnificent behaviour. As Norman Luck recalls, Heorshe put it this way:

"People know her as the Monarch, as someone they like to look up to. They also know she's reputed to be the richest woman in the world, with no problems about shopping or suchlike. In other words she has the kind of life we'd all like to lead, though we're not sure we could handle it if we did. But how many people could have behaved the way she did with this fellow? It showed up a whole new facet of her character."

Apparently this aspect seemed to Heorshe almost as important as a disclosure of the scandalous state of security at Buckingham Palace. But it needs to be added that Heorshe, according to Fleet Street practice, was handsomely paid by the *Daily Express* for the tip-off. Norman Luck, for a story that added greatly to both the prestige and the circulation of his paper, received a bonus of £250, but turned down an offer to go to the *News of the World* as chief investigative reporter at a salary a third higher than he was getting at the *Express*.*

---

* Norman Luck, Percy Hoskins and John Warden won the Scoop of the Year award in Granada Television's *What The Papers Say* presentations in February 1983.

He made a few extra pounds through being interviewed on no fewer than forty-eight radio and television news programmes around the world. In some of these interviews he was asked about the words said to have been used by the Palace chambermaid when she first saw Fagan in the Queen's apartments, words that are now part of Royal folklore: "Bloody hell, ma'am, what's he doing in here?"

The memory of how he first came across this 'quote' still makes Norman Luck chuckle. In his interview in the pub with Heorshe, his informant related how the Palace maid, Elizabeth Andrews, encountered Fagan. But Heorshe couldn't quite remember the actual words she'd used at the time. He could remember it was a north country expression.

"Bloody hell?" volunteered Norman. "That's it!" said Heorshe.

Norman experimented further: "Bloody hell, ma'am, what's he doing in here?" "That's it!" said Heorshe. In such a way are 'quotes' sometimes discovered.

Norman Luck deliberately placed the sentence in his paper as a 'plant', to see which newspapers were 'milking' his exclusive material, but he was amused later to hear a rumour that the Queen, in relating her harrowing experience to friends, was herself ascribing the words as precisely those used by her maid!

As public disquiet over the whole affair continued, a thought uppermost in many minds was 'What would have happened if the *Daily Express* had not published its report of the intrusion into the Queen's bedroom?' It was the question that *The Times* decided to ask in its first leader on July 14, five days after the event, when security precautions at the Palace had already been tightened and when there had already been demands made for the resignation of both the Home Secretary, Mr William Whitelaw, and of the Metropolitan Police Commissioner, Sir David McNee. If the *Daily Express* had not published its report, *The Times* demanded to know, "would the Home Secretary have made his statement to the House of Commons? Would the incident have been disclosed at all? Above all, would there now be the same sense of national outrage, the same urgency in the determination that this time adequate security measures must be devised and implemented? It is bad enough that the episode occurred at all. But it is even more disturbing that all the signs suggest that, but for the happy chance of a Press disclosure, there would have been an official conspiracy of silence."

Would there? The Queen's Press Secretary, Michael Shea, stoutly maintains there was never any attempt, no consideration given even, to hushing up the matter. But other sources at the Palace are not so adamant. It is known that the Queen herself wished the whole incident should be forgotten as quickly as possible, but this expression of feeling – a very natural one in the circumstances – came after some newspapers had delved into the Queen's private life in an attempt to come up with descriptive details of the Queen's bedroom, even to the kind of nightdress she wore in bed.*

The editor of the *Daily Express,* Christopher Ward, was not alone among Fleet Street editors in believing that although the facts would almost certainly have become public knowledge eventually, it was the intention of both Scotland Yard and Buckingham Palace that they should remain secret – if this were at all possible.

The truth of the matter probably lies in the private view of a senior Member of the Queen's Household, couched in words that seem to epitomise the shrewd cautiousness of the Palace in practically all matters. "I think when such an incident does happen, there is no immediate urge in an organisation like ours to rush to the public prints with it because in many ways it can be best and most reasonably investigated and any fault in the system put right in private rather than in public."

Unfortunately for everyone directly concerned (though not for newspapers and their readers who thrive on scandal) the sensation of an intruder at the Palace – albeit by no means for the first time in history** – was compounded by the almost equally astounding announcement made just eleven days later that the Queen's personal police officer, Commander Michael Trestrail, aged fifty-one, and single, had resigned his post following an admission to a homosexual relationship with a male prostitute.

Friends of the Queen say this sudden and totally unexpected departure of one of her most trusted servants caused her even more distress than the business of Fagan. Trestrail, a Cornishman, had been involved in Royal protection since 1966 and the Queen's police officer for ten years. In 1977 she had shown her appreciation of his loyal service by making him a member of the Royal Victorian Order,

---

* One newspaper, *The Sun,* quoted Fagan's wife, Christine, as saying her husband had described the Queen as wearing a cream shortie nightie, pins in her hair, and with a wig on the bedside table. All the claims were dismissed by the Palace as 'figments of a weird imagination'.

** In June 1981, the Home Office acknowledge, three young German students spent the night in an area immediately within the Palace wall. Two months later a man was found inside the grounds. And there have been several other similar incidents over the past 150 years. In December 1840 a seventeen-year-old youth, Edmund Jones, was discovered hiding in Queen Victoria's dressing room, only a few feet away from where the young Queen was sleeping. Another boy, aged twelve, lived undetected in the Palace for almost a year around 1838. Like Jones, he had originally entered in search of scraps of food.

one of the few honours that is her own personal gift.

In accordance with her preference for having familiar faces around her, the Queen had been guarded by Mike Trestrail during thousands of miles of home and overseas tours.* He was a well-known, well-liked and a highly respected figure in Palace circles. Though the subsequent report of the enquiry into the security aspects of his employment referred to a police colleague's suspicions, everyone else at the Palace appears to have been totally unaware of Trestrail's proclivity. Indeed, he had quite a reputation amongst the staff for popping into offices to chat up the secretaries. And at the end of a long day of Royal engagements on an overseas tour he seemed thoroughly to enjoy relaxing with a pretty girl over dinner.

Lord Bridge, chairman of the Security Commission, found in his investigation that no breach of security had been caused by Trestrail's behaviour, and security was not put at risk. Why, then, did the Commander see fit to offer his resignation so promptly? Could it not have been avoided altogether? These were questions asked both inside and outside the Palace, among members of the Royal Family and the public alike, immediately after word of his resignation was made public.

Once again, it's worth noting, it was a newspaper that alerted the world to what was going on. On July 16 1982 *The Sun* was approached by a man claiming to have had a sexual relationship with Michael Trestrail. The newspaper's editor decided that Scotland Yard should be informed immediately, and that no report of the man's allegation should be carried by the newspaper in its next issue. The following day, Saturday, as a direct result of *The Sun's* action, Trestrail was seen by Sir David McNee, the head of the Metropolitan Police, and on being confronted with the allegations offered his resignation, which was straightaway accepted.

Quite extraordinarily, however, especially as the resignation followed hard on Fagan's intrusion at the Palace, Home Secretary William Whitelaw, in overall charge of the Metropolitan Police, was left uninformed of the matter until the Monday morning. Officials at the Home Office had apparently decided to take most of the weekend to prepare a report before approaching him. It's well known among civil servants that government ministers, like most people, are best not approached at weekends with bad news. Even so, in the special

---

* The policemen who guard the Royal Family at Buckingham Palace, both plain-clothes and uniform, are the same who protect them at Windsor, Balmoral and Sandringham. At the Queen's express wish, they move from place to place, wherever she is in residence, even though officially all are members of either A1 Branch or A Division of the Metropolitan Police.

201

circumstances, the delay in telling Whitelaw at least *something* appears curious to say the least.

What Members of Parliament, assembling after the weekend, were most concerned to hear from Mr Whitelaw was whether anyone in the Police or at the Palace had known all along that the Queen's police officer was a homosexual. Had he been subjected to "positive vetting", the form of questioning that is supposed to leave no stone unturned? It transpired that he had been, some three months previously, when new tighter security measures had been introduced at the Palace. Before that time he had evidently not qualified for special scrutiny of his private life because he was not among those with access to secret documents.

Trestrail, in a statement issued through his solicitor, claimed his relationship with a male prostitute had been "casual, only occasional, and three years ago," which, coupled with the fact that he had obviously been discreet, led some people to wonder whether his resignation had been really necessary.

Letters to *The Times,* which probably did not reflect the views of the great majority in the country,nonetheless raised reasonable arguments. "Commander Trestrail's job has not been to set a standard of sexual morality for the Queen or for the rest of us, but to guard the Queen outside the Palace. This, by all reports, he has done in an exemplary fashion over a long period, earning the Queen's high regard in the process. So why did he have to resign?"

"He is a homosexual; are we now going to decimate public life by firing all homosexuals in positions of responsibility?"

A homosexual relationship between consenting adults is not a criminal offence in Britain, but in some professions − such as the police − it can be safely assumed to carry a social stigma, and is a hindrance to promotion prospects if discovered. Trestrail's private liaison with a male prostitute, it could be argued, made him susceptible to blackmail.

Whether or not this was the conclusion drawn by the Queen − and it seems likely that it was − she was immensely saddened at the collapse of her police officer's career, and regretful that his resignation had been pre-empted by *The Sun* newspaper's tip-off. Almost certainly she would have preferred that little or no publicity be attached to his going, if go he must. As with Fagan, it would have been infinitely more agreeable from the Palace's point of view, and certainly from Trestrail's, if there had been no 'rush to the public prints'. At the same time it should not be forgotten that in the case of both sensational revelations − Fagan's intrusion and Trestrail's homosexual relationship − the *Daily Express* and *The Sun* were tipped off by outsiders, and in the latter instance *The Sun* chose to inform the authorities first, knowing full well, admittedly, that it could publish later.

In the view of at least one journalist, Alexander Chancellor, writing in his weekly column in the *Daily Express, The Sun* "was right not to buy the prostitute's story, but it was wrong to report the affair to Scotland Yard. The decent thing, given that Trestrail had committed no crime, would have been to inform him, and him alone, of the prostitute's allegations. He then might have been able to resign in a more dignified manner and, perhaps, with less scandal." Chancellor argued that by going first to the police and in due course publishing a picture of the prostitute and "the full fascinating story", *The Sun* had "managed in the end to have its cake and eat it." Something that most organisations and individuals, in and out of Fleet Street, have aspired to at one time or another.

By the time August 1982 came around the Royal Family, and everyone involved with administering the machine of Monarchy, was more than ready for a summer holiday. Though, as usual, she betrayed little of her innermost feelings and continued to carry out public engagements with her customary charm and dedication to duty, the Queen was undoubtedly in need of rest. The strain of the past few months sometimes showed up in her face, and while she tended in company almost to laugh off the dreadful episode in her bedroom no-one, not even a person as self-composed and common-sensical as the Queen, could undergo such an experience without any after-effects. She had borne the brunt of the summer scandals that at one time seemed to fill the newspapers day after day. In addition, along with several thousand other mothers, she had experienced all the worries attached to having a son on active service in the Falklands war with Argentina. (When he returned safely home with his shipmates in September, Prince Andrew's bubbling presence acted like a tonic on the Queen.) She had shared the country's deep shock and anger at the murder of eleven of her soldiers in Hyde Park and Regent's Park by I.R.A. bombs — a tragedy which came just the day after Commander Trestrail's resignation. Her last act before stepping onto the Palace lawn for a formal garden party for 8000 guests was to send messages of sympathy to the commanding officers of the Household Cavalry and the 1st Battalion, the Royal Green Jackets. In addition, but unknown to the majority of the public, in the midst of all the outcry over the Palace intruder, the storm over Trestrail, and the outrage at the I.R.A., the Queen had suffered a deep private grief with the death, at the age of 59, of one of her and Prince Philip's closest and dearest friends, Lord Rupert Nevill.

As a young Princess Elizabeth, she had been escorted to her first charity ball by Lord Rupert Nevill. In World War II, while serving as a Guards Officer, he had been assigned the duty of speeding King George VI and Queen Elizabeth out of London in a bullet-proof car in the event of a successful German invasion. During the 12 years he had been Prince Philip's Treasurer and then his Private Secretary, Lord Rupert had become known to his staff as 'Prince Charming'; his office at the Palace was renowned as one of the happiest in the building. The Queen and Prince Philip were frequent guests at Lord and Lady Nevill's country home in Sussex. A small but telling instance of the esteem and affection in which Lord Rupert was held: when the Queen learned that his heart ailment might benefit from regular but gentle exercise she gave instructions for the temperature of the Palace swimming pool to be raised a few degrees for the benefit of her friend.

At the start of August, when they travelled up to Balmoral for their annual holiday, the Queen and Prince Philip shared their sadness along with a profound relief that the quite terrible events of the past three months were at an end. Norman Luck, whose year of professional glory it had been, took a holiday before returning to the reporting of more mundane matters.

As a direct result of what he had reported, security measures at Buckingham Palace were closely examined and greatly overhauled. A number of police officers employed there were either suspended or transferred to other duties. Additional higher ranking officers were drafted in. Sir David McNee, the Metropolitan Police Commissioner, who was due to retire in the autumn, did so. And Mr William Whitelaw lived on to fight another day.

One evening in November, as he drove round Buckingham Palace in the rush hour, Norman Luck suddenly experienced a sharp pang of guilt as he counted altogether thirteen uniformed policemen standing guard at various points around the perimeter of the Palace, stamping their feet to keep warm and looking glum with cold. "I felt like stopping the car, getting out and saying 'Sorry, fellows, it's all my fault'."

It is said, though it has never been officially admitted or substantiated, that soon after Fagan's arrest, when time had allowed a tightening up of security, a team of men belonging to the S.A.S., acting on a proposal of the Prime Minister herself and with the knowledge of the authorities, made five attempts to enter Buckingham Palace undetected. On each occasion they succeeded in their mission, and in one 'raid' they even took away a silver trophy. All efforts to return the trophy to its rightful place have failed because the Palace is quite insistent that it was never stolen in the first place. It denies all knowledge.

13. PRINCE CHARLES – IMAGE AND MAN

"I have no particular profession or special experience except perhaps as a representative of one of the oldest professions in the world – the monarchy, I hasten to add."
The Prince of Wales, addressing a Parliamentary Press Gallery luncheon, March 1975

"He is only a few years younger than I am. Some people say we even look alike. I longed for the opportunity to say directly 'Look, let's be friends. Tell me what it really feels like to be the Prince of Wales. Would I like it?"
Peter Osnos, in a preamble to an interview with Prince Charles in the Washington Post, August 1982

"Ought we to inflict on a young man of Prince Charles' calibre (or anybody) a lifetime dedicated to what in essence is a non-job?"
The Guardian, June 27, 1969

"It is not enough for a Prince of Wales to be democratic, to 'go walk-about' and smile and handshake on all possible occasions. He has to show that royalty is relevant to present-day Britain and that it has a worthwhile role to play in the future. If any man can do this, it is surely the Prince of Wales."
Wynford Vaughan-Thomas, 'The Princes of Wales'

At thirty-five – he was born at Buckingham Palace on November 14, 1948 – the Prince of Wales reaches that certain stage where he seems quite old to the very young, and still youthful to the quite elderly. An age when there are still plenty of people around who can remember clearly the night, even the time (9.14 p.m.) when he was born. An age which, to those under twenty, still seems an unimaginably

205

long way off. An age, even so, that marks the halfway point in the proverbial life span of three score years and ten.

In common with most men in their thirties Prince Charles is self-conscious about how the years race on. ("Don't remind me," he responded to a woman in the crowd who called out "Many happy returns" on his thirty-fourth birthday.) He is sufficiently vain to regret the growing spread of baldness on the crown of his head (he wasn't fully aware of the first signs until he saw a press picture taken while he was swimming in the Australian sea in 1977) but not so conceited as to try to hide one of the side-effects of ageing. (The Princess of Wales persuaded him to change his hairdresser and hairstyle soon after they were married, and so she may be more concerned about her husband's hair loss than he is.)

Caring for one's 'image', either in the literal or the advertiser's sense, is not the kind of thing Prince Charles thinks about much, in any case. "I couldn't care less about my image," he has said. "I don't believe in fashion, full stop. I cannot understand the idea that one year you think one way and another year you think something else. Things do go in cycles and they do go in fashions, but so often they come back to the same thing all over again." He puts much more store on values than on images, on principles than on popularity. His wife may have effected a change in his hairstyle and persuaded him to wear 'casuals' instead of 'lace-ups' on formal occasions, but it is extremely unlikely that she could change his attitude to things of deeper significance in life, even if she wanted to. By the time she came to marry him (she was twenty and he was thirty-two) he was not set in his ways, but his ways were set. The process had begun before Diana was even born.

Literally millions of words have been spoken and written about the influence of the Queen and Prince Philip on the formative years of their eldest son. "I'm very lucky because I have very wise and incredibly sensible parents," he once told the author. In his childhood and youthful days his father's influence was most apparent − in the way, for instance, he encouraged, quite forcefully at times, a boy who was shy and a slow-developer, to face up to challenges that he might otherwise have preferred to side-step. Some of these challenges − like bumping and boring in the very male-orientated sport of polo, and pulling the trigger on live animals − he came to enjoy more and more until, as his wife discovered, they became an essential part of his life. Other outdoor activities favoured by his father − sailing, for instance − he lost interest in. Prince Philip's intention was never to make his eldest son a keen and proficient sportsman, but through sport to help prepare him for the role that lay ahead. As both men grew older, Prince Charles became more and more his 'own man', listening to, but not always taking, Prince Philip's advice. However, even after Prince Charles had entered his thirties his father evidently saw the need on occasion to steel his son against events. On the day the body of Lord Louis Mountbatten, assassinated by the I.R.A., was flown across the Irish Sea to England, Prince Philip kept up a taunting match with his eldest son over lunch, until Charles finally got up from the table and left the room. Others present, knowing the deep grief felt by both men for Lord Louis, gauged the purpose of Prince Philip's otherwise quite extraordinary behaviour was to stiffen the sinew before they both had to appear in public, before the cameras of Press and television, to witness the coffin of the great man carried from the aircraft and borne past where they stood in solemn respect. Prince Philip betrayed no emotion, but the cameras picked up Charles brushing a hand across an eye.

The person with the greatest, or at any rate the most lasting, influence over Prince Charles has been the Queen, his mother – and that is the order in which, if required, he would probably put it. He is her subject, and so it is fortunate that he not only has an admiration as great as anyone's for the way in which she carries out her role as monarch, but also that he dearly loves her.

It is from his mother that Prince Charles inherited the gentler side of his character, and the part of him that spurns personal extravagance and values thrift.* From both his parents he has learned about diligence and plain commonsense. If he is ever apt to cogitate at length about 'the role of the monarchy' the Queen is likely to interrupt: "There's no need to talk about it. We just get on and *do* it." More and more, as he grows older, Prince Charles takes on the mannerisms and to a certain extent the appearance of his father, but he has more of his mother's sweeter nature. He has his father's wit, though not as caustic, and his father's energy – though he sometimes overdoes it, flakes out, and dozes off, even during a meeting. Desmond Morris, author and expert on body language, was once asked by the *Daily Mirror* what he could surmise from Prince Charles' well-known mannerisms and concluded that:

"Touching his tie is a self-comforting device and reveals a human being who is apprehensive. Fiddling with his cuff-links, wrist-watch, clasping one hand with another are all very defensive postures. They signal that unconsciously Prince Charles feels threatened."

---

* A story often told relates how the Queen sent Prince Charles, when still a boy, to search for a lost dog-lead in the grounds of Sandringham, with the reminder that "dog-leads cost money". Not nearly so well known is the fact that the full-length morning coat worn by Prince Charles on such occasions as State funerals was tailored originally for his grandfather, King George VI, and handed down to his grandson.

One of the few occasions when Prince Charles has been visibly apprehensive occurred when he made his first visit to Wales — in 1969 — and was confronted by Welsh nationalist demonstrators. On another occasion, a few years later in America, he faced up to I.R.A. supporters with placards showing crude drawings of his mother captioned 'The Queen of Death', and others describing him as 'The Prince of Torture'. He was incensed, not by what he was called, but by the insult to the Queen. His first thought was to confront the protestors and argue it out with them. But his aides gently urged him in another direction, away from the jeers and towards the cheers of the great majority of the crowd. Asked if he ever worries about the possibility of being assassinated Prince Charles responds with a quietly spoken "No," before adding, "There's no point in worrying. Otherwise I'd give up and go away."

The picture the world has of Prince Charles today — a picture that journalists and biographers alike have done little to adjust with the times — is of a man still fonder of sport than thought, who seeks out physical challenges in order to prove himself. Though these assessments were never entirely true of Prince Charles, they are even less of the whole truth than they were ten years ago and, one suspects, will become increasingly inapt as the Prince grows older.

Someone whose early guidance has had a lasting influence on the Prince of Wales, and who has quietly slipped astern of the Royal armada in the last few years, is Squadron Leader Sir David Checketts. A bluff, cheerful, family man, a keen ornithologist and a sailor, he moved from being an equerry to Prince Philip to being a mainstay to Charles when he was seventeen. He subsequently became the Prince's first Private Secretary and was his mentor for thirteen years. He remains a firm friend.

It was Squadron Leader and Mrs Checketts, with their three eldest children, who accompanied Prince Charles to Australia in 1966 — his first trip abroad without his parents — to spend a spell at Timbertop, the up-country branch of Melbourne's Geelong School. The Checketts set up house some 120 miles away from Timbertop, at Devon Farm, and for seven months it was Prince Charles' home at weekends when he mucked in with the family, making his own bed, sharing chores, enjoying the outdoor life. Checketts has said of that time in Australia: "I went out there with a boy and came back with a man." And Prince Charles himself has affirmed that his feeling of close affinity with Australia and Australians dates from that time.

In subsequent years it was Checketts, in the pipe-sucking style of a friendly housemaster, who helped steer Prince Charles through the confusion and self-examination of early manhood. The basis of his advice was always the same: If something's worth doing it's worth doing properly. Don't *play* at things. Go to university — to read for a degree. Go into the Royal Navy – with the aim of having your own command within five years.

One of the most obvious differences between Prince Charles and practically any other young man is that it has always been known which job he will end up in. The problem in his case has never been *how* will he get to the top, but what will he do *before* he arrives there. David Checketts, aware that many inside and outside Buckingham Palace frequently addressed their minds to this question, saw his job partly to draw out the potential he recognised in his young boss from an early age, and bolster the self-confidence of someone who by nature – despite his established position in the world – is sometimes diffident and often surprised by his own popularity.

On overseas tours Checketts was there at Prince Charles' side – along with a man from the Foreign Office – to check and advise on the after-dinner speeches which Prince Charles insisted on writing himself, sometimes allowing no-one else to have even a glimpse until the Royal aircraft was on its final glidepath to landing at the town where he was to make the speech. On occasion Prince Charles would argue strongly against the blue pencil crossing out some of his lines ("I'm afraid, Sir, you will offend several influential politicians if you say that") and with his penchant for starting a speech with a joke and finishing with a *bon-mot* he would, just occasionally, forget a facet of protocol, causing the man from the Foreign Office (overseas Royal tours are carried out largely under the aegis of the Foreign Office) to feel suddenly cold.

On his tour of America in 1977 (ten cities in eleven days) the Prince of Wales omitted on two occasions to finish up his speech by proposing a toast to the President of the United States in the traditional manner. On the third occasion, at the urging of the Foreign Office, he promised faithfully to remember, and even showed aides what he had written in large letters on the last page of his prepared speech: DON'T FORGET TO TOAST THE PRESIDENT. But he did, and he didn't.

It was on that same trip, incidentally, at the revered Alamo in San Antonio, Texas, that Squadron Leader Checketts (he had not yet been knighted) unconsciously committed a gaffe that has not gone down in Palace folklore but deserves to. Because of lack of space, a severely restricted number of Pressmen were allowed into the actual building, and to tour the museum that contains relics of the famous last stand of Texan volunteers against General Santa Anna's Mexican force. As Prince Charles drew abreast of each exhibit and a dignitary came forth with information, the gist was passed down the line to those following, ending up with the Pressmen at the rear.

Among the glass display cases there was one particularly prized exhibit: the actual fur hat worn by the legendary Davy Crockett at the Battle of the Alamo. Prince Charles bent down to have a closer look at it, quite fascinated. Spotting this from a distance, and realising it might be of Press interest, Squadron Leader Checketts – when he drew level with the display case – glanced over his shoulder at the reporters in train, pointed and remarked: "There's something for you – Davy Crockett's cat."

Failure in communication and being ill-prepared for eventualities (often amounting to the same thing) are among the few things almost guaranteed to irritate Prince Charles. He dislikes having things sprung on him – whether it's being asked to wear a silly hat, or "to say a few words". Whenever it is required of him to don a 'hard hat' (on a building site) or dress up as a cowboy (both he and Prince Andrew succumbed in Canada in 1977) his head and shoe sizes are supplied to his hosts in advance. But occasionally – knowing full well the cameras are on him – he will disappoint someone in the crowd who is longing for him to wear a bowler decorated with the Union Jack. He enjoys a meal much more if he knows he's not required to make a speech afterwards. Unlike the Queen, however, who will not compromise in these matters, he may be prevailed upon to crack a joke, express his thanks, congratulate the organisers, say a few words without prior notice, especially if he thinks it might be discourteous not to. However the biding rule for his aides remains the same: "Brief me well." Only by knowing in advance precisely what's *supposed* to happen can any member of the Royal Family hope to get through the endless days with assurance, dignity, and an apparent degree of interest. "He seemed to know so much about me/us" is a remark frequently expressed, with a hint of surprise in the voice, by those who have exchanged only a few words with a passing Prince. The Royal Family's back-up teams, from Private Secretaries to equerries and civil servants working in regional branches of the Central Office of Information, by and large do a grand job of spadework.

After thirteen years devoted service to his Royal master, Squadron Leader Checketts left his desk in Buckingham Palace to work in public relations. During those years he had watched "the boy" – the way he sometimes affectionately referred to Prince Charles – develop from a slightly gauche and introspective youth into a lithe young man with a degree from Cambridge university,* a grade A pilot's licence, and the command of a Royal Navy minehunter, H.M.S. Bronington. But Checketts had never intended his job with

---

* Prince Charles, with two GCE A-levels from Gordonstoun, joined Trinity College, Cambridge, in October 1967 to read archaeology and anthropology and, later, history. He won a half-blue at polo and in June 1970 graduated with a Bachelor of Arts (Honours) degree.

the Prince to be a life's work. He was forty-eight when he vacated his desk at the Palace, and "the boss" (the appellation still used in the Prince of Wales' office) was twenty-nine.

Despite a knowledge and breadth of experience that far surpassed that of practically any other man of a similar age, Prince Charles was only just reaching full maturity. Over the years he had given great weight to the advice of his father and his great-uncle, Lord Louis Mountbatten. He had learned much about statecraft from the Queen, and had confided often in Queen Elizabeth, the Queen Mother, for whom he has always had a very special love and respect. But it was always clear that once he left the Royal Navy (which he did in December 1976, with the rank of Commander) a whole new chapter of his life would open up. The formula that had been proposed by Lord Mountbatten at a gathering called by the Queen in December 1965 to discuss her eldest son's future had been adopted and carried through – "Trinity College like his grandfather, Dartmouth like his father and grandfather, and to sea in the Royal Navy ending up with a command of his own." Now it was time to look ahead another twenty, thirty years.

The man who replaced Squadron Leader Checketts as Prince Charles' Private Secretary and closest professional confidante, the Hon. Edward Adeane, possesses a somewhat more rigid personality than his predecessor. It may be that Checketts' more avuncular approach was appropriate for a young man growing up whereas Adeane, also a powerful influence, has the qualifications and the temperament to stand at the side of the man who one day will be King. Both Prince Charles and his Private Secretary are basically traditionalists, but Adeane is by instinct probably more conservative than his employer. He is extremely punctilious, whereas Prince Charles is not renowned for being speedy with paperwork. Charles tends to be generously impulsive with promises. Adeane sometimes has the task of finding a way out of his keeping to them. Critics, mostly civil servants, or those with civil service minds, are sometimes annoyed that Edward Adeane does not consult colleagues as much as they think he should. Instead, he is inclined to go ahead on his own, which is what Prince Charles often does too. And though this may mean they are slightly at odds at times, it also partly explains why the two men get along so well with one another. Prince Charles likes and respects his Private Secretary, and Mr Adeane is loyal to the Crown and his master beyond all else.

Fleet Street, and the media in general, have always shown affection for Prince Charles, as well as respect. But some editors and Royal-watchers alike are inclined to draw breath and reserve judgement when asked about his Private Secretary, even though they have seen his influence in operation for some years now. (The Hon. Edward

Adeane took up his appointment as Private Secretary to the Prince of Wales officially on May 1, 1978.) Adeane's overall attitude to newspapers, Fleet Street generally believes, is none too favourable. In fact, like many of his colleagues in the Royal Household, Prince Charles' Private Secretary is strongly disapproving of certain sections of the popular Press, for what they do and what they print. He abhors gossip but also, one suspects, sees no very good reason why anything more than the skimpiest information about the private life of the Prince and Princess of Wales (or of himself for that matter) should ever need to be published. He is of the old school that, by and large, believes the Royal Family is best protected, and conserved, behind a shield of silence.

However Adeane's influence is discernable in the way that Prince Charles has become a much more serious minded and soberly behaved person, compared with even five years ago. An examination of the speeches that the Prince of Wales has made in recent times shows a depth of research and understanding not so apparent in earlier days. The tag, 'Joker Prince', has been removed. If tags are needed, 'The Caring Prince' would seem more appropriate. Much of the change that has taken place can be attributed simply to the fact that, as he gets older and more experienced, Prince Charles, like most men, has become somewhat more sober-minded. Fortunately he is never likely to lose entirely his undergraduate-style sense of humour, but equally it is less than likely that he will ever again appear in a documentary film, as he once did, acting the fool and mimicking the voice of Peter Sellers in the famous Goon shows. You can have a king who is a comic, but a comic king is to be avoided. The appointment of the cautious, sombre Edward Adeane was almost certainly the first move in a long term plan to place around Prince Charles men (and women?) who will serve him well for many years, even into his reign as Charles III. Machiavelli once wrote: "The first opinion which one forms of a Prince and of his understanding is by observing the men he has around him; and when they are capable and faithful he may always be considered wise, because he has known how to recognise the capable and faithful."

The nineteen-seventies were peppered – much more than the 'eighties look like being – with television appearances by Prince Charles, book prefaces by Prince Charles, magazine and newspaper interviews with Prince Charles. Some of these were linked with unique national events, such as the Queen's Silver Jubilee in 1977, or fund-raising appeals. But a minority of the interviews allowed the viewer or the reader a rare insight into the mind and thinking of the man.

Until 1981 probably the most often quoted interview was the one that first appeared in *Woman's Own* magazine in November 1975. It was during this interview, given to me, that Prince Charles gave such headline-catching replies as: "I've fallen in love with all sorts of girls, but I've made sure I haven't married the first person I've fallen in love with." And: "I personally feel that a good age for a man to get married is around thirty." The latter quote, in particular, as Prince Charles later admitted with wry regret, was to hang "like a millstone round my neck" until the day he did in fact marry – aged thirty-two.

Because of publishing schedules, Prince Charles' words did not actually appear in *Woman's Own* until several weeks after the interview – based on questions sent in by the magazine's readers – had taken place at Buckingham Palace. On the day of publication whole passages were picked up and 'splashed' across the front pages of every popular national newspaper and prominently reported by other papers in Britain and around the world. The Prince of Wales was totally unprepared for, and none too pleased by, the degree of exposure given to his thoughts and opinions, even though he had been shown the article before it was published and had been prepared to answer every question put to him bar one.* Presumably he had imagined his frank and open responses would be read only by the magazine's six million readers. In any event, he has been careful ever since – and his advisers even more so – to guard against spending an hour or more talking to a journalist about his private life and feelings. Such interviews as he does give nowadays are strictly confined to subjects in which he has a personal interest – such as the raising of the 'Mary Rose', King Henry VIII's flagship, from the seabed off Portsmouth – or causes close to his heart, such as racial integration and opportunities for young people, which he has made his special concern.

Of course, the great majority of people – not just journalists – would be fascinated to hear Prince Charles talk about his married life and the kind of way he would like to bring up his son. If the Princess of Wales were to join him in such a public *tête-à-tête* public curiosity – to say nothing of newspaper sales – would be immense. However, such an interview is unlikely to take place in the foreseeable future, if at all. In the past two and a half years, scores of formal requests have been made to the Palace for an interview with the Princess of Wales,

---

* The only two questions a *Woman's Own* reader from Shanklin, Isle of Wight, had wanted answered were these. "Does Prince Charles have clean sheets on his bed every day, or does he, like me, have to put up with them being creased for the rest of the week? Also, does he wear pyjamas in bed?" Prince Charles read out the letter with fascinated amazement, then told the interviewer: "You can tell her I don't have clean sheets every night. But I'm *not* saying whether I wear pyjamas or not!"

and all have been flatly declined. Informal attempts have also been made to persuade the royal couple to talk about their relationship with one another − most notably by reporters following the tour of Australia and New Zealand earlier this year.

Even a formal interview with a member of the Royal Family is extremely difficult to arrange, and usually happens, if at all, only after months and sometimes years of patient waiting. In the first instance an application is made in writing, to the Queen's Press Secretary, and must include the name of the person the interviewer wishes to speak with, the subject he wishes to talk about, and the name of the publication he represents. A reply usually arrives by return − in one of Buckingham Palace's envelopes which, being part of the Royal Mail, requires no stamp. Nine times out of ten the reply is couched so that "regrettably there is no prospect of an interview such as you envisage in the foreseeable future."

If there *is* a faint hope of the interview taking place then the matter will be raised with the appropriate Private Secretary. If he thinks there's a chance, he will probably ask for the proposal to be considered again at one of the future-programme meetings that take place at the Palace twice a year, normally in July and December. These meetings, which last all day, are attended by Private Secretaries, Press Secretaries, and equerries. Their purpose is to collate and then short list the hundreds of requests that arrive at the Palace for one or other member of the Royal Family to attend, open or visit a function, factory, hospital, gala evening, or whatever. The 'Principal' − i.e. Prince Charles or Prince Philip − usually joins the meeting in the afternoon, after the requests have been reduced to a manageable number.

(The one sure way of *not* being granted the presence of a senior member of the Royal Family at a ceremony, incidentally, is to suggest a date that coincides with one or other of the immovable annual engagements on the Royal calendar − e.g. the Remembrance Service at the Cenotaph in November; the State Opening of Parliament in the same month; the Trooping the Colour ceremony, that marks the Queen's official birthday in June. Dates that cross with Royal Ascot, Royal Family summer and winter holidays, and Royal tours abroad, announced well in advance, are also inadvisable as suggestions.)

As a matter of deliberate policy, the Queen does not give interviews. Neither does the Queen Mother − although shortly before her seventieth birthday, great efforts were made, from inside the Palace, to persuade her to agree to at least one of several alternative types of interviews suggested. Curiously, considering all the electronic options available, none of the Royal Family has so far agreed to record on tape or film unique memories that could be locked away in the archives for the benefit of future biographers and historians.

The Queen does keep a diary, but unlike her ancestor, Queen Victoria, she relies less on words and more on photographs, most of them taken with her gold Rollei. Under each picture she writes her own long captions. Albums of these pictures, stretching back to the earliest years of her reign, are catalogued and carefully preserved.*

But to return to the hopeful journalist seeking an interview with a member of the Royal Family, other than the Queen herself or Queen Elizabeth the Queen Mother. If he, or she, is lucky, a date, time and place for the interview will be arranged – sometimes up to a year after the original application – and a request made for a list of questions to be submitted in advance. Depending on the journalist, this list will either be deliberately short and the questions fairly general, or will be long and detailed. Next, the proposals will be 'sent upstairs' by the Palace Press Office and, usually, returned with only one or two deletions, or sometimes none at all. (If the latter happens, the journalist kicks himself for not including the question he didn't dare ask!)

When the day finally arrives, the interviewer presents himself at the pre-arranged rendezvous feeling as nervous as a cub-reporter sent on his first assignment. It is arguable whether the television interviewer, accompanied by technicians and probably a producer, has a less nerve-wracking job than the lone journalist who suddenly finds himself seated opposite the Prince of Wales in the Prince's study or sitting room. In either event, once the first question is put the interviewer is very much on his own. (Sometimes, but not always, someone from the Palace Press Office sits in on the interview.)

Fortunately, interviewing Prince Charles is invariably a pleasant experience, as those who have had this privilege will testify. He is courteous, friendly, amusing, and goes out of his way to put the interviewer at ease as quickly as possible – from his point of view, it can be no fun being interviewed by someone who looks like remaining a bag of nerves throughout! Prince Charles seems actually to

---

* Robert Lacey, whose 'Majesty' (published in 1977) was one of the most well received and financially successful books ever written about the Queen, scarcely glimpsed the subject of his biography, except in pictures, while he was researching his book. However, he did have off-the-record interviews with, amongst others, Prince Philip and Sir Martin Charteris, the Queen's Private Secretary at the time. When this author, interviewing Prince Philip on the occasion of his sixtieth birthday, asked if the Queen was ever likely to grant an interview to a biographer or journalist, he was told: "I should think probably not." Prince Philip's opinion was that the risks of mis-understandings, or running counter to official attitudes, would be greater than the benefits.

enjoy being asked questions, even if at times he thinks some of them are slightly daft. He has become adept at side-stepping, usually with a joke, the questions he has no intention of answering. His sister, Princess Anne, on the other hand tends to give short shrift to anyone who puts a question that she thinks a waste of time. On one occasion, shortly before several members of the Royal Family were to appear in public, a journalist asked Princess Anne – more or less as an opening gambit – how the ladies in the Royal party decided what clothes and colours to wear, so they didn't clash. "What a stupid question," replied the Princess.

Interviewing Prince Philip can be a daunting adventure too, though the highly complex personality of the Queen's husband also makes him an extremely intriguing person to talk to. Attempt to meet the challenge he throws back at his interrogator with practically every question, and it will become noticeable how much he enjoys an invigorating discussion – even though he still tends not to suffer too well those who are not altogether fools.

For any interviewer, almost as interesting as the thought of spending an hour putting questions to a member of the Royal Family, is the prospect of seeing inside the private apartments of a Palace and being able to report on items of special interest – with, it might surprise some people to know, the forbearance of the owners. How, otherwise, would one be likely to discover, for instance, the wholly unimportant fact that the Duke of Edinburgh has numbers pin-pricked on the insoles of his shoes – presumably for identification? Or that Princess Anne places mementoes, handed to her on world-wide walkabouts, on a ledge running round the walls of her sitting room at Gatcombe Park?

The author, interviewing Prince Charles in his study at Buckingham Palace – this was before the Prince's marriage – thought he was showing off his keen powers of observation when he wrote in the first paragraph of his article that "there is a large desk facing the door, and on the left a glass cabinet, next to a grandfather clock (stopped at 3.20)."

As promised, the completed manuscript was posted to the Prince of Wales' Office for checking and returned a few days later with an amendment, in Prince Charles' own handwriting, in the margin: "It is not stopped – it is a 24 hour clock!" On reflection, this still didn't make sense!

Reporters are not renowned for being mechanically minded, and the presence of a tape recorder has nearly ruined more than one Royal interview. Most journalists still prefer to rely on a notebook, memory, or, in a few cases, speculation, when it comes to 'getting a quote' but a long and rare interview with a member of the Royal Family demands accuracy, and might provide an excuse to purchase a handy-sized tape recorder.

Christena Appleyard, of the *Daily Mirror*, tried out her new tape recorder at home the evening before she was due to interview Prince Charles about the Tudor warship, the 'Mary Rose'. She pushed down the 'Record' button to test the machine and in self-conscious jokey style asked: "What about this f---ing old ship then?" Unfortunately although she ran the tape back to the start, when she was about to begin her interview in Prince Charles' sitting room the following morning, she pressed the 'Play back' button instead of the 'Record' and suffered the embarrassment of hearing her own voice repeating the question.

On another occasion, Grania Forbes, the Press Association Court Correspondent, arrived at Windsor Castle for her interview to discover that the B.B.C. had not quite finished making a short film with the Prince. Miss Forbes was shown into an adjoining room, a bedroom as it happened, to wait her turn. As she had officially taken up her appointment as Court Correspondent only that morning she was more than usually nervous. Compounding the stress was the realisation that the tape recorder, hired specially that day, wasn't working properly. An inveterate smoker, she craved a cigarette but, knowing Prince Charles' strong disapproval of the habit – especially in a bedroom, she presumed – she managed to desist for several minutes before giving way. As she exhaled the first plume of smoke a head popped round the door. "Next please," said the Prince of Wales.*

Fleet Street has always had a soft spot for Prince Charles. To middle-aged fathers he is the sort of man many wouldn't mind having as a son – especially if he brought home a girl like Lady Diana. For his part, he has shown a fairly constant tolerance of the media – amounting at times almost to a mutual conspiratorial affection – even towards those who have unashamedly played tricks on him in order to obtain pictures. On one of his annual skiing holidays in Switzerland a beautiful young woman suddenly careered out of a wood and crashed into the Prince, entangling them both in her skis. As she struggled to her feet a voice from the wood shouted, "Again Barbara, again!" The young lady, a former Miss Switzerland, obliged by sinking to the snow once more, and as Prince Charles bent down to give her a lift his detective raced up, calling out "It's a

---

* In the author's case, his first interview with Prince Charles was held up for some minutes while a search was made of the Prince's study for a missing tape recorder. It eventually transpired that while photographs were being taken the black box had been inadvertently kicked out of sight under a settee. Retrieval required an undignified scrabble on hands and knees . . .

set-up, Sir." Charles looked round smiling, and declared "I don't care, she looks lovely." Again, in 1979, when a bikini clad beauty pounced on the Prince as he emerged from an early morning dip in the Indian Ocean, his comment to the preying photographer was: "I'll say one thing, you certainly know how to pick them."*

In the past he has put on a funny mask to please photographers, written a funny ditty about them (two of the lines read: "Insistent, persistent, the press never end,/ One day they will drive me right round the bend") and, in one instance at least, apologised for getting in the way.** Of late, however, he has been much less inclined to become involved in Press capers. It was noticeable that on the two occasions he went for a swim during his most recent Australian tour he was surrounded by an unusually large number of Royal protectors and frolicking damsels were kept well away. The likelihood is that any changes in the Prince's relationship with the media are to do with age (Prince Charles, as he has no need to be reminded, is no longer a very young man); stage (he has left a Naval career behind him and could be said now to be well and truly involved in the full time responsibility of being heir to the Throne); and above all, marriage. His young brother Prince Andrew can be left (none too safely) to provide trivia for the media in future. The two men have a genuine love and respect for one another, but Prince Charles has always known that Andrew, a natural extrovert, bombastic at times, was likely to upstage him in some respects.***

Today the Prince of Wales is moving towards the period in his life when increasingly he can be expected to take a larger share of the duties and responsibilities of the Monarch, as the Queen's chief representative at some State occasions, and as her ambassador abroad. Beside him will be the Princess of Wales — the young

---

* Both incidents were pre-arranged and were not the accidents they were meant to appear to be. In the first case the photographer had rehearsed his model for two whole days to ski and crash at exactly the right angle and the right spot to give him the best shot.

** A freelance photographer who has never met Prince Charles received a call at his home late one evening in July 1982. The caller claimed to be Prince Charles, and, once he had convinced the person at the other end that he was indeed the Prince of Wales and not Mike Yarwood ("I'm always having this trouble") apologised for any inconvenience he'd be causing the following morning by flying a helicopter to join the P & O liner 'Canberra' as it returned from the Falklands. The photographer had been commissioned to fly the same route to obtain aerial pictures of the liner's triumphant homecoming, but would be prevented if the usual 'purple corridor' was reserved for the Royal aircraft.

woman who has done more to popularise the concept of monarchy throughout the world than any other member of the Royal Family in the last ten years. At home will be their children. By her marriage to Prince Charles and through the birth of Prince William, the person whom half the world still thinks of as 'Lady Di' gave the Prince of Wales the one state that above all others he has always cherished and in which he feels the most secure: that of family man. As it does with most people, marriage and parenthood have brought about a change in him, and in his beautiful wife also.

*** A few years ago, when the two brothers were receiving instruction simultaneously in parachute jumping, Prince Andrew was called ahead of his brother by the R.A.F. instructor to practise a jump. As he moved away, Andrew made a facetious, cocky remark, ending up with "I am a card aren't I?" "One day," remarked Prince Charles, without the trace of a smile, "somebody will teach that young man the meaning of modesty."

14. THE FAIRY PRINCESS

"If Lady Diana Spencer is to be the future Queen of England, she cannot expect to be Greta Garbo as well."
Daily Mirror, January 1981

"If she'd been a model, and had been paid for every picture that's appeared of her, she'd have been able to buy Buckingham Palace."
Auberon Waugh, on the BBC-TV Terry Wogan Show, February 19 1983

"No court astrologer would have ever advised them to be married in July, since Prince Charles *and* Lady Diana have strong Uranus transits on their charts. In addition, the last week in July is sandwiched between two eclipses, and those are not good auspices under which to enter any permanent relationship."
'Svetlana' of the Washington Post

"It is interesting that the most popular woman in England today is the gentle, ultra-feminine Princess Diana, who chose looking after children as a career, the one pastime the women's movement claim is boring and demeaning."
Jilly Cooper, the Mail on Sunday, May 9 1982

"The ninth Princess of Wales is a perfect blend of regal and real — the only sort of Princess the British could have accepted in the 1980s."
Penny Junor, 'Diana, Princess of Wales'

It is hard to believe that until the autumn of 1980 the name of the future wife of the Prince of Wales was utterly unknown to the great majority of people. Today there is no-one who is photographed more often, and there can be few celebrities more photogenic. Her picture has been cut out of magazines and pinned up on more walls of more houses in more parts of the world than any other living person, with the possible exception of the Pope. As in his case, the charisma has almost as much to do with her own personality as with her position. She is immensely popular in her own right. However, unlike the Pontiff, in the very few years since she entered the public domain, the Princess of Wales has had to contend with intense speculation about what goes on in her private as well as her public life. In some ways she has been treated by the popular Press like a movie star in the hey-day of Hollywood — boosted when she was tipped for stardom, adulated when she married the world's leading man, very nearly crucified by rumours, based on fairly flimsy evidence, of an unhappy first year of marriage.

Fortunately, though members of the public may often *treat* Princess Diana like a film star, they do not think of her as such. Her position in the scheme of things is much more important to them than that, and so there has to be an extremely good and proven reason produced before they will even consider changing their good opinion of her. As the media has discovered, through postbags and 'phone-ins, the fairy-tale princess of folklore is still a very popular conception, and no-one wants a dream shattered. Practically everyone, it seems, has empathy with the Princess, and the great majority have a genuine liking for her. It is no exaggeration — it is a cliche, however — to say that, almost from her first unscheduled appearance on television, people took her to their hearts.

Lady Diana Spencer might quite easily have been just one more addition to the fairly long line of girls who had been wined and dined by the Prince of Wales. Two years earlier Diana's eldest sister, Lady Elizabeth Sarah Spencer, had accompanied the Prince on a skiing holiday,* and there had been several other girls he liked well enough. But, to give the Royal watchers their due, a number of them very quickly surmised that Lady Diana might be the one who eventually became the Princess of Wales. "Is this the real thing?" asked Harry Arnold in *The Sun* on September 8 1980, hinting with more conviction than before that it might indeed be.

Figuring in the match-making calculations of the reporters was the fact that, as their research quickly discovered, the 19-year-old Lady Diana had apparently had no serious boyfriends before now —

---

* Subsequently, in an interview with James Whitaker for *Woman's Own*, (he was using the pseudonym of Jeremy Slazenger on this occasion) Lady Sarah was careful to insist that the relationship was platonic. "I am not in love with him . . . and I wouldn't marry anyone I didn't love, whether it was the dustman or the King of England."

unlike some of Prince Charles' previous girlfriends. On his side, they reckoned, he was becoming increasingly anxious to find the right girl and settle down − it was something he *had* to do.

Just three months before Lady Diana was invited to Balmoral by the Queen (in September 1980) Prince Charles had been rejected by Anna Wallace, the 25-year-old daughter of a Scottish landowner, following a spectacular scene at Windsor Castle* and this, the Charles-watchers again surmised, made him all the more vulnerable.

It seemed extremely unlikely that Prince Charles and Miss Anna Wallace would have married one another, even if they hadn't fallen out, just as it seemed quite possible that Charles and Diana would. Accordingly, for practically the whole of the next five months, almost until the very eve of the announcement of their engagement to one another, Diana endured the Press and televison at her door, *inside* her door, on the 'phone, on the pavement, at the kindergarten where she helped out. No other member of the Royal Family, before or after marriage, has ever had to contend with such a degree of Press curiosity without police protection. Diana battled through it bravely, and, to begin with at any rate, apparently found it all quite amusing. This was not as surprising as at first it might seem. Here she was, after all, a quiet-living girl, excited by having her first flat in London (shared with three other girls) and suddenly she comes face-to-face with quite famous journalists from popular papers, whose stories and tittle-tattle she's enjoyed reading ever since schooldays. They send her flowers, they have a way with words, they smile at her a lot and are courteous. And when she insists that she is sorry but there is nothing she can possibly tell them, they still hang around. They really are rather like children waiting to be given a treat.

For their part, the reporters took a shine to Diana immediately and − more important in some ways − went on liking her even after her own attitude to them had undergone something of a change. Never rude nor pompous (two forms of behaviour which infuriate most reporters more quickly than any other) Diana enchanted them with

---

* According to Penny Junor, amongst others, in her biography 'Diana, Princess of Wales', Anna Wallace, known to her friends as 'Whiplash', took grave exception to being left alone much of the time when she was Prince Charles' personal guest at the Queen Mother's eightieth birthday ball at Windsor in June 1980. Charles felt obliged to spend time with other guests on such an important family occasion, and Anna was overheard to rage: "Don't ever ignore me like that again . . . No-one treats me like that − not even you." That same month, she became engaged to and then married the Honourable John Hesketh. Charles was said to have been clearly besotted by Anna.

her fresh looks, her coy glance, her giggle, and her accent which was not 'counties-posh', more Kensington-Cockney. They marvelled at the way this young girl, totally unused to being 'staked out' by the Press, continued to live her life as normally as possible. They decided, perhaps even before Prince Charles did, that this was the person the heir to the Throne would do well to marry. "She'd bring a breath of fresh air to the Palace," was a conclusion reached by many, and by passing on their feelings and, even more influential, their pictures of the lovely Diana to their millions of readers and television viewers, they made it possible to judge that the world was of a like opinion. Diana herself was never in doubt about what she wanted. But then, she was madly in love.

It was when she felt that she had been badly let down that problems arose.

On November 16 1980 the *Sunday Mirror* ran the story of The Royal Love Train on its front page, claiming that Lady Diana had twice had a secret night-time rendezvous with Prince Charles on board the Royal train as it stood in a deserted siding near Holt in Wiltshire. The first occasion was supposed to have taken place on the night of November 5th when Prince Charles did indeed sleep on the train, on his way to an official visit to the West Country. But Lady Diana was at home in bed. She told a Press Association reporter twelve days after the allegations had appeared in the *Sunday Mirror* (the Palace had already protested that they were 'totally false') "I want to get the record straight. The story was completely false. I was not on the Royal train when they said, and have never been on the Royal train . . ." Unfortunately the same interview quoted her as saying "I'd like to marry soon," and she denied ever having said *that*.

As speculation about the Royal romance increased the conduct of a few journalists was unforgivable. A photographer pushed his way through a lavatory window to get inside the Young England Kindergarten where Diana worked. A reporter attempted to conduct an interview through the letterbox of her flat in Coleherne Court. The attention of other representatives of the media, including television news units, was unremitting. Even when she went to stay with her mother and step-father on the Shand Kydds' sheep-station in Australia (Prince Charles had already proposed marriage, but the world had yet to be informed) the so-called secret holiday was rudely interrupted by a helicopter loaded with Australian Pressmen squat-landing a few yards from the house.

Looking back, it seems slightly surprising that Lady Diana and Prince Charles were permitted any respite for courtship. But Prince Charles, through long experience and with some help from his friends, is adept at giving the Press the slip when he means to. At weekends both the Prince and Lady Diana were guests on occasion at the homes of friends, such as the Parker-Bowles and Tryons. He took Diana to Highgrove and, as he was later pleased to tell reporters, his grandmother, the Queen Mother, had loaned them Birkhall, her lovely home near Balmoral, for a very happy weekend.* He still had his work to get on with, but he gave instructions that Lady Diana should be kept informed of all his forthcoming engagements — something he had never done with any other girlfriend.

Within hours of the announcement of their own engagement, to one another, Lady Diana had to face up to her first Palace-arranged interviews and photo session. She made a success of both by appearing — as she has appeared on many occasions since — carefree and at the same time careful. The questions had been agreed beforehand — some had even been suggested to the interviewers as the kind Charles and Diana would prefer to be asked — but even so the prospect of the interview especially must have been something of an ordeal.

Interestingly, when the television interviewers (Keith Graves of the B.B.C. and Anthony Carthew of I.T.N.) asked the Prince and Lady Diana to sum up their feelings on that day and touched on the subject of love — "And I suppose in love?" was the slightly laconic way the question was actually posed — Lady Diana agreed immediately. "Of course!" Her fiancé, however, was circumspect. "Whatever 'in love' means," he replied. Which, for the author at least, brought back a memory of what Prince Charles had said to him in an interview in 1975:

"I think one's got to be aware of the fact that falling madly in love with someone is not necessarily the starting point to getting married. Marriage is a much more important business than just falling in love — as I think a lot of couples probably find out. I think one must concentrate on marriage being essentially a question of mutual love and respect for each other. Creating a secure family unit in which to bring up children, to give them a happy, secure upbringing — *that* is what marriage is all about. And essentially one must be good friends, and love I'm sure will grow out of that friendship and become deeper and deeper."

Prince Charles dislikes being requoted on something he spoke about years before, in case his opinion has changed in the meantime, but in this instance it would seem that his views had altered little, if at all.

After the splendour of their wedding — surely the happiest national

---

* It is often suggested that Queen Elizabeth the Queen Mother and Ruth, Lady Fermoy, her Lady-in-Waiting who is also Diana's grandmother, played a combined game of match-making where Charles and Diana were concerned.

celebration in Britain since the end of World War II – the first year of the Prince and Princess of Wales' marriage was, like that of so many other newly-weds, largely one of adjustment. And it was so not only for them, but also for those in close working proximity to them. Those more entrenched at Buckingham Palace, accustomed to a quiet and most orderly life, were enchanted by the arrival in their midst of such a comely, lively girl but were a little mystified, if not slightly put out, by a Princess of Wales who walked around with earphones on her head listening to pre-recorded music – apparently the contraption was known as a Sony Walkman and was available, at discount price, in the Tottenham Court Road.

They were not used, either, to serving a Member of the Royal Family who went down to the kitchens herself to fetch an apple, or a Princess who rat-tat-tatted on the parquet floor of the Music Room in attempts to master the intricacies of tap-dancing. One or two of them were *really* taken aback, 'rocked on their heels' as one aide put it, by the intentions of independence displayed by the young lady. They had imagined that, once she had become the Princess of Wales, the former Lady Diana Spencer – not a total stranger to custom and tradition, after all* – would be willing to fit in with the long established Royal way of going about things. And so she would, but not it seemed without asking questions and not without querying some of the arrangements made on her behalf.

By no means everyone was surprised by Princess Diana's determination from the outset to protect her independence and prevent herself becoming smothered by protocol; the great majority who came into contact with her at the Palace admired her and had every sympathy with her views. But "anyone who did not appreciate that she had a will and a mind of her own, and would be her own person totally, misestimated her," comments someone qualified to know.

In her day-to-day dealings with staff her manner was easy-going, but never over familiar. She disliked signs of familiarity towards herself, and more especially any displays of chumminess where her husband was concerned. She disapproved strongly if she overheard anyone refer to him as 'the young man', no matter how long they had known and worked for the Prince of Wales.

Prince Charles himself may have been slightly surprised, even irritated, on occasion, by his wife's behaviour. This was not the image of the coy, shy Diana that the Press had portrayed over the months. However, if he was annoyed at times, he took care not to betray his feelings in front of others. The likelihood was that he

---

* The Princess of Wales' father, Earl Spencer (then Viscount Althorp) was acting Master of the Royal Household at the time of his marriage to the Hon. Frances Roche, future mother of Lady Diana.

recognised and approved of Diana's determination to retain as much as possible of her old style of living; she would simply have to come to terms with the fact that she couldn't just slip out to the shops whenever she felt like it. But *would* she?

Adjusting to a new style of life was necessary for Prince Charles, too. He realised that his careworn days as a bachelor (he hadn't always been happy, often quite lonely in fact) were over and that some of his small circle of close friends would not necessarily go on to become friends of his wife also. He was aware that his wife did not share his enthusiasm for polo, for hunting, for horse-riding and certain kinds of dogs even – but he was not ready to give up his hobbies. He was not prepared to give up very much, in fact, though he was happy to talk things over and give his wife (he had never been a 'women's libber') as much freedom as possible. If she became bored by Balmoral in the rain, then why shouldn't she fly down to London? If he talked almost incessantly about the problems of raising one of his ancestor's battleships from the seabed, then she knew that she ought to show interest. This, they had both heard often enough, was the stuff of marriage – in the first few months it was a case of give and take.

As the two of them made plans to move to Kensington Palace, away from the vast sombre spaces of Buckingham Palace, Prince Charles was prepared to see some of his staff take their leave; Stephen Barry, for example, who had been his valet for 12 years and Paul Officer, the policeman who had once saved his life and who had been assigned to the protection of Princess Diana. In the months to come others would move on in furtherance of their careers, among them Francis Cornish, the Prince of Wales' Assistant Private Secretary, a Foreign Office diplomat who had given sterling support to the Princess from the moment of her engagement.

The public's fascination with the Princess of Wales seems boundless. They could not see enough pictures or read enough stories, and when she began undertaking official engagements they turned out in their thousands to line the streets in the hope of a glimpse of their fairy Princess. "She's so beautiful." "She's so natural." "Oh, she's *gorgeous*." The signs of slight nervousness and shyness that were apparent in the early days only enhanced her attractiveness. She so excelled at walkabouts and at meeting Lord Mayors that she might have been born and trained to the job. As it was, she had benefited from tips passed on by other members of the Royal Family. For instance, she had learned the Queen Mother's habit, whenever she was about to sign a Distinguished Visitors Book, of asking onlookers "Does anyone know the date?" (By lifting her head to enquire she gave the photographers a chance to get a good picture for the local archives.) The Queen had impressed on her the Royal maxim,

"Never stand when you can sit, and always glance down on a stairway to make sure of your footing." (She still has to master the Queen's discipline of walking slowly, however.) Prince Charles had shown by example how to throw out a general question on a walk-about — "Do you all come from around her?" — in order to get individuals talking, and how to use a smile to get you gracefully out of one *tête-à-tête* and onto the next.*

Naturally, Diana was flattered and slightly overwhelmed by the extent of her popularity — even though she carried it off so well. (At the end of her first tour of Wales with Prince Charles she was physically and emotionally exhausted.) But for some reason she had always believed that public interest would fall away soon after the tumult of her wedding had passed, and she would be left more or less alone, in her private life at least. When this didn't happen, she seemed to go through a gamut of emotions ranging from surprise to resentment, and on through nervous tension to fury. A large part of her resentment, which could take the form of unpredictable moodi-ness, appeared to be directed towards the media, especially towards the photographers who pushed and shoved to get their pictures, or hung around like vultures or skulked like private detectives on a divorce case. Once or twice everything became too much for her to bear, and on at least one occasion it was *not* the photographers who were to blame.**

News, in November 1981, that the Princess of Wales was expecting her first child increased Press — and public — interest to such a degree that within a month of the announcement serious concern was being expressed inside Buckingham Palace not only about harass-ment but about whether relations between the Princess and the Press might not be permanently impaired, to the detriment of the Mon-archy itself, if something were not done to restore a balance. The meeting of editors at Buckingham Palace in December, called by Press Secretary Michael Shea, undoubtedly eased matters — though

---

* Princess Alexandra once complimented a woman on "your wonderful baby", then realised the person holding the child was at least seventy. "It taught me a lesson. You should always look at the woman first, and then at the child. In that way you have a better idea about guessing the relationship."
** A few days before her wedding, attending a polo match in which her fiancé was playing, Lady Diana had been asked to present a Cup, and had declined the unofficial invitation even before play started. However a persistent Club member had attempted several times to change her mind as she sat watching the game — cameras focused on her all the time — until, feeling pressured on all sides, she fled the stand in tears.

the pictures taken of Diana in a bikini in the Bahamas two months later did *not*. Following on the editors' meeting Shea thought it might be of help all round if Princess Diana were to be offered the opportunity of seeing how the media works from its side of the camera, so to speak. A private and informal visit to the Independent Television News studios was secretly arranged. David Nicholas, the Editor-in-Chief of I.T.N. entered the cryptic letters BUPTV in his diary for February 11th, and on the day before conducted Michael Shea and the Princess of Wales' detective on a tour of the building without any of his news hawks realising who the visitors were. At five o'clock on the 11th, thirty minutes before she was due to arrive, Nicholas advised his staff over the Tannoy: "You may be interested to know that in about half an hour we are to receive an informal visit from Her Royal Highness the Princess of Wales. Sorry for this late announcement, but it is at the Palace's request." The early evening news bulletin was due on the air in forty-five minutes' time.

The Princess enjoyed every minute of her hour long stay. Her Private Secretary told David Nicholas that afterwards she was bubbling over with excitement. The editor had purposely arranged that she should be shown round by Selina Scott, a newscaster not unlike Diana in appearance, and should meet people of her own age group. It was altogether quite fortuitous, and not an example of Nicholas at his most wily as some suspected, that both the newscaster and the programme director doing duty that evening were also pregnant. When she spotted a notice on the door that read "Royal Birth Unit" – it was outside the room used to prepare special projects – the Princess smiled coyly.

Some five months after Prince William's birth the Princess paid a visit to Capital Radio, London's most successful pop-music station, and once again it was apparent that she was completely at ease in a world that was very familiar to her. Diana is an avid Capital Radio listener – her husband much prefers B.B.C.'s Radio 4 – switching on her transistor in the morning when she hears Capital's traffic-spotting 'plane flying over Kensington Palace (i.e. around 7.20 in the summer, and 7.45 in winter) and very often bathing Prince William to a background of pop music. She is mortified, it is said, when, driving down the M4 motorway to Highgrove, her car radio runs out of range of Capital, around Exit 13.*

---

* Capital Radio enterprisingly invited Prince Charles and Lady Diana to make separate lists of their Top Ten favourite records for broadcasting on the eve of their wedding. They willingly complied, but almost at the last moment Buckingham Palace requested that the idea be dropped. Classical music made up the bulk of Charles' list, while Diana's was comprised entirely of pop music and evergreen melodies.

As she toured the radio station, disc jockeys and executives alike were surprised, and naturally delighted, that Princess Diana knew so much about them. She had obviously studied her briefing beforehand – due to an oversight one executive's biography had been omitted and he was the only one for whom she didn't have a question ready. But staff and bystanders alike were equally intrigued by some of Diana's remarks. A disc jockey who stubbed out his cigarette and apologised for smoking (the management had asked everyone not to) had the Princess's sympathy. "Sometimes smoking does help to reduce tension," she said, adding "there are some moments in married life when I feel I'm going to have to take it up in a *big* way." She had a long conversation with a 20-year-old Cockney D.J. who was new to the station. When asked where he had come from he replied "the gutter". Diana appeared genuinely surprised, and pleased that someone from a background without money or education could become a disc jockey. "Isn't it nice," she commented to a head of department, "that people can just be themselves. Most of life is not being able to be yourself."

Quite conceivably, not far from her mind were the astonishing reports that had appeared in some newspapers just eight days earlier. The *Daily Mirror,* under a front page banner headline – CONCERN FOR DI'S HEALTH – said fears were being expressed over her diet. "The greatest concern," wrote James Whitaker, "is that Princess Diana could fall victim of the dreaded slimmers' disease anorexia nervosa." On the same day Harry Arnold, in *The Sun,* claimed that Prince Charles was so seriously concerned that his wife was showing all the symptoms of the disease that he had sought medical advice. (Arnold maintains that at one stage his paper intended publishing the name of the specialist who was treating the Princess, but, for undisclosed reasons, decided not to.) *The Standard* that evening quoted "a source close to the Royal Family" as saying the Princess of Wales was being affected by stresses and strains caused largely by "grossly exaggerated" reports of her health. Claims that she was suffering from anorexia nervosa were "unsubstantiated speculation". Michael Shea thought that "the fact that the Princess of Wales was in sparkling form on two public occasions yesterday for millions to see speaks for itself". But an examination of newspapers around that time appears to show that the Palace never once categorically denied that the Princess was suffering from anorexia nervosa, or was in danger of the disease through losing too much weight. Perhaps she was not. Or perhaps it was just that, as a Palace spokesman said at the time: "We do not get involved with the personal affairs of the Royal Family every time a distasteful rumour is started."

Sadly for her, Diana had to endure the spreading of other unpleasant rumours during the course of the next two months. By far the most startling allegations were those that came from Nigel Dempster, gossip columnist for the *Daily Mail* and author of a biography of Princess Margaret. On a London Weekend Television late-night chat show excerpts were shown of an interview he had given in New York to A.B.C.'s "Good Morning America". According to Dempster "Shy Di becomes a wilful and spoilt girl. She knows she is the Princess of Wales. She knows she can do what she wants." He told his audience: "Suddenly, getting this enormous power, having people curtsy and bow and do everything she wants, she has become a fiend. She has become a little monster." He claimed that Prince Charles was desperately unhappy, firstly because he knew he could never divorce Diana, and also because Fleet Street had forced him into the marriage. Buckingham Palace dismissed the Dempster claims in one word. "Ridiculous."

The Palace was even more contemptuous of an American psychiatrist's warning, in January 1983, that the Princess of Wales stood an 80% chance of becoming ill through the strain of Royal life. "An obsessive compulsive illness could definitely be a possibility," claimed Dr Thomas Holmes, Head of the Department of Psychiatry at Washington Medical School. Deviser of the Holmes-Rahe stress scale, he scored Diana at an alarming 417 – anything between 150 and 300 indicating a 50% chance of illness in the near future. Dr Holmes, it needs to be added, having never actually met the Princess, apparently based his calculations on "known facts in the Press". (He later denounced the Press for distortion of anything he may have said.)

In all fairness, Royal watchers were genuinely concerned about the change they thought they detected in the Princess of Wales towards the end of 1982 – it was not just a matter of looking for a new angle to the continuing story of Kensington Palace. They – and a good many of the public as well – thought she *was* much thinner than a healthy person should be. They wondered *why* she had arrived five minutes late at the annual Service of Remembrance at the Albert Hall, attended by the Queen herself, after Prince Charles had told one of the organisers that she would not be coming. They heard rumours that away from the public eye, the Princess was proving 'difficult', but they could not fault the manner in which she carried out all her public engagements. They sensed an antagonism building up between the Princess and themselves which, they told one another, would bode ill for everyone. Perhaps the Royal watchers, reporters and photographers alike, read far too much into what they saw and heard. Perhaps, for a time at least, they should have restricted their reporting to official Royal occasions. But it is easy to talk after the event, just as it is very hard to explain to an editor why your rival has a story and you have not . . .

On January 9 1983 the Prince and Princess of Wales flew to Zurich, Switzerland, for a skiing holiday. It was supposed to be a private holiday, if not actually secret. (Buckingham Palace Press Office did not tell the Press where the Royal couple were going.) On the same day a local reporter phoned the residence of Prince Franz Josef II in Liechtenstein: "What will happen when Prince Charles stays with you this week?" he enquired. Came the astonished reply: "How did you find out?" Within hours all local hotels were booked out with reporters and photographers from the rest of Europe and from Britain.

Steve Wood of the *Daily Express* and James Whitaker are probably the only two Royal watchers capable of skiing well enough to keep up with the Prince and Princess of Wales. On his first day, Steve skied close to Diana, photographing as he went along. At one point she fell down almost directly in front of him but, because of the angle, Steve knew he couldn't get a good shot – though he would have liked to have. "I'm glad you didn't take that picture of me falling over," the Princess told him a few moments later. "We do have our rules," Steve almost lied, with a wicked smile.

There are invariably arguments between Palace and Press about the ground rules on occasions like this. The Prince and Princess of Wales were on a private holiday, but they were skiing on public slopes. Scores of holidaymakers were just as anxious to get photographs of the couple as were the Press – though admittedly they stood to make less or no financial profit from so doing. Prince Charles has a dislike of being 'ripped-off' and his wife showed increasingly that she did not wish to have pictures taken. Interestingly, Steve Wood had shot several pictures of a smiling Diana, but the ones that Fleet Street chose to publish showed her doing her best to hide her face from the cameras. She was 'SULKY DI' according to *The Sun,* but Harry Arnold, who filed the story, would have much preferred that the picture had shown a Princess up-ended in the snow. "The caption would probably have read 'Oops-a-Di-sy', and readers would have loved it because it showed Diana enjoying herself." Instead as a Member of the Household said, SULKY DI would only serve to put the clock back in Palace efforts to bring Diana to terms with her role in life.

At one point the Press thought they had made a deal (through Prince Charles' personal detective) whereby the Royal couple would be left alone to have their lunch in peace in return for a posed picture later in the day. But Diana emerged from the restaurant with her head down, a frown on her face. No amount of pleading from Prince Charles – "Please, Darling, please Darling" – could persuade his wife to relent her frozen attitude. If she had agreed to stand and smile for, say, five minutes perhaps photographers — whose presence had attracted hordes of inquisitive holidaymakers — might have left her alone for the rest of her holiday. The trouble was, there were certain Pressmen she no longer trusted, and there were plenty of photographers who had never completely trusted one another. Bargains? What's a bargain?

Jean Rook wrote in her column in the *Daily Express:* "Not to put too fine an acidless point on my pen, she behaved like a little Madam . . . Tender as Diana is, she should realise that, at times, she must make long-suffering Charles very sore. Unlike her, he may have been trained for the job, but unless his wife grows a thicker skin, and a stronger sense of humour, his job could be hard work for them both." An American magazine quoted the opinion of a London psychoanalyst: "If one is barely out of adolescence, one wants adulation, glamour, indulgence, but there is also the adolescent yearning for privacy, which is encroached on. Some can solve it. Some cannot."

On February 3 1983, just when things were beginning to simmer down, the *Daily Star* (one of the two newspapers that had brought its readers the Bikini pictures a year before) ran no fewer than six pages on THE TRUTH about Diana's marriage, her life, her relations with the Press, and called for an end to intrusive journalism into the lives of the Queen and the Royal Family. It described Charles and Diana's marriage as rumbustious — "but they are still very much in love." And it promised to continue to report and photograph the Royal Family's movements, but only with their knowledge. "We will still be telling you about their plans, their hopes, their lives, and, yes, their loves and disappointments . . . without intrusion." To back up its headline, 'Charles and Diana — The Facts' it quoted at length "one reliable source close to the Palace" whose turn of phrase bore strong resemblance to the way Michael Shea talks. The *Daily Star* called for a new understanding between the Press and Buckingham Palace, and the Queen's Press Secretary, the paper duly reported, praised the *Star*'s declaration of fair play: "This is a development to be welcomed." And so it was. At the same time no-one was under any illusions. So much depended on the Princess of Wales herself: on whether she continued to adapt successfully to the role she had taken on, or persisted in demands for a degree of privacy and personal freedom that could never quite be met.

On March 20 1983, the Prince and Princess of Wales, their nine-month-old son Prince William beside them, flew to the small town of Alice Springs at the start of a six-week tour of Australia and New Zealand. There to meet them — almost inevitably blocking the view initially of the couple of hundred townsfolk who had come out to greet them — were about sixty reporters, photographers and television crews from Australia, Britain, America, Europe and Japan.

The Prince and Princess of Wales descended the steps of the aircraft smiling broadly and waving to the crowd at the conclusion of a flight that had lasted some thirty hours. A few moments later Nanny Barnes emerged from the aircraft carrying Prince William, blinking in the bright midday light. She placed him in his mother's arms and for several minutes the group of three stood on the tarmac, turning first this way, then that — Diana relaxed and smiling all the while; her husband making a joke about the first Australian fly to land on Prince William's face — while cameras clicked and slicked on motor drive. Then, with baby William safely returned to the aircraft, the Royal couple turned towards the waiting crowd of well-wishers.

During the next forty-five days the Princess of Wales travelled 30,000 miles, shook at least six thousand hands and had her photograph taken a million times. She wore fifty different outfits in almost as many days, and moved from rain to blistering heat and on again to cold and rain. She was never once heard to complain. She never once looked bad tempered and hardly ever slightly bored. She even ate up everything that was placed before her. If she had set out deliberately to confound her critics and to please her innumerable fans she could not conceivably have done so to better effect. The 1983 tour of Australia and New Zealand was a huge success for both the Prince and the Princess of Wales. And for the Press and television. But for Diana personally it proved to be nothing short of a triumph.

15. A NEW TEAM IN THE NEW WORLD

"Close-up, Diana is as beautiful as her photographs. Charles on the other hands is growing ugly in an unspectacular way."
David Marr, The National Times March 25 – 31 1983

"The present Royal tour of Australia is not just about pomp and glitter and trivia and spreading goodwill among people. Behind Buckingham Palace's agreement to the tour by Prince Charles, Princess Diana and little Prince William there was a serious political purpose."
Geoffrey Barker, The Age, March 1983

"The tide of history, however slowly it might move, is against the survival of Australia's royal links with Britain.
Red Harrison, B.B.C. correspondent in Australia speaking on International Assignment, B.B.C. Radio, April 28 1983

"The Prince and Princess of Wales – or perhaps one should say the Prince and Princess of Australia or New Zealand, because that is what they are too – came with their baby; they were seen by multitudes, and by all accounts they conquered."
The first leader in The Times, May 2 1983

Things did not get off to a particularly good start. Just as, a month earlier, it had been expected that the Queen and Prince Philip would tour California in sunshine so, too, did it seem practically guaranteed that the Prince and Princess of Wales would arrive in the red heart of Australia in broiling heat. Instead, fourteen inches of rain fell in the three days prior to their arrival, flooding the normally parched lands and sending torrents of red muddy water over broken bridges and through many houses in Alice Springs.

The British media, coming from winter conditions and relishing the thought of sun and blue skies, arrived in advance of the Royal Party and squelched around their motel complex like boy scouts and girl guides at summer camp in the English Lake District. (Anthony Carthew, I.T.N.'s Court Correspondent paddled through the giant puddles in flip-flops and blue jeans rolled up to his knees, while James Whitaker surveyed the wet scene in a ridiculous-looking straw hat purchased in Swaziland.)

Even as their Royal Australian Air Force Boeing 707 was flying them out from London, contingency plans were being hurriedly made in case the weather precluded the Royal visitors landing at Alice Springs. As it was, arrangements for the Prince and Princess of Wales to stay at the luxury Federal Hotel (a casino was one of the advertised attractions) were abandoned because the approach road had been washed away by the floods.* Instead, Charles and Diana would be put up in a suite at the newly opened Gap Motor Hotel which — the media was delighted to discover — boasted a circular wooden bath tub. Predictably, Harry Arnold's description in *The Sun* the following morning had an eye-catching headline to go with the picture: RUB A DUB DUB, THIS IS DI'S TUB.

He may have missed the notice at Reception: "Neat, clean and tidy dress at the discretion of the management is a requirement to gain access to this hotel", and the sign on the rear of a truck clearing away debris caused by the flooding: "Reality is an illusion caused by lack of drugs."

After proudly showing off their son to photographers, mostly to please Australians and partly to ward off any possiblity of Press intrusion later, Charles and Diana went to their hotel and inspected their rooms. Then, since the weather had reverted to sun and clear skies, settled for a few hours by the pool of a house lent them by a local businessman with interests in shops and car sales. (Ironically it was a travelling group from Mitsubishi, whose franchise he holds, who happily agreed to move out of their rooms at the Inn in order to make way for Prince Charles, Princess Diana, and their entourage of fifteen.)

That evening the lounge bar was cleared of tables and chairs so that the Prince and Princess of Wales, wearing TI and DD respectively

---

* The original plan was for Prince William to stay overnight with his parents before being flown on to Woomargarma in New South Wales where he would remain for the rest of the Royal tour of Australia. However "rather than unpack everything just for one night" it was decided that he and those looking after him would fly straight on from Alice Springs to Albury, the nearest adjacent town, via Canberra.

could meet representatives of the media, the majority of whom were also wearing either TI or DD. (One of the few exceptions was Ashley Walton of the *Daily Express* who wore LS, possibly to conceal a small tear in his trousers.)

The official programme for each Royal tour devotes a glossary to "Suggested Dress", indicated by symbols.

"DJ   – Dinner Jacket, Black Tie
LD   – Long Dress
U   – Uniform
LS   – Lounge Suit
DD   – Day Dress
TI   – Territory Rig (Slacks, Shirt and Tie)
CAS – Casual
d   – Decorations
T   – Her Royal Highness wears a Tiara"

Princess Diana's DD at the reception was the frock she wore at the start of her honeymoon. During the next two days, as the temperature soared into the nineties, she wore dresses just as informal but less colourful – and, ladies noticed, she went bare-legged!

The attention paid by some reporters, most of them British, to what Diana wore, or didn't wear, and the question of whether she had caught too much sun lying by the pool, and how she would face up to the rigours of her first overseas tour, at first puzzled and then vexed some of their Australian colleagues.

"The truth about the Press obsession with Diana," wrote David Marr in *The National Times,* "is that their fascination is mixed with hate. They want to break her. The tabloids have her always on the verge of collapse from nerves, the sun, and obsessive dieting."

The accusation was well wide of the mark, even absurd. The truth was, and still is, that popular papers always need an angle to go on, a quote or a change from the normal, on which they can hang a headline, usually next to a picture. Especially during the first few days of a tour, reporters can become almost neurotic about "not missing out". They pounce on the smallest detail, dreading a "callback" from their office about a story – usually quite inconsequential – that has appeared in the first edition of a rival newspaper. News photographers (known as "smudgers") spend several additional hours at the end of a normal twelve hour day "pinging" (wiring) pictures back to their papers or agencies. Television reporters, who edit tape and write commentaries in hotel bedrooms cluttered with equipment, often have to travel many miles to the nearest satellite transmission point. Magazine photographers, shooting in colour, have to be experts in international airline scheduling if they're to get their film back in time to stand a chance of it being selected.

Even those who write for weekly newspapers and magazines

agonise over what they can say that is not too near to what has already been said. While they rarely ask for sympathy (and never expect to receive it) those who choose – indeed clamour sometimes – to be sent on Royal tours by their offices can never be said to have been given the easiest of journalistic assignments.*

On the tour of Australia and New Zealand problems of communication were increased because of the time difference. What was late night in Sydney was early morning on the same day in London. But, largely because the Prince and Princess of Wales had wisely insisted on frequent "days-off" in their exhausting schedule, the media had slightly more chance to relax than usual. Even so, they still had to be always ahead of the Royal party, to await their arrival, and so spent many hours checking in and out of hotels and waiting around at airports.

The behaviour of British media representatives, both at work and on the rare occasions they could relax beside a hotel pool, seemed to infuriate one or two Australians assigned to cover the tour. Geoffrey Barker, a columnist on *The Age,* a prestigious newspaper, wrote: "After only three days on the Royal tour even a staunch republican has to sympathise with Prince Charles and Princess Diana in their unequal and unending contest with the Fleet Street Press."

While agreeing that there would be little point in a Royal tour without massive publicity, Mr Barker complained that Fleet Street photographers have "shoved local people and tourists aside with rough contempt; they have had to be restrained from sticking their lenses right into Royal faces." This was not true.

But even Mr Barker could not get everything right. He spelt James Whitaker's name incorrectly when he launched into personal abuse. "Among the reporters, the herd leader appears to be a certain Mr James Whittaker of the London 'Daily Mirror'. Mr Whittaker is one of those fat, pink Englishmen of overbearing manner who brays rather than speaks, who laughs a lot and who smears himself with suntan lotion."

David Marr, of *The National Times,* who also spelt the name wrongly, thought "James Whittaker speaks like a suburban major-

---

* After a week or more of photographing Royalty almost non-stop most photographers have nightmares about their job. On the Australian tour one newspaper cameraman dreamt of not being able to get Princess Diana's hair in focus, and when eventually he did and she turned full-face towards him, there were sockets where her eyes should have been! In his recurring dream another, internationally famous, photographer saw Diana giving a cabaret performance in a mini skirt. But he suffered nightmares through not being able to locate the right lens amongst all the equipment strung round his neck!

general with deaf daughters to raise."

Interviewed on A.B.C. Television's Nationwide programme, Whitaker himself appeared to be trading insult with insult. Happily unable, he said, to remember Geoffrey Barker's name, he was irritated that somebody such as he should use British journalists to try and make a sort of name for himself. "I believe he works for some paper in Melbourne. My guess is he will remain on that newspaper for the rest of his life, and having written this ridiculous article he will disappear back into oblivion."

"What I find fascinating about this part of the British National Press," responded Barker on the same television programme, "is how seriously they take themselves."

"Well, I've always described myself as the Master of Trivia," said Whitaker. "What I write is usually totally unimportant, but it's very, very readable." He argued that if a very serious political story appeared on the front page of any Australian newspaper with, next to it, a story about the condition of the Princess of Wales' skin then most people would read the story about the Princess of Wales first. This, he emphasised, was not to underestimate the serious element in the tour − "After all, Prince Charles is going to be the King of Australia one day" − but a Royal tour should be fun.

There were certainly moments of light relief. Like the occasion when a gigantic member of the Northern Territory police force approached Anthony Carthew of I.T.N., a compliant man, and expressed the hope that he, Carthew, was not going to give him a hard time. "Not at all," smiled Carthew nervously. "In that case," said the policeman, thumbs tucked into his belt, "why are you parking an Avis car in a Hertz parking place?'

But after a few days of sizing-up and settling down, Australians were happy enough to drink with Brits and policemen started smiling − very occasionally.*

Looking after British media arrangements on the tour was Victor Chapman, one of the Queen's two Assistant Press Secretaries, ably assisted in Australia by Graeme Wicks, the Commonwealth Media Liaison Officer from Canberra. This was only the second overseas Royal tour that Chapman had undertaken and he quickly

---

* It's worth pointing out, perhaps, that during the Royal tour *The Bulletin,* an Australian current affairs magazine ran a colour picture of Princess Diana when five months pregnant, and claimed that Buckingham Palace referred to the Press as "reptiles" − an unlikely word. *Truth* ran an article about the Queen sub-headed "A penny-pinching eccentric". And, until it was banned, there was a poster on sale in Sydney purporting to show Princess Diana topless. The British Press, it seemed, could not alone be blamed for trashiness.

established an excellent relationship with reporters and photographers. A fifty-two-year-old Canadian, former professional football player and one-time Press liaison man for Pierre Trudeau, Chapman arrived at Buckingham Palace in September 1982 and immediately made an impression with his burly form, his rolling gait, and his no-nonsense approach. Most Pressmen felt an instinctive rapport with him, at the same time wondering to what extent traditional Palace thinking might alter his refreshingly open-minded outlook.

They were soon to learn that Chapman is not the kind of man to be easily pushed around by anyone, and unlike some of his predecessors he is at ease in a bar like most Fleet Street men or women are — which was definitely a mark in his favour.

Chapman is chummy, but not over familiar, with Pressmen. He can see through most of their ploys, in the same way that they are aware that the reason he slips away from private functions often has as much to do with the fact that he is dying for a cigarette (he is a thirty-a-day man) as with wishing to keep reporters briefed on what is going on behind closed·doors. On a number of occasions on the Australian tour he came to the aid of the media when over-zealous officialdom looked like queering the Press pitch. Equally, his wide footballer's shoulders loomed up to block the view of those photographers who encroached too close on the Royal couple. It was Ashley Walton of the *Daily Express* who aptly nicknamed Chapman "Rowdy Yates" — the cowboy in the old TV series 'Rawhide' whose job it was to "round 'em up, and move 'em on".

Most of the time the Prince and Princess of Wales appeared well enough pleased with the arrangements — though metal barriers rather than plastic ribbon would have served better to hold the crowds in check on walkabouts. Reporters and television cameramen who infiltrated the crowd to get better pictures and sound recordings were now and then stung to blushing by the Princess. "Are you trying to hear what I'm saying?" she asked, knowing that they shouldn't be. Prince Charles, who can usually spot a television camera and microphone, even when they are half-concealed in a crowd several yards away, makes sure he has something vaguely amusing or obliquely pointed to say when he draws level. Accepting a boomerang from a schoolboy at Tennant Creek he remarked: "This will come in handy for dealing with the Press."

Very rarely were either of them caught out by the unexpected, but two examples illustrate the super awareness required of any member of the Royal Family in public. At Alice Springs the Prince and Princess were scheduled to have a dialogue with children in the outback over the two-way radio of the School of the Air. Ushered into a studio only a few minutes before transmission, twenty reporters watching through a glass partition, they sat down with the head-master and went over some of the questions the pupils were going to ask. Without any warning their concentration was broken by the background sound of the National Anthem relayed through loud-speakers. It was a moment before Prince Charles realised. He tapped his wife's knee: both of them rose and solemnly stood to attention, looking slightly sheepish.

Flying south from Tennant Creek to a day-off at Woomargarma, they were due to stop briefly at Alice Springs to take farewell of Northern Territory dignitaries. However, due to a misunderstanding, the Princess of Wales was unaware that the Press were to be there also. In fact the journalists, as weary as the Princess probably at the end of a day's work, were only hanging around in the terminal building for their own aircraft to be given clearance for Canberra. But as the Royal plane taxied-in the photographers could not resist rushing outside for yet another arrival picture. The Princess descended the steps from the aircraft, a cardigan draped casually over her shoulders, and hardly a trace of a smile on her face. With justification, and even more than most women, Diana does not enjoy having her picture taken before she has had a chance to do her hair — and her hairdresser, Kevin Shanley, was already on the ground.

But this was a small incident, remarkable mainly because it demon-strated how completely in control the Princess appeared to be throughout the tour. Journalists were impressed — and delighted — by the twenty-one-year-old Diana's composure. The thousands who turned out to greet her (in Brisbane crowds were estimated to total 100,000 — twice the number that had lined the streets the previous year to cheer the Queen) were thrilled to discover that she was every bit as beautiful as she was in her pictures. It was her complexion that impressed most Australian and New Zealand women, and the depth of her hemline that was remarked upon by many older women — "far too long for out here."

She was rarely at a loss for something to say — especially where children were involved. And often it was the children who asked the first question.

"Do you like dead horse?"

"What on earth's that?"

"Tomato sauce," hooted the small boy, swinging the Princess by the hand.

She must have accepted literally thousands of posies, thrust at her by children darting out of the crowd. When a little girl failed at first to get near enough and burst out sobbing, the Princess went over to her, bent down to take the flowers and reassured: "Agony over." Her youthfulness, the complete absence of pomposity, and a kind of demure dignity — these were the attributes that won the affection of the crowds. It became increasingly difficult to believe that this was the same young woman who had glowered at people on a Swiss mountaintop only a few weeks earlier; even harder to think of her in terms of being a fiend.

Prince Charles had known from the outset that provided his wife wasn't overawed by the size of the crowds – always a fear in Palace minds – or became exhausted by the inevitable repetitiveness of Royal tours, then she was bound to be the star attraction, with him in the best supporting role. When it happened exactly this way, he was plainly delighted, ready as ever to turn any twinge of discomfiture he may have felt (after all, he himself had been the star attraction up until now) into a joke.

"It would have been far easier to have had two wives to have covered both sides of the street," he commented at a banquet in New Zealand. "And I could have walked down the middle directing the operation."

At moments throughout the tour Charles and Diana showed signs of the affection they both obviously feel for one another – moments recorded by nimble fingered photographers. His hand resting on hers, her glance towards him – those sort of telling things, so beloved of Press and public alike. Once, though, Diana appeared to bridle at one of her husband's gestures. As they were making their entrance at a glittering evening function, Prince Charles placed a hand on his wife's back. "Will you not *do* that," she was heard to remark, or something similar.

This minor marital disagreement apart, the Prince and Princess of Wales showed every sign of being an excellent Royal partnership – "a new double-act in the Royal Road Show," was how one Australian journalist dubbed it in passing.

Much harder to gauge was the long term effect of the Australian section of the tour on that nation's attitude towards its Monarchy. Judging by the number of occasions Prince Charles made oblique or open reference in his speeches to the historical ties between Australia and Britain and to the joint futures of the two countries, an important aim of the tour was to bolster Commonwealth relations – and, in private conversations, to test out the strength of republican leanings.

The tour – the longest since the Queen's 1977 Silver Jubilee tour – originated through an invitation of the then Prime Minister of Australia, Malcolm Fraser, at the Commonwealth Games in 1982. (An earlier invitation had to be postponed when Princess Diana became pregnant.) But just fifteen days before Charles and Diana's arrival, Australians had voted in a general election for a Labour government with a republican platform commitment. Ironically, some observers believed this Labour victory improved the chances of

241

Australia remaining a Monarchy for a good many more years. Suddenly, with so many other matters to attend to – notably the state of the national economy – the desire for republicanism receded in importance. And the bitter taste left by the sacking of the Gough Whitlam Labour government in 1975, by the Queen's Governor-General in Australia, Sir John Kerr, was assuaged.

"Royal tours," claimed one of Australia's national newspapers, "provide circuses for people who are a little short of other things to keep them subdued and compliant in times of severe recession." But opinion polls showed that 60% of Australians – no longer predominantly descended from Britons – would prefer that things remained as they were.

Although the fundamental reason for Prince William's presence in Australia and New Zealand was because his parents did not like the idea of leaving him at home for six weeks, one effect of transporting him 12,000 miles across the world was to delight thousands of young mums. Another was to convey very strongly the idea of continuity. "I hope his presence here," Prince Charles told one of his audiences, "is to revive that family feeling which I know my wife and I think is so important."

"The Prince and Princess of Wales have set back the cause of republicanism in Australia by 50 years – and Prince William has probably set it back a hundred," proclaimed the *Daily Express* in London at the close of the tour.

On the same day, in the last paragraph of its main leader, *The Times* declared that the tour had revealed a new maturity in the Prince and Princess of Wales "moulded together now more as a partnership in the public imagination than has always been the case in Britain . . . In another hemisphere, but so also thus in the Britain to which they will return, the promise of that wedding, with its music, its bunting and the acclamations, has now been confidently returned."

What's more, when Charles and Diana departed New Zealand for nine days of holiday on the Bahamian island of Windermere – arranging for baby Prince William to return home to London via Los Angeles – not a single British newspaper photographer or reporter was sent on the story. For a whole week the most photographed couple in the world were to be left alone to enjoy idyllic seclusion. Was this the start of something new? Not really. European photographers turned up, and *Paris Match* ran four pages of fuzzy pictures showing Charles and Diana cavorting on the beach. But, to their credit, British newspapers and magazines declined to buy any of the photographs. So the Palace was pleased.

It was most displeased, however, a month or so later by an incident at the start of a seventeen day visit to Canada by the Prince and

Princess of Wales.

A reporter from a small local paper in Halifax, Nova Scotia, came ashore from 'Britannia' after the customary welcoming Press reception and – like her colleague from American television reporting on the Queen's tour earlier in the year – blabbed in print what she'd heard supposedly in confidence.

Apparently the Princess of Wales had remarked on how she gets a "horrible feeling" in her chest and wants to stay indoors after reading nasty stories about herself in the newspapers. And she talked about the wolf-pack tabloids – a description most of the mass selling papers in Britain omitted to pass on to their readers in their reports of the Canadian journalist's account of her conversation with the Princess.

Diana's father, Earl Spencer, also provided an insight when he gave an interview to the *Chronicle Herald* of Halifax, which was published just before the start of the Canadian tour. He confirmed what many Royal watchers had believed for a long time: that the Princess of Wales is "a very determined woman indeed". Diana's father was making the point – just a few days before Prince William's first birthday on June 21st, 1983 – that his Royal grandson will be brought up close to the Spencer side of the family, and be influenced by it as much as by the House of Mountbatten-Windsor.

In his bluff, friendly way he was quoted as saying: "I know the Royals can appear to swallow people up when others marry in, and the other family always looks as if it has been pushed out – but that could never happen to us.

"We can cope with the pressures. We have been brought up with Royalty and there is no question of us being pushed out. Diana would not permit it to happen. And she always gets her own way. I think Charles is learning that now. Marriage has changed her. She is not shy any more, and knows her own mind."

The Canadian tour certainly served to underline the fact that after two years of marriage the Princess of Wales has imprinted her own individual style in public and private, and overall to good effect. The Royal Family has always possessed an almost uncanny ability to adapt to changing circumstances outside the Palace walls so that it has not only survived into the last quarter of the twentieth century but has become, if anything, even more universally popular in recent years. Now it has learned to adapt to the inclusion among its top echelon of a quite extraordinary young woman who will one day be Queen.

16. M.F.

"We live in radical times and the more People see the Sovereign the better it is for the People and the Country."
The Prince of Wales, later King Edward VII, in a letter to Queen Victoria

"It is the aim of all individuals and organisations to present their best case to the world, consistent with their long-term credibility."
Bernard Ingham, Press Secretary to Margaret Thatcher, addressing the Guild of British Newspaper Editors, April 30, 1983

"Do you think, after 30 years on the throne, the Queen is still doing a good job for the country?" Yes: 94%. No: 5%. No answer: 1%.
Result of a poll carried out by Woman's Own, June 1983

"The fascination of a constitutional monarchy to its people will always be less to do with a Prince's role than what, if anything, he wears in bed."
Anthony Holden, 'Charles, Prince of Wales'

When King George IV died in 1830 *The Times* had this to say in its obituary of the monarch: "There never was an individual less regretted by his fellow creatures than this deceased King. What eye has wept for him? What heart has heard one sob of unmercenary sorrow? . . . If George IV ever had a friend — a devoted friend in any rank of life — we protest that the name of him or her never reached us."

When the name of the future King Edward VII was linked to a certain Society lady's divorce case, the Prince of Wales was booed in the streets and *Reynolds News* believed that "even the staunchest supporters of monarchy shake their heads and express anxiety as to whether the Queen's successor will have the tact and talent to keep royalty upon its legs and out of the gutter."*

George V, early on in his reign, was accused of drunkenness because he stumbled on mounting his horse, and was said to have left a morganatic wife and two children in Malta, and to have married the fiancée of his elder brother too soon after the unfortunate man's early demise.

Even the present Queen's much loved father, George VI, did not get off to a particularly good start apparently. A reporter from the *New York Herald Tribune,* observing the departure of the King, by train, for Christmas holidays at Sandringham in 1936, wrote: "King George VI, hat in hand, bowed right and left automatically as he drove up. Scarcely a hat was raised in reply. King George VI and his family walked bowing across the platform. Perhaps half the men in the little throng raised their hats. There was a subdued murmur which might have been a suppressed cheer – or might not. In short, on his first public appearance after his successsion to his brother, King George VI was given an extremely cold shoulder."

It seems almost superfluous to point out that things have changed somewhat since all those far-off days – today's gossip is much less damning by comparison.

The present-day popularity of Britain's Royal Family, in widespread areas of the world, is due in no small part to the millions of complimentary words and thousands of flattering pictures that are devoted to them each year. Hardly a word of criticism is heard, let alone written, and any unflattering pictures that are used are generally captioned 'Caught Off-Guard', or something similar to make sure that nobody is left with the impression that an attempt is being made to depict members of the Royal Family as undignified, moronic, or downright ugly. (Interestingly, although some of the famous Bikini pregnancy pictures of Princess Diana were shot of her sideways-on, none of these was selected for publication in Britain.)

A century and more ago, cartoonists lampooned the Monarch without mercy. Today fun is sometimes poked, but not maliciously. One of the reasons for this gentler treatment is the fact that the sovereign no longer holds the political power that her ancestors did. The Queen still has the right to advise and influence, yes. To alter, no. Therefore she cannot, off her own bat, make decisions, pass laws, which might prove unpopular, especially among those with power of their own to protect. She is free, of course, to behave disgracefully, to be profligate with the money that taxpayers, through Parliament, set aside for Royal use each year, or even to take herself a lover – all of which her ancestors did, bringing the steel nib

---

* Certainly until comparatively recently, allowances were paid out from a special Royal fund to the illegitimate children of Edward VII still surviving.

of cartoonists and commentators down upon them like daggers. But the Queen is not like her ancestors.

The calculations of editors and proprietors, almost as much as anything, may be said to be a reason for the sparsity of criticism of monarchy in recent years. Kingsley Martin, editor of the *New Statesman* in its heyday, made the comment in his book *The Crown and the Establishment (1962),* that British monarchy was never criticised. "Broadcasters may argue about socialism, birth control, and even homosexuality, but I do not recall republicanism being discussed or even mentioned on the B.B.C. . . . In the 20th century anyone can question the divinity of Christ, but no-one attributes faults to the Royal Family." Perhaps he should have asked himself, in regard to newspapers at least and possibly the B.B.C. as well, whether questioning the divinity of Christ had the effect of reducing sales or the number of listeners. Because promoting the idea of a republic, or harshly criticising the conduct of members of the Royal Family, can turn out to be a fairly disastrous course of action for mass selling newspapers, leading to a worrying scale of cancelled orders at newsagents.

Experience has taught Fleet Street that a tricky balance needs to be maintained between providing readers with news and gossip about the Royal Family (which the majority clearly love − even though not all readily admit to the fact) and pursuing one aspect or one person to the extent of "overkill". When the adventures of Prince Andrew and Koo Stark were just beginning, the editor of one of Britain's biggest dailies ran the story prominently for several days running, until he noticed a dip in sales and an implied yawn in readers' letters. For a while after that − the Prince and Miss Stark may just conceivably have noticed − they were left fairly well alone, by that particular newspaper at any rate. However, there may have been another factor in readers' reactions which the editor missed.

Whether for personal reasons or, more likely, because he judged most people would not approve of the relationship, there was just a hint of disapproval in the pictures his paper used to illustrate the racy romance of the sailor Prince. Yet, only a few months later, in April 1983, the *Sunday People* published the results of a poll which showed that a majority of its readers were actually in favour of the relationship. To the question: "Do you approve of Prince Andrew's friendship with Koo?" 52% of the men who answered voted "Yes", and so did 40% of the women readers (the rest had no firm opinion either way). However, in June, in answer to a questionnaire in *Woman's Own* magazine, 60% of readers (the great majority women presumably) disapproved of the relationship.

A hundred years ago, or less − at any rate before television and accountants held sway in Fleet Street − editors expounded their personal views in hard hitting editorials, or commissioned famous writers to do the same, without too much attention being paid to the opinion of readers. Today, with circulation figures hard to hold, greater emphasis is placed on reader reaction. Consultation, through polling, plays an increasingly important part in helping editors discover the views of their millions of readers on a wide variety of subjects ranging from unilateral disarmament to whether or not the Princess of Wales spends too much on clothes. (For some reason – perhaps it's the influence of football pools – thousands of people don't seem to mind finding the time to do other people's market research by filling in forms.) Sometimes the questions are more illuminating than the replies – "Would you willingly wait in the rain for two hours for a chance of glimpsing the Queen on a walkabout?" Yes 56%; No 43%; – but as an expresssion of how a large number of people currently feel about Royalty (*Woman's Own,* for instance, can claim some six million readers) they are a useful indicator. It may come as no surprise that 94% of that magazine's readers who replied to the survey thought that, after thirty years on the throne, the Queen was still doing a good job for the country. But Buckingham Palace might not have been quite so happy to read that over half were of the opinion that it was "part of Princess Diana's job to be photographed wherever she goes".

Questions such as "Do you think the Royal Family should be given more privacy?" are recent inclusions, an outcome of controversy. It is very unlikely that the question would have even been considered for use in a poll conducted in 1964 which showed that there were still 30% who believed that the Queen was someone specially chosen by God, and therefore on a very high pedestal indeed.

Popularity ratings are always a favourite with readers, and can also result in surprises. Again to quote *Woman's Own,* 32% of the respondents chose the Queen as their favourite person among the Royal Family, but only 2% chose Prince Philip. (A poll published in the *Daily Telegraph Magazine* in September 1969, which asked who would be the best dictator, put Prince Philip at the top, with Enoch Powell in second place.)

The Prince and Princess of Wales came out neck and neck in *Woman's Own*'s popularity stakes (15% and 16% respectively) but a *Sunday People* poll placed Prince Charles as the clear favourite at 72%, with the Queen at 67%, Princess Diana at 51%, and Prince Andrew at 24%. (For some reason, unexplained, Prince Philip did not figure at all in this particular questionnaire.)

People may no longer need to be asked whether they think the Queen rules by Divine Right, but the Royal ratings underline another change in attitude – one which some find disturbing. The idea of The Royal Soap Opera has taken root in the public mind just as firmly – and perhaps just as temporarily – as the latest pop television serial. The characters are not hard to place. The Queen (Brenda, as she has long been known to the readers of the satirical magazine *Private Eye)*, is the matriarchal figure – Miss Ellie of "Dallas" – who has a nice son and a not-so-nice son who goes out with "the wrong sort of girl". There is Anne, the grumpy daughter, and Edward the brainy son. There is the foreign beauty who likes the limelight, and the English rose who married the handsome Prince and then becomes a source of worry because she doesn't eat enough or because, rumour has it, she gives her husband a hard time.

The demystification of Royalty began with the television film *Royal Family* and has progressed apace since the arrival of Prince Andrew and Princess Diana on the grown-up scene. Both have a way of behaving very naturally in public. Even on solemn occasions one looks for the moment when either one of them finds it impossible not to let the mask slip. There was a moment, for instance, at Princess Diana's wedding when, immediately after the ceremony, Prince Andrew crossed the aisle to have a cheerful chat with the three pretty girls who had been the bride's flatmates. It seemed in character.

Princess Diana is constantly, and presumably quite unconsciously, endearing herself even further with the public by speaking in a fashion that they are not used to hearing where Royalty is concerned. Before her marriage admittedly, at her first public engagement with Prince Charles, she was overheard telling one wellwisher: "I've got pins and needles in my bottom – I've never had to sit still for so long!" And to a tearful old lady who clutched her hand, remarking the while that she had waited all her life for this moment, Diana quipped: "Well, you'd better make the most of it while you have the chance."

Even after two years of subtle and well intended Palace pressure, capable of smoothing public utterances to the neat shapes of word processors, Princess Diana can still surprise and delight by saying the first thing that comes into her head. "Oh God, *he's* not here is he?" she exclaimed when informed that a person she didn't particularly wish to meet would be in a receiving line.

Long-distance microphones as well as long-distance lenses can nowadays pick up the quietest aside; and while most are never broadcast, enough are transmitted to enable more and more pieces to be added to the jigsaw picture of a Royal Family that is becoming less and less a private firm and increasingly something akin to public property. It is not just a hard act to follow. It's a hard act to be *in*.

The situation is unlikely to change. A recent poll indicated that 86% of those questioned would not like to see a return to the days when Royalty was shrouded in mystique.

Even in Queen Victoria's reign it was necessary for the monarch to be seen to be believed. "If you sometimes even came to London from Windsor — say for luncheon," suggested the Prince of Wales in a letter to his mother, "and then drove for an hour in the Park and then returned to Windsor, the people would be overjoyed — beyond measure." But in those days they would also have bowed or curtsied, and the men would have doffed their caps as the Queen passed by. Today their descendants would be as likely to put an Instamatic up to their faces and hope that the Queen, on a walkabout or at the Windsor Horse Show, would pause to pose for a moment. Her Majesty would be unlikely to; Diana might.

Largely because the Royal Family are seen and written about so much, a feeling almost of mateyness has developed, certainly on the public's side. The Queen's subjects have become more like her supporters, and the Princess of Wales — the future Queen — is sometimes treated like a megastar of the pop world, with teenage shrieks greeting her as she steps glamorously from her limousine to attend what otherwise would be a staid and probably quite boring banquet.

Many see danger in all this showbiz adulation. As Nicholas Wapshott pointed out in an article in *The Times* in July 1982: "There is a delicate balance beyond which the Queen, once revered, becomes a celebrity like any other, open to abuse and ridicule like the rest. Familiarity can lead to more than just contempt."

Alongside the new familiarity, however, there remain those occasions — such as the State Opening of Parliament or a gathering of Commonwealth Ministers — when Royal pageantry and a sense of cohesion demonstrate to millions of people, in and far beyond Britain, a degree of stability and neutrality that many find reassuring in a world increasingly riven by ideological divisions. The Queen may not *be* Britain — indeed, as anti-monarchists would be quick to point out, in many regards she is no more than a figurehead — but for the great majority she and her family are not only the longest serving but also the *most reliable* ambassadors Britain has. In addition, as any travel agent will tell you, they are a marvellous tourist attraction.

Buckingham Palace has never liked the idea of the words Public Relations and Royal Family being linked together. The Queen does not have a Public Relations Department, and would probably be dead against the idea of a Publicity Office. Equally her Press Secretaries might cringe if they knew how often they are referred to in newspaper and television company offices as "the Queen's PRs". And yet, at first glance it is hard to see grounds for objection. A very large part of the Royal Family's public engagements are very much to do with public relations — whether it is through giving patronage to a charity, publicity to an industrial concern, or support to a particular sport or leisure activity. The presence of a member of the Royal

Family at a function, or an agreement to tour a factory or visit a town is worth a very large sum of money in terms of free publicity, as any organiser will affirm.

Of course Palace officials would be right to point out that it is the people and the places accorded a Royal visit, not members of the Royal Family themselves, that benefit from the publicity. Their job is to give recognition to what is deemed worthwhile, and in the course of so doing to meet as many people as possible.

The Queen does not need publicity, the argument goes. She and her family attract more than enough free space in the Press and on television without their Press Secretaries having even to lift a 'phone. She *is* the Monarch, and the Monarchy shows little or no sign of crumbling through lack of interest.

As to safeguarding the image, the media sees to this too. Ninety-nine per cent of its coverage is favourable to the Royal Family. The institution of Monarchy in Britain has not been under any serious threat since the abdication crisis of 1936, and carefully orchestrated events like the Queen's Silver Jubilee and the Royal Wedding serve to increase its popularity.

Certainly, if Fleet Street, or the media in general, were ever to see reason for making a deliberate and concerted effort to denigrate the Royal Family at every opportunity — with or without truth — then it could quite conceivably create a crisis in which the very existence of the Monarchy was threatened. But at present the Press is far too well-disposed towards the Queen and her family for anything like that to be even remotely considered, and the situation seems unlikely to change in the foreseeable future. The only real argument is over privacy and access to information.

Addressing the Guild of British Newspaper Editors in Cardiff on April 30 1983, Michael Shea quoted an anonymous member of the media as saying that if Fleet Street did not give the range of coverage to the Royal Family that it does "then the very position of the Monarchy would be threatened and the Royal Family themselves would be the first to complain." "Is that a blinding truth, or is it an absurdity?" asked Mr Shea of his audience.

It is probably neither. More likely it is a view fairly widely held among journalists, one which contains more than a grain of truth. Of course the position of the Royal Family would not be put in jeopardy, not immediately anyway, if the Press stopped publishing stories and pictures and continued with this policy for a matter of months. But after a few months, who's to say what the effect would be? Who's to say that the Queen wouldn't enquire of her Press Secretary why the crowds coming out to greet her were much smaller than they had been hitherto? Would there not be many more questions in Parliament than there are now about the cost of maintaining a Monarchy? If there were no stories printed about the private lives of members of the Royal Family wouldn't interest and affection begin to evaporate? Prince Charles once commented to the present author that the size of crowd he could expect to see at the start of a provincial tour was directly commensurate with the amount of publicity he or other members of the Royal Family had received in the day or two prior to the visit. The value of Press coverage on an overseas tour is immense. Indeed there is good reason for believing that the President of an African state who intended banning overseas journalists from reporting a Royal tour of his country a few years ago was advised quite specifically: No Press, No tour.

The point Mr Shea was making – or, rather, the warning he was issuing – was directed at those in the media who believe they have a right to free-range over both the Royal Family's public and private lives.

"What has to be assured," said the Queen's Press Secretary, "is that all concerned understand and accept that there is a limit to what is acceptable. That there is a *line to be drawn*. Is it really reasonable to say – as one or two extremists do – that 'the Royal Family has no right to privacy', that they are 'fair game'?"

No, it is not reasonable. But where is the line to be drawn and who is to draw it? The Palace, the Press, or the People? Is the Press to be regulated by an outside body with greater powers than the present Press Council, or by new restrictive laws? Is the Palace to be allowed to proceed "with all severity and rigour", as James II wished to do in 1688, "against all such who shall be guilty of any such malicious and unlawful practices, by writing, printing, or other publications of such false news"? In the end surely it must be the people – the readers and the television viewers – who are the arbiters of what is acceptable and what is not. After all, the Queen and her family are very much *their* Royal Family.

However, just as reporters tap out MF at the foot of each page of copy to indicate that there is more to follow, so it is pretty safe to assume that in the long fluctuating relationship between Palace and Press the story is by no means over yet. The bond is still fragile.

But, even in the space of writing this book, and especially after the success of the tours of Australia, New Zealand and Canada, there are hopeful signs of a possible change on the way. A closer collaboration; and more informal, off-the-record get-togethers, possibly, between the Prince and Princess of Wales and the media. The Palace and the Press need one another's co-operation. And the People, by their adulation of the one and their avid readership of the other, express a desire that both should continue to please and to provide.

BIBLIOGRAPHY

ARNOLD, Harry: Charles and Diana, New English Library 1981

BAGEHOT, Walter: The English Constitution, Chapman and Hall, 1867, Longmans Green, 1915

BOOTHROYD, J. Basil: Philip: An Informal Biography, Longman 1971

CAMPBELL, Judith: The Royal Partners, Robert Hale, 1982

COOLICAN, Don and LEMOINE, Serge: Charles, Royal Adventurer, Pelham Books, 1978

COUNIHAN, Daniel: Royal Progress, Cassell, 1977

CRAWFORD, Marion: The Little Princesses, Cassell, 1950

DUNCAN, Andrew: The Reality of Monarchy, Heinemann, 1970

EDWARD VIII: A King's Story, The Memoirs of H.R.H. The Duke of Windsor, Cassell, 1951

HOLDEN, Anthony: Charles Prince of Wales, Weidenfeld and Nicolson, 1979 and Their Royal Highnesses, Weidenfeld and Nicolson, 1981

JUNOR, Penny: Diana, Princess of Wales, Sidgwick and Jackson, 1982

LACEY, Robert: Majesty: Elizabeth II and the House of Windsor, Hutchinson, 1977

LICHFIELD, Patrick: Royal Album, Elm Tree Books/Hamish Hamilton, 1982

MARTIN, Kingsley: The Crown and the Establishment, Hutchinson, 1962

MORRAH, Dermott: To be a King, Hutchinson, 1968

MORROW, Ann: The Queen, Granada, 1983

SCOTT, George: Reporter Anonymous, Hutchinson, 1968

TALBOT, Godfrey: Ten Seconds From Now, Hutchinson, 1973

VAUGHAN-THOMAS, Wynford: The Princes of Wales, Kaye and Ward, 1982

WHEELER-BENNETT, John W.: King George VI: His Life and Reign, Macmillan, 1958

ZIEGLER, Philip: Crown and People, Collins, 1978

BLACK AND WHITE ILLUSTRATIONS